THE
DANNY
KAYE
STORY

BY KURT SINGER

Duel for the Northland, 1943
Spies and Traitors of World War II, 1945
3000 Years of Espionage, 1951
Story of a Hypnotist, with Franz Polgar, 1951
Charles Laughton Story, 1954

THE
DANNY
KAYE
STORY

×××

by
KURT SINGER

THOMAS NELSON & SONS
Edinburgh   **NEW YORK**   *Toronto*

DESIGNED BY FRANK KARPELES

Library of Congress Catalog Card No.: 58–13652

Printed in the United States of America

Acknowledgments

Cast of Characters
of the story behind the story of *The Danny Kaye Story*

Time: 1956–58   **Location:** Terra Firma

DANNY KAYE........... the modest guy who feels he is too young to write his own biography and will be too young until he is "an old and doddering fool"

SYLVIA FINE........... who "always makes sense" and therefore had no hand in the writing of this book

DENA KAYE............ a charming young lady challenged by her parents' success

ROBERT HALE.......... British publisher who suggested this book because "no one has ever made me laugh as much as Danny Kaye"

DR. IRVING SOMACH...... who gave many psychological insights into the world of Danny Kaye

A PRIEST.............. who calls Danny "the Juggler of God"

A MINISTER............ who tells of Danny's missionary work in Assignment Children

A RABBI.............. who knows Danny's belief in *one* God

RUTH BARTH........... a UNICEF "Lady in the Dark"

NINA SHERROD......... who accidentally burned the first chapters

TOM BLEDSOE.......... who insisted on social and religious implications

v

EDDIE SHELLHORN....... Paramount publicity man who shelled out releases, pictures, and invaluable data

JOHN MASON BROWN.... the first drama critic to predict Danny's great future

PAUL MEYERS.......... consultant to the Theatre Collection of the New York Public Library who labored for the sake of this book

EDITH CURRIE.......... who retyped the book four times

JANE SHERROD SINGER.... a wife who gave two and a half of her "best years" to this book

KEN SINGER............ 13-year-old who loves Danny Kaye because he is a "cool cat"

AGENTS HARRY WALKER,
MAX PFEFFER,
SOL SHIFRIN,
AND OTHERS............ who promoted the book

Contents

I.	Tears in the Cup of Fame	13
II.	Kid From Brooklyn	24
III.	Kominsky Island	32
IV.	This World Is a Difficult Place	40
V.	Kaye-San	52
VI.	Ping-Pong on a Rhinoceros Hide	59
VII.	Sylvia	67
VIII.	Her Head on My Shoulders	75
IX.	Pure Nonsense Can Be Funny	87
X.	Okaye	94
XI.	Sam Goldwyn's Office Box	104
XII.	"I'm a Wife-Made Man"	124
XIII.	"Danny Walked Out on Me!"	138
XIV.	"My Second Home"	145
XV.	Seeds for Mighty Enterprises	169
XVI.	The Prankster	177
XVII.	The First Fourteen Pictures	184
XVIII.	The Private World of Danny Kaye	202
XIX.	"I'm Their Kind of People"	215
XX.	Ambassador-at-Large	225
XXI.	Juggler of God	233

THE
DANNY
KAYE
STORY

I

Tears in the Cup of Fame

ANY NUMBER OF REASONS HAVE BEEN SET FORTH TO EXPLAIN Danny Kaye's success story, but few have done him justice.

Danny is more than the sum total of the factors to which he gives credit: hard work, long hours, know-how and the great talent of his musical wife.

"To be funny is no joke," Danny once said to Sam Goldwyn while discussing the secrets of comedians.

No, it is not a laughing matter to keep humor from becoming stale, to remain fresh, new, youthful, to reach the minds and hearts of millions year after year.

The detonator of the human bomb that is Danny Kaye is Danny himself. He is as adaptable as a chameleon, as flexible as a rubber band and as sensitive as a sea anemone. This "bundle of complexes" draws energy, ideas and motions from a bottomless well of intelligence, wit, humanitarian ideals, emotions and human sympathies.

The serious comedian knows that laughter is a world of its own, sometimes filled with true humor and often salted by the tears of Chaplinesque pathos.

"There are children in the world who have never laughed at all," Danny Kaye said recently when he decided to dedicate his life to the advancement of the forgotten children in the world. "How does one make people laugh who have not much to laugh about? I would like to find out."

For twenty-five years Danny Kaye has entertained millions of his paying fans on Broadway, in London, San Francisco and Hollywood, the glitter cities of the world. He has frisked his way across so many stages that the hardwood floors are more familiar to him than his own home's wall-to-wall carpeting.

But for almost four years, Danny, like the mythical Peer Gynt, has traveled around the world spreading smiles among forgotten children, searching for the truth that comes from giving, for the hidden joys lying behind a new kind of laughter.

As the first United Nations ambassador to the world's impoverished kids he has faced war orphans, cripples, malnourished and diseased children who had never giggled before, had never seen milk, penicillin, modern medical techniques, and had never blossomed from the warmth of human understanding.

With Danny Kaye there travels a brigade of United Nations doctors in a crusade to bring modern hygiene, medicine and twentieth-century nutrition to the obscure corners of the world.

Danny Kaye has always believed that "kids are kids," and that the youngsters of Asia and Africa are not basically different in their reactions and needs from children in Europe, Australia or America.

But there *was* one great difference: the underprivileged children in Asia and Africa had never seen television or a motion picture, had never heard a foreign language, knew nothing of Hollywood or Danny Kaye. They were gaunt from hunger and pierced with diseases. But they all understood Danny Kaye, although he spoke only English or the garble of nonsense he is prone to make up on the spot. They understood his funny faces, his antics, his dances and his open gestures toward them. They understood he liked them, wanted them and was reaching out to them through the medium of laughter.

These children in the remote parts of the world may not have had much to laugh about, but they smiled, chuckled and gave way to solid laughter when they realized, or sensed instinctively, that this was a strange man who had come from far away to help. He was, therefore, their friend.

A new Danny Kaye has emerged out of the luxuries and extravaganzas which make up the Hollywood dream factories. The United Nations ambassador visiting Nairobi, Ghana, Thailand and India has come to realize that bowing before plush royal audiences cannot constitute all the meaning of life.

One of the United Nations staff members watched Danny Kaye slide behind a thatched hut and wipe tears from his eyes. The indescribable poverty and illness of so many children pierced his heart.

"I am not ashamed of these tears," he said quietly to his friend. He rubbed his nose and went on the stage, a cleared section of adobe field, and entertained in the style of a great clown.

The second man inside Danny Kaye is very much awake. It is he who discovered that the old and young people of any nation, race or creed possess an immense will to laugh and that they have found a common bond: all people on earth are the same in the great wide world of humor.

Children are greedy for play and laughter. Actors are greedy for fame. Humanitarians live for the satisfaction that comes from helping the unfortunate. There is a little bit of all these elements in this complex man, Danny Kaye.

His is the greed of giving—a life of contradictions.

Behind the mask of laughter throbs a drumming heartbeat of paradoxes.

He is shrewd and naïve.

He is brash and modest, intellectual and frivolous.

He can be as warm and sensitive as Florence Nightingale, as hard-boiled as a Brooklyn mobster. He is serious and trifling, thoughtful and forgetful in spite of a wizard-like memory.

His greatest love lies among the children of the world, but still he has been called "high-hatted."

He laughs with his friends, with a heartiness few people are capable of conjuring—and he often withdraws, yogi-like, into himself.

Since he never settles down long enough for anybody to determine what he really thinks, he is often misunderstood. Whatever his schizoid tendencies may be, he hypnotizes the millions in his audience into helpless laughter. He has learned the secret of pitching a tantrum of heroic dimensions, of performing with never tiring and almost furious intensity, of elevating an audience with unforgettable inner merriment.

The children of the world who have accepted him as their ambassador sense the secret of his soul. Now in his forties, Danny Kaye is one of them, a grown-up boy who will never grow up.

The rest of us who try to understand this highly intricate personality realize Danny Kaye is as difficult to analyze as the labyrinth of the human brain.

There are many Danny Kayes. There is the highly sophisticated entertainer, who, with the gestures of a Shakespearean buffoon, plays a baby in diapers. There is the sheer comedian who will never forget the apprehensions of failure in his early years and is still convinced that his success is a bubble that may burst at any time.

There is a Danny Kaye who is bemedaled, awarded, applauded, honored, the United Nations ambassador who often thinks the best place in the world is alone in his desert retreat.

There is the man of many moods, the egomaniacal, complicated star. He can be utterly urbane, aloof and cold, but underneath there shines the glistening of a golden heart and the warmth of loyalty.

There is a Danny who has not always been the best husband—but respects his wife more than anyone else. There is Danny the lover whose deep romance is with his daughter, Dena, who reminds him daily that he is really not merely a funny man.

There is Danny Kaye, one of the great clowns of history, who refutes his reputation with the words, "I don't want to be a clown at all."

And there is the worrier—the man surrounded by millions, who is alone.

The ballet dancer, the singer, the pantomimist, the boy-man who is jazz-crazy, kid-crazy, cartoon-crazy and medicine-happy: these are also Danny Kaye.

He is a nitwit and sage all in one breath. He is a perpetual student who might have been a great doctor had he ever conquered the one beloved mistress he never had time to subdue—medicine.

While filming a silly scene in which he loses his sequined pants in *The Court Jester,* his dressing-room table was piled with books on psychiatry and psychosomatic medicine. Paradoxical? Not

more than his medal from Frank Sinatra which has on one side
Saint Christopher and on the other the star of David.

The man on the stage is high pressured, completely zany, hyper-
tense, driven by nervousness. The man in the dressing room is
relaxed as a rag-doll.

He will compromise, but not about his art, where he is a stub-
born perfectionist.

Fearful of success, he waves his arms with a wide gesture that
seems to embrace Hollywood, New York, London, the whole wide
world, his family, home and personal goods and says: "The bubble
will burst. All this will pass away. And when it does, I'll hear
voices saying: 'We're on to you, feller—the jig is up.' "

"Don't mention the word 'success' to me," said Danny recently.
"Why, only a few years ago I was the world's greatest flop. I laid
an egg bigger than a dinosaur's at the Dorchester in London in
1938. What happened? I went to London as a stooge for Nick
Long in a saloon act. My part was to cut up in the back of the
club, and I was so unfunny one confused Englishman yelled out
while I was singing my version of 'Dinah,' 'I say, what's that
infernal din back there?' I didn't last long.

"Success? . . . I'll never forget the twelve long and hard years
I spent playing every whistle stop in the United States. I played
from beer brawls in Brooklyn to wine suppers on the Borscht circuit.
I played at sugaring-off parties in the Vermont maple-country and
at masked festivals in the Louisiana bayous. I've beat my brains
out all over the world.

"I wasn't born a fool. It took work to get this way. And I'm
not a clown. I'm just an entertainer. I've spent many years learning my trade. All I want to be is funny. I never aspired to play
Hamlet; I leave this to the great actors.

"So when you talk about success and ask how it feels to sit on
Olympus, my answer to you is, 'What is Olympus, anyway? A
mountain in Greece, a city in the state of Washington?' Whatever
it is and wherever it may be—it is not for me.

"Naturally, I'm aware I've been lucky, but I sincerely believe
that if I ever succeeded in feeling I have reached success, success
will succeed me.

"You ask what was the greatest single break in my career?

"I wouldn't say there has been any one break. Anything the world might call success has come from an endless series of wonderful and helpful people. I still see much work ahead, and I don't believe there will ever be time to sit back and to feel successful.

"In my opinion there's no such thing as an overnight sensation in show business. I say it is impossible. Oh, some get up the ladder quicker than others—and they are lucky. But I claim show business is like medicine. Look at the years of study, internship and perhaps specialized training a doctor has to spend before he can nail up that shingle. And even after that he has to wait more years before he develops a thriving practice. It's exactly the same with an actor.

"All my life I have loved nothing else as much as standing before an audience, feeling one with them while we enjoy each other. Sometimes I get so carried away I forget people have to go home. Then I apologize and explain, 'There is nobody, but nobody who enjoys listening to me entertain as much as I do.'

"This matinee today was one of the most difficult performances I have given in my entire career. Do you know why? Didn't you see it?"

There was silence in Danny Kaye's dressing room.

A slim, thin-faced young man spoke these words thoughtfully in answer to remarks and questions from the backstage crowd of reporters, visitors, agents, autograph hunters and gapers at San Francisco's Curran Theater. It was the fall of 1952.

The house was still vibrating from the applause of an enthusiastic crowd of conservative San Franciscans. It is seldom one hears loud "bravos" in the city by the Golden Gate, but Danny Kaye had taken the city by storm. The audience loved everything he did. They laughed at his imitations, applauded his mimicry and were touched by his songs from *Hans Christian Andersen,* which had not been introduced before.

San Franciscans, accustomed to high standards of performances, expected good entertainment, but this exceeded their expectations and forewarnings. The *San Francisco Chronicle* quoted the British press, which called this young man "the only satisfying idiot in show business in thirty years."

This engagement meant a lot to Danny Kaye. First, he loved the beautiful Bay City in which he had played before as an obscure and unsuccessful vaudevillian. This return saw him as an entertainer who had charmed nations, kings and presidents. But, more important, on this trip he brought Sylvia and Dena with him.

To travel with Danny was not new for Sylvia, his wife. She had toured with him for years as his accompanist, his co-pilot, the discoverer of his fantastic art of scat-singing and the predictor of its success.

But to Dena, the Kayes' five-and-a-half-year-old daughter, this was an unaccustomed and exciting experience, for her parents, very wisely, had sheltered her from the dazzling and dizzy world of the theater with its glitter and false glamour.

And Dena had still another new experience awaiting her. For the first time she was to see her father on the stage. The Kayes were a little apprehensive, a little concerned, for Dena never shared the laughter of the audiences when she saw her father in motion pictures. "I hate it," she said to Danny. "In every movie you are chased, locked up, and made fun of—I don't like it when those people do nasty things to my Daddy."

Danny was nervous. This was like an opening night, or a command performance. He would play before a great and important person—his daughter. What he did was important and how he did it was more important. And Dena's reaction was the most important thing of all.

Dena and her mother, unrecognized by the buzzing, rustling audience, took their seats fifth row center and settled themselves. Sylvia read the program to Dena, who sat very straight and starched in her taffeta pinafore, matching blue bobby-socks and shiny Mary Janes. Occasionally she felt to see if the big white bow was still at a proper angle on the back of her head. The house lights dimmed, the curtain was raised and Sylvia reached for Dena's hand as the anticipatory applause began.

To the majority of the audience it was just a very funny Danny Kaye performance, but those who had seen Danny before noted that he told animal stories, sang about children and confided he was just a "sort of kid" himself.

He worked hard. Kaye was not only Kaye but any number of

other people—a gesticulating conductor who was replaced by a pompous master of ceremonies, and then a speechifying politician, an Italian singing teacher, and a Wagnerian prima donna. He broke into "Minnie the Moocher" and easily lured San Francisco's fur-bedecked society matrons into responding to his directions with weird cries, yodeling, bogus Russian, notes somewhere around high c and nonsense like "ti-ti rereta-dena—tete-ta—reetledee-reetle—beetledeebet—dena." The audience was with him. They loved him and thought his show was wonderful fun.

And all the time his blue eyes moved through the crowd and sought out Dena. What he saw was not a happy sight. In desperation he sang his famous "Deenah, is there anything feenah in the State of Caroleenah?"

"I watched Dena during the performance," said Danny. "She stared wide-eyed while I ran about, waving my arms and twitching my face. When the audience roared with laughter, Dena closed her eyes and clapped her hands over her ears. She could not stand the laughter of the people—but if she only knew how much her Daddy loves that laugher . . ."

Danny, seeing her tears, tried to be funnier, warmer, kinder, but all his efforts were in vain. Dena cried without a sound. There were no audible sobs, no wails, but Dena's cheeks were coursed by huge salty tears. "All through the first part of the show she was impatient to see me perform, but, in spite of our efforts, she wasn't really prepared to see me alone on the stage. And each time the audience laughed, little Dena cried. Her behavior was incredibly good, but she was upset—terribly upset."

Stanton Delaplane, San Francisco's most celebrated columnist and one of America's wittiest, was sitting directly behind Sylvia where he could watch with half-sad, half-amused eyes the drama that was taking place in the audience, in the heart and mind of a little girl who loved her father so much she did not want people to laugh at him. Delaplane, a warmhearted father himself, was a sympathetic observer of the scene.

"Danny," recounts Mr. Delaplane, "came down and sat with his feet dangling over the footlights. He told the matinee audience his daughter was in the house and had never seen him act like this before. He called to her, 'Dena, are you out there, honey?'

"The young lady answered 'yes' in a very small voice. Mr. Kaye asked, 'Do you like the show?'

"Dena said an even smaller 'yes' and promptly burst into tears. The ladies nearby clucked sympathetically."

Danny was miserable. Why could he make everyone but his own daughter laugh? Was this the deadly reaction of a child to a comedian father and a mother who wrote these nonsense songs? The critic he wanted most to please had turned thumbs down. Danny completed his last number. The curtain was lowered and raised, lowered and raised by the demanding applause of a bewitched and enthusiastic audience.

Seconds later a huge crowd invaded Danny's dressing room. They milled about, laughed at incidents remembered from the show, asked endless questions, and offered their congratulations.

But Danny kept waiting for Dena. Where was she? Where was Sylvia?

With a touch of panic, Danny excused himself from his visitors and stepped out on to the empty, half-darkened stage. A slight sound in a corner led him to a sobbing bundle that was his daughter, crying as if her heart would break.

With his arms open he walked toward her, and she flung herself into their embrace. With jumbo tears dropping onto her white blouse-front, she choked out her grief: "They just shouldn't laugh at you."

Sylvia, a tiny, elfin-like woman with beautiful eyes filled with warmth and understanding, had tried to comfort Dena during the performance by explaining "those people" were all her Daddy's friends and their laughter meant his success, but her words had failed. Now Daddy tried his paternal talents.

Danny took her into his dressing room, fighting his way through the crowd and suggesting they leave.

Danny had had enough. He didn't want to hear another word or answer one more question. This afternoon he didn't feel like a funny-man; he wanted to be alone at the Fairmont with Dena and Sylvia. His daughter was tired and upset, and he was exhausted.

The not-too-gentle hints to go home were ignored by the reporters. They hungrily took note of every detail of the scene so they could spread it in the columns for public consumption in the morning papers. They asked more questions . . . and more questions.

Danny whispered something in Dena's ear. Her face lighted, and she laughed for the first time that afternoon. It was a Japanese nursery rhyme the two had rehearsed in the morning.

"You know," said Danny to the crowd in general, as if he were thinking out loud, "I'm not the most patient man in the world, but among the many things Dena has taught me, I have learned it is impossible to be impatient with a child without being cruel. Adults can learn so much more from children than children from adults."

With Dena still in his arms, Danny stood in the center of his dressing room—a good-looking, tired man of thirty-seven, six feet tall, with fair skin, reddish-blond hair that sweeps thickly back from his high forehead. Through his thin dressing gown showed a strong chest, hard arm muscles and legs like steel cables.

And then one of the reporters made the statement that was to stick. Someone in the crowd said, "He is another Al Jolson." Jolson had died at the St. Francis Hotel, only a stone's throw away from the Curran Theater.

San Francisco is a romantic city, and even the hardest of the local reporters has a large part of sentimentality in his soul, so the idea captivated them. They imagined that sparks from the fallen star, Al Jolson, were on the shoulders of Danny Kaye. They wordlessly agreed that Jolson had bestowed his light, talent, genius and kindness on this young man in the very same city where the famed minstrel man had died.

As flattering as the compliment was meant to be, Danny was unwilling to accept comparison with any actor, comedian—or any other man. What did these reporters really know about him?

And by now Danny was ready to fight, if necessary, to get rid of the crowd. He literally pushed the visitors out of the room. One die-hard reporter insisted on a last question: "For my paper may I quote you as saying this first performance for your daughter was the most difficult you have ever played?"

Danny laughed. "It was certainly easier to make the entire frightened audience laugh last night in the middle of an earthquake than it was to get my one little girl to smile today."

"What did you do when the earthquake hit San Francisco last night? Wasn't there panic in the theater?" asked the reporter.

"No," answered Danny innocently, "I told them not to worry . . . it was just a cable car passing by."

II

Kid From Brooklyn

"I DON'T KNOW HOW IT HAPPENED THAT A SKINNY KID NAMED David Daniel Kominsky from a polyglot section of Brooklyn was fortunate enough to become known and liked throughout a sizable portion of the world. Or what good fortune gave me such wonderful friends and family. These answers I will probably never know.

"When I was growing up in the Brownsville section of Brooklyn, the toughest district in all New York, I loved being the neighborhood kid who sang and cut up. I got a great kick out of making people laugh. Later, when I became a professional entertainer, times were often difficult, but the sound of laughter from an audience always made hunger easier to bear."

Danny Kaye knew austerity before he was nine and accepted the conditions of poverty while growing up. To him life never seemed like hardship nor did he feel his plight was tragic. His own immigrant family, the Kominskys, was better off than many of the families in homes which he visited.

The skinny six-year-old knew the warm devotion of a family whose poverty never affected their emotional relationships. A sly glance at the table indicated the state of the family finance, and his father's hearty laughter or tired silence was another barometer. Goose and chicken fats, sprinkled with salt and garlic, were steady fare. They lasted longer than butter.

The Kominsky family lived in one of the typical Brooklyn red brick tenement houses. Mother Kominsky was particularly careful to keep the two long narrow windows overlooking the street spotlessly clean. Apartment on apartment placed side by side and separated by thin walls made the entire block almost a single family. Everyone knew each other, and each tenement window stared into the face of another directly across the street. It was difficult for the young Danny Kaye to know which he should dread more: the stifling heat and humidity of the summers which brought the strong scent of cabbage and gefüllte fish, mingled with the spicy aroma of garlic and onions and Italian cheese; or the winters, when he awakened tired every morning from sleeping under the three heavy cotton-filled comforters in the underheated apartment.

When his neighbor Ryan died, Danny attended the wake; when Mamma Rosa had her sixth child Danny took a home-baked cake to the family; and when old Schmul from Russia moved into their block the boy carried the salt and bread as a welcoming gift so that this Jewish home might never be without it.

In the Kominsky home the kitchen was the center of social affairs. It was here that Pop Kominsky received his guests and read books aloud. It was here they ate during weekdays, and it was here they sang and here they cried.

The Brownsville section of Brooklyn was a jumbled, crowded area which drove kids into the streets. There were narrow, dark alleys filled with garbage cans, empty liquor bottles and old clothes. The kids could play cops and robbers, stage their revolts, learn about sex and plan for their futures—gang wars, great wars and love affairs.

When the United States entered World War I, Danny was four years old. While American soldiers were putting on their khakis, Pop Kominsky shook his head and took his youngest son on his knee, gathered his other two boys around him and said, "War is a terrible thing. We left Russia to be away from wars. Poor people are cannon fodder. Our young men die. Wars never bring peace. War is a monster."

Danny grew up with this philosophy and believed it.

Brownsville was the most poverty-stricken and crime-riddled section in Brooklyn. "Duvidl," as his parents called him, played with all the kids on the block. Many of them were dead-end waifs, and some died later as full-fledged members of "Murder Incorporated" in Sing Sing's death chamber.

The streets of Brownsville served the growing boys as baseball fields, and the lids of gray garbage cans marked the bases during the spring training. The neighborhood children called Danny only "Kominsky." He knew all the kids, but he had very few close friends.

Many of Danny's playmates were constantly on the street, swiping apples from the pushcarts, plaguing shop owners or huddling in small groups scheming plots. Mother Kominsky felt her share of apprehensions. As she looked out of the window she could watch the young boys climbing on the roof tops, scaling lamp posts, clustering in doorways and prowling through deserted buildings. With anxiety she watched them hanging around the musty pool halls. Danny, she knew, was familiar with boys in trouble, but he kept silent. She sensed he was aware of their families' personal and financial problems.

Mother Kominsky prayed, as her youngest son grew up, that he would avoid the bad girls of the neighborhood and find a really fine wife.

Before Buchhalter became one of America's most celebrated killers and panderers, ending his life as the leader of "Murder Incorporated," he was one of the Brownsville kids Danny had played with in the flowerless streets of Brooklyn.

Some of young Danny's acquaintances became a part of the underworld at an early age. In many cases they were trained by their families to be experts in the questionable arts of carrying guns, manipulating lotteries, delivering narcotics and bootleg liquor.

Danny, bewildered, shy and frightened, was introduced to some of his friends' mothers who wavered out of bedrooms in alcoholic hazes, and some of the fathers who at the end of the day's work sat with dulled eyes ripping newspapers into shreds.

Danny had heard of the "shikorim," the "goyim" who were drunk. His first experience was unforgettable. On the floor above lived a struggling artist, Adolph. The two spent many hours together and Danny was happy when his new-found friend permitted him to play with his oils and brushes and palettes. To the youngster the ability to materialize one's own inner thoughts was next to a miracle. Adolph, of course, never had money and always appreciated it when Mother Kominsky invited him to share a scanty boiled beef and potato dinner.

Then came the night when the taxi screeched to a halt in front of the Kominsky door. Danny was sitting on the cement steps outside and saw an angry cab driver push his friend out of the cab. Adolph lay prone on the sidewalk, his nose bleeding and his full lips already taking on the mottled hue of purple grapes.

"Who is going to pay this drunk's fare? Let me at him. I'll find his wallet," shouted the driver.

Danny suddenly felt an unknown power. He simply had to get his friend away from the derisive laughter of the neighborhood adults and kids, had to pay off the noisy driver and get his bleeding friend upstairs to bed.

Almost without thinking he yelled "Mother! Mother! Mother! Come down fast. We need you."

Danny took over. The cab driver was willing to wait until Mother Kominsky got her month's savings out of a marmalade jar while young Danny hoisted, step by step, the destitute artist up the stairs and lifted him onto the unmade bed. After taking off Adolph's shoes and wiping his face with cold water Danny slowly went downstairs, peered through the door into his mother's kitchen and found her ironing his and his brother's clothes. She looked over her left shoulder and gave Danny a smile of approval.

Against such a depressing background Danny began to dream about the great things he was going to do when he grew up and how he would help his family to get out of this poor and gloomy neighborhood.

David Daniel Kominsky was born in New York on January 18, 1913. His parents had immigrated with their two young sons, Larry and Mac from Ekaterinoslav in Russia. They spoke not a single word of English when their small ship docked in Brooklyn harbor. There, on the wharf of the East River, Jakob Kominsky, a horse dealer from czarist Russia, stood with his awed wife, Clara, and their two small children, greeted only by two relatives.

The day the Kominskys landed in New York was never forgotten by the family. Mother Kominsky's account became legendary, and each time it was told she added further embellishments:
"Jakob was holding my hand very tight—so tight it hurt. 'Look,
Mama,' he said, 'this is the Statue of Liberty. This sight I wanted
to see all my life. It means you, the children and I are safe. No one
will harm a Jew in this country.' It all sounded very fine, but I was
scared. I had never seen such tall buildings, so much traffic, so
many people. The children were crying, and all I was wondering
was where we would sleep that night. But Jakob was sure the
streets of New York were plastered with gold. I held on to my boys
and prayed."

Most of the family money had been spent for passage. They
found a small apartment with other immigrants in Brownsville.
Jakob found a job sewing saddlebags, eventually graduated to sewing corsets and, slowly but surely, worked himself into a secure
but scarcely lucrative position in New York's garment industry.

Clara Kominsky met many other mothers in the neighborhood
who had not yet learned to speak English. Yiddish, Russian and
a smattering of Italian were the dominant languages in this crowded
tenement district where the old European customs and dress were
still very much alive.

Brooklyn seemed kind and comfortable to the newcomers. It
promised a new life to be paid for by hard work. For Clara and
Jakob their cold-water flat seemed far better than their small home
in Russia where every rap on the door could mean either a friend
or the agents of a vicious, anti-Semitic pogrom.

America, the promised land, had been reached.

From Clara's standpoint, as she gazed out the narrow windows
of her new Brooklyn apartment, the streets appeared to be tre-
mendously wide, and if she peered to the left she saw the rounded
top of a synagogue and if she craned her neck to the right she could
see the lofty spires of a church.

Clara and Jakob were determined to build their own gracious
island in the land where houses of worship could stand peacefully
side by side.

Jakob Kominsky felt the sanctity of his new household and held
firmly to his Russian-Jewish traditions. In the gray of the morning

during the leaden winter months he crept silently into the cold kitchen to pray to his Maker and to give his thanks. Summer was not different, as far as his living schedule was concerned, except it was more difficult because of the enervating humidity.

Every Friday at four o'clock Jakob Kominsky put away his needles and spools of thread and mentally closed his ears to the grinding noise of the subway which took him from Manhattan's garment district to Brownsville. He gave a smile of approval when he entered his home and saw his three boys, each ready to receive the Sabbath. Jakob, a kindly man, kissed his wife on the brow and washed his hands while chanting his "brochah."

Danny remembers to this day his mother's gleaming white linen table cloth and her gentle beauty as she leaned over to light the seven candles of the "Menorah." In meager weeks the Sabbath meal consisted only of gefüllte fish and the traditional "Challeh," which Jakob had to break first, saying his prayers before the family was allowed to eat. The Sabbath was always a close family affair. Jakob looked forward to prayers at "schul," and he expected his sons to accompany him there. Saturday nights were party nights filled with laughter, music and dancing, half-Russian folk dances, half-American fox-trots. Mother Kominsky knew most of the songs. She had the musical ear in the house. Tailor Kominsky led the festivities, for he possessed a strong love of life, a deep appreciation of music, an inborn sense of rhythm and a great gusto for humor. Danny anticipated with pleasure the end of each week and remembers "there were always enough potatoes and whisky to go around."

Danny Kaye's success can only be understood if X-rayed on the screen of his background and religious philosophies, the humility needed to be a good Jew.

Mother Kominsky, a devout Jewess, had come to America to find freedom from religious persecution. But she still lived in her all-Jewish world, and it seemed so strange to her that Danny could be at home in a neighbor's house where they washed down a bite of meat with a gulp of milk and even dared to serve ham and other "trefe" food. Danny had also gone to a Protestant wedding reception when Pa Miller, two doors down, gave his daughter away.

But Danny had his quota of uncomfortable experiences, too.

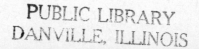

Some of his playmates were gentiles and, one afternoon in the heat of anger, called him the nastiest things they could think of: "Christ killer" and "kike." Danny ran home in tears to ask his mother, "Why did they do it? Aren't they my friends? And Jesus, wasn't he a Jew, too?"

His mother wrapped him up in her skirts and told stories of old Russia where life was much more difficult. "In Russia," she said, "Jews were not insulted. They were killed."

Danny fought back but was often beaten up by other kids.

Each time he brought home a purple eye he felt not only anger, but his own weakness. There were times when he wondered if he were a "sissy," who couldn't fight well enough to get the respect of the other kids.

Jakob Kominsky was sensitive to his son's thoughts and problems. Danny, his skinny, carrot-topped, long-nosed son, was a susceptible creature to be carefully nurtured. Jakob hoped his boy would learn to use his hands, his brains, . . . to be an American boy.

One night after an alley skirmish there was an abrupt rap on the door. Mac, the oldest Kominsky son, opened the door to find a delegation of three boys. "Sorry we hit your brother. Can we talk to him?"

Not waiting for an answer the three boys pushed their way through the small living room and blustered into the kitchen where Danny was silently eating his soup. Without greeting the parents they stood back a pace, their hands on their hips. The spokesman issued the pronouncement: "I just talked to Father O'Brien, and I guess you guys didn't kill Christ after all.

"Bring your mitt. We are having a game in front of Mrs. Kowalsky's house."

On the next Sabbath Father Kominsky philosophized. Through the closed windows came the distant rumble of wagon wheels, the yelling of noisy and impatient mothers and the faint tinny tunes of an organ grinder.

That night Jakob and Clara invited one of the old and learned rabbis from Ekaterinoslav and described, in front of Danny, the entire scene when the kids had burst in with their apologies. The rabbi, still dressed in his "Kaftan" garb, with long black beard and the "payes," the ear curls hanging down at his temples, looked at all three sons and said slowly, as if he wanted to underline each of his Yiddish words: "You are living on a small Jewish island. You, Duvidl, have just discovered a larger island. Always remember that the larger the island, the longer the shore line of learning. Man is never limited to the tiny island of his own ego. The spirit of forgiving is the elemental bond which binds man to his Creator."

III

Kominsky Island

IF A MODERN PSYCHIATRIST ATTEMPTED TO ANALYZE THE YOUTH
of Danny Kaye he would look back to a warm September day in
1919 when Clara Kominsky put on her best black silk dress, to
take her scrawny big-eared boy to school. It was with some hesita-
tion that she approached the double doors with their frightening
appearance of authority. "Duvidl" hung back. He could not understand all the words, the forms, the business that was going on.

Clara Kominsky was lost in the registration office, and Danny
was equally lost in the new world of rules and discipline.

Danny was pushed into a line and found himself the tallest boy
with the narrowest shoulders in the group. He felt his ears were
waving like butterfly wings.

That day, uncomfortable as it was, was Danny's first totally
American contact. His family still spoke only Yiddish at home
and had preserved all the Russian-Jewish customs.

But he was not alone. His first-grade teacher had come from
immigrant stock herself, a bright-eyed Scandinavian who asked the
class to excuse her, if she made errors in speech, because she had
not spoken a single word of English until six years before when she
immigrated from Oslo.

A new era was beginning in America. Women had won the
right to vote, and a new crop of teachers with high ideals and great

hope for an era of brotherhood and peace held forth in the class-rooms.

Some of Danny's teachers were determined to help this young boy who came from a non-English-speaking home. They remember him as a shy, quiet, intelligent boy who looked lost and tiny in his older brother's hand-me-down clothes. "In the classroom," remembers one teacher, "David was good as gold, but on the playground he would break out with the most ridiculous antics, making funny faces to the great amusement of the older boys whom he was trying to attract. Even we teachers were often convulsed by his nonsense, but none of us ever dreamed that frail, white-faced boy would become a world-known comedian."

Another of his teachers commented that Danny's subtle humor was well developed when he was seven. "The last day of school," she tells, "I asked a prissy little girl what she was planning to do during the summer vacation. Linda, in a snobbish tone, said she was 'going to camp and ride on a horse and fish.' David's blue eyes twinkled, pulled up into triangles with amused wrinkles at the corners and he said to me in a loud aside, 'Say, how do you think she'll look on a fish?' None of the children got the joke, but I nearly collapsed."

Laughingly the teacher remembers how she had dropped a full jar of paint. "It broke and spattered red muck over floor, desk legs—and me. I stood there, wanting to walk out of the room and never come back. David grinned, went for the mop and shot back over his shoulder, 'Teacher, don't you wonder sometimes why you are a teacher?' That was all it took to roll the clouds of anger away. David and I cleaned up the awful mess."

From the anecdotes told by all the people who remember Danny's early days at school one can paint a portrait of a sensitive, shy youngster who entered a new world with some fears and uneasiness. He wanted to be liked, but wasn't quite sure how to achieve affection. The girls made fun of his red mop of hair and gangling arms. The boys admired the class members who were sent to the principal's office for misconduct and those who could fight the toughest on the way home from school. Danny was not popular. He could fight—as a matter of protection—but he basically didn't like roughness and was often licked by the more rugged boys his own age. Then, too, Danny as a child was skinny, disjointed, topped by a wad of pinkish-orange hair. It took him some time to grow to fit his long, dangling hands, his oversized white ears, long nose and kangaroo feet.

The psychiatrist would never miss the scarecrow effect young Danny Kaye made. His older brothers' hand-me-down coats floated like a cloak about him as he walked. His father's remade shirts flopped around his neck like an unfastened noose.

Danny spent many after-school hours in the house, following his mother through her household duties and listening to her sing old Russian folk tunes. Soon Danny knew the songs by heart, and often surprised his father at the Saturday night parties by breaking into a solo.

Danny Kaye the adult would likely tell his psychiatrist of the times when he helped his mother clean the house, scrub the floors, polish the silver and dust the furniture. He would probably confide that Clara's meticulousness has been an influence in his life. He would remember the afternoons when she carefully washed the old elegant pieces of Meissen and Dresden porcelain, bought at the pawn shop around the corner, and dusted the secondhand piano.

Mother Kominsky's goal was to send her three sons to college. She felt strongly that they should be doctors or lawyers. At any rate they should be more important people in America than their parents.

As Danny grew up, his mother never relaxed her vigil. She insisted that her sons listen to her. She told Danny what to wear, supervised his manners and code of behavior and required an accounting of every hour of the day and evening.

She inquired about his school work, what he saw in the streets and in the park, whom he visited and what he did. She gave advice and oversaw his lessons. She told him with whom to associate, whom to avoid and warned him about the questionable boys and girls in the neighborhood. Clara Kominsky, however, was convinced she never dictated to Danny. She thought she merely advised.

"Mother was a wise woman," says Danny Kaye.

Mother Kominsky was more interested in Danny's being a great man, noble, learned, profound, kind and gracious, than in his being a rich man. She saw in Danny a dreamer. Matriarch that she was, Clara prayed her youngest son would fulfill her own dreams.

"As a kid, I was scarcely the model for a well-behaved child, but I wasn't really bad either. For instance, as a teenager I was the kind of guy who stood behind the guy who whistled at the girls," he remembers.

Scholastically, David did only fairly well. He was intelligent, and profited from the maturity of his older brothers and the painstaking care given by his father and mother.

Danny comments, "I had a fly-paper mind, but also a loving and understanding home. My parents always encouraged me. They were wise people in handling kids. And after Mom died, Pop dedicated his life to bringing up my two brothers and me. He was a great man who always understood me emotionally and let me grow in my own way. In later years he never opposed my career, which must have often seemed foolish and impractical to him.

"On the other hand," continues Danny, "Dad was a great comic himself, so maybe I'm just a little splinter off a great block. One of the things I remember as a kid was the night Pop took out the dog for a walk. A few minutes later he came in looking as if Rockefeller had just given him a ten-dollar gold piece, and proudly announced, 'You should have seen the big mutt. Is he smart? The minute I took him out, he made a beehive for the lamp post.' "

What sort of man was Jakob Kominsky? A rare man with great loyalties and limitless faith in his sons.

Father Kominsky was never forced to face the great abyss which so often yawns between American-born sons and their immigrant parents.

The first American-born generation tends to move toward American patterns and customs and is often sharp and aggressive toward its parents' European past. In the case of Danny Kaye, there appears never to have been that abrupt chasm of misunderstanding between father and son.

Perhaps Danny never fully comprehended his father's often exaggerated Jewishness but he felt the warmth and sanctity of his home life. Danny was always aware of a deep respect for his father and an enormous love which he could not always understand, nor which he wished to analyze.

After each day's hard work Father Kominsky dug out old, dilapidated books from a bundle still wrapped in yellowed Russian newspapers. Danny would watch him sit down and pore over the pages until fatigue finally closed his eyes. The young impressionable boy developed an acute respect for books.

Danny understood his father's frequent weariness, for on many occasions, as a special treat, he was permitted to meet his dad on Friday in the bustling, teeming, exciting garment district on Manhattan's east side.

One of the witnesses to this close relationship, Dr. Irving Somach, a lifetime friend and doctor of the Kominskys, reminisces, "I watched those two for many years, and sometimes I actually thought old man Kominsky was funnier than Danny. Several times I saw Danny rolling on the floor of my office, holding his sides with laughter at some of his father's cracks.

"The old man always spoke Yiddish because it was easier for him. Once when father and son came into the office, I asked Mr. Kominsky if he had a headache. He looked at me with a bit of bewilderment, then glanced at Danny and answered dryly, 'Doesn't everyone have a headache—somewhere?'

"Danny was absolutely convulsed.

"Of course," continues Dr. Somach, "in the early years no one knew Danny would go so far in the world, but it was very impressive to me that even after Danny had gained prestige, the two men, father and son, continued to make their visits together for check-ups, pills and just for talk. Danny would do anything for his father, and vice versa.

"Toward the end of Mr. Kominsky's life, we had to remove part of his stomach. Danny sent him to Florida to recuperate, but they stopped by my office for a final examination. I commented to Mr. Kominsky, 'Within a month you can eat anything again—even nails with catsup.'

"Danny's father snapped back to me: 'Dr. Somach, I despise catsup!'

"And again Danny was laughing with gusto. Yes, he was fortunate to have had such a father!"

While Danny may be remembered by his teachers as a retiring boy, his late father remembered with a chuckle his son's first public appearance as an entertainer, at the age of four. The scene was a busy, crowded Brooklyn shoe store. Danny was sitting well back in a worn leather chair with his legs stretched out straight in front of him, when suddenly, for no apparent reason, he leaped into the seat and began to sing a silly, incoherent ditty called "Fifty Fifty." The startling rendition in his shrill little voice caused a complete panic. Customers gathered round, laughed and applauded, but the clerks, failing to appreciate the fact they were witnessing the premiere performance of the great Danny Kaye, patted him soothingly on his carrot-top and emphatically nudged him to the door and onto the street with admonitions to wait outside. But Danny knew his performance had been a success.

Danny's second, and this time authorized, performance came when he was in kindergarten at P.S. 149 in Brooklyn. "I did my first bit of real acting on a school stage," he reminisces. "I had the magnificent and illustrious role of a pickaninny, representing a seed in a big slice of watermelon. I was somewhat dubious about the success of my role, for at that moment my hair was uncompromisingly red and my ears snowy white. The teachers told me I did quite well and that scarcely anyone noticed that the third pickaninny from the end in the last row had red hair and white ears."

Once when Danny joined a handful of Brownsville kids for a rare and eventful trip to the Barnum and Bailey circus Danny became lost in the crowd. When one of his companions finally found him, Danny was staring, as if under the spell of hypnosis, at the gaudy posters on the side of a candy stand. It was as if he were completely absorbed by the courageous animal trainer, dressed in his immaculate tight white trousers, whip in hand, facing the bank of three ferocious lions. The next picture showed an exquisite young wasp-waisted lady reaching for an elusive trapeze bar. The last poster showed the sad face of the circus' most famous clown.

His friend Mike pointed to the clown, "That is what I would like to be."

Danny didn't answer. He didn't want to be an acrobat, a clown or anything in the circus. His mother had told him so many times he should be a doctor or a lawyer. He had to be someone of importance. He liked the idea of being a physician, a doctor to help all people: Dr. Kominsky.

So the years rolled by for Danny on the Kominsky island in Brooklyn. He attended Thomas Jefferson High School and found baseball, basketball and swimming were sports well adapted to his lean, lengthening frame. He worked hard at sports knowing that, while he would never be an outstanding football player like Johnny Mack Brown, he should make use of every muscle in his body. The hours in the gym and on the field helped him to build sinewy strength, and developed his inordinately fine coordination and sense of timing. During one period he was sorely tempted to join the school's dance class but reconsidered on the grounds that the other teenagers would call him a "sissy."

His grades still fluctuated from B's to D's and Mother Kominsky wrung her hands with worry each time examinations neared.

When Clara fretted about Danny's academic achievements Pop Kominsky would pat her affectionately and say, "Duvidl is a good boy. He has a good voice. He will do well as a 'chasen' [cantor] in the temple. His sense of humor will always help him over the hurdles of life."

The financial problems of the family had not diminished with the passage of time. As a matter of fact, the Depression had added severe strains.

Songs and love and fun and laughs and friends kept the adolescent boy healthy and content.

But Danny's fourteenth birthday was filled with a new uneasiness. It was not that he knew anything was wrong—he received his usual quota of presents; he cut the customary chocolate cake his mother had baked for him; but he noticed the weary stoop in Clara's body and deepening lines on her face. For three days in a row she had stayed in bed until eight in the morning, a time far too late for his energetic mother to arise.

A week later her strength appeared to have completely dissolved. She spent even more time in bed. Coming from school each day Danny found her rocking in front of the window looking at nothing in particular.

She tired easily from the effort of cleaning and dusting. The three boys took over the chores. No longer did Danny hear her hitting the old yellow keys of the upright piano. Clara moved to the chaise longue in the front room.

Jakob was silent. It was as if the five of them were in a secret pact not to admit what each one knew.

The night Clara Kominsky died the block was palled in gloom and busy with action. Everyone remembered what the wise, stout little woman had done for him or her. Mrs. O'Brien hurried to the house with food for the boys and sent her husband for the priest; Mrs. Miller came in to do the laundry; Mrs. Riskin had called for the rabbi and came to give feminine comfort to the paralyzed sons.

Jakob was in a helpless world of his own. Within a short time his nine best friends gathered for the "minjon," wearing their "jamakes" (skull caps) and "talles" (prayer shawls) and prayed . . . prayed . . . prayed.

Danny's mouth was dry. He tried to swallow but knew he couldn't. He lived through a vacuous, detached daze. It was only after the funeral that Danny could hide himself and cry.

IV

This World Is a Difficult Place

THE FIRST FRIDAY NIGHT AFTER CLARA KOMINSKY'S DEATH, JAKOB said the blessings and greeted the gentle angel who entered his home on the wings of the Sabbath.

"Whatever happens to us," he told his three sons, "in this family the Sabbath is the Sabbath. We'll observe it as we always have. Your mother would have wanted it that way."

Jakob filled the silver cup with wine, saying his prayers as he glanced up. It seemed to the three boys that their father prolonged the ritual as if in a vague hope his wife would materialize before him and take the empty chair at the foot of the table.

With a nervous rap on the table, the master of the house brought an end to the ceremonies, declared the blessings of the Lord for the meal and served his oldest son the soup and chicken Mrs. Kowalsky had prepared.

Danny was first to leave the table. An uncomfortable feeling had overwhelmed him. It was not until the next day that he could tell his father the leading question in his mind.

"Look, Pop, people like us are poor. We never have enough money to pay the rent without worrying about it. I have watched you work, day after day, in the sweatshop, coming home tired and worried. I want to make money, too. When I bring my first pay check home, I'll celebrate the Shabbes with you."

Pop Kominsky had nothing to say. In his mind he felt his

Duvidl's statement was close to heresy but an inner voice seemed to say his son was wishing to fill, in some way, the gap made by the loss of a beloved wife and mother.

Mac and Larry were earning money. It was only natural that David Kominsky wanted to help, too.

For one of the few times in his life, Pop Kominsky didn't tell his sons where he was going. He slowly descended the steps of the house onto the littered pavement of the street, threaded his way through the crowds of kids, oblivious of their shrill laughter and shouts, and walked meditatively to the brown doors of Rabbi Rosenzweig's one-family home.

"I want to thank you for my wife's funeral. I wished I could have paid you more but I'm a poor man. Our house is empty now without Clara but filled with many great problems. My boys are wonderful young men, but Duvidl, the youngest one—he refuses to accept the shabbes until he can pay for its food. He wants to quit school, and I fear he may also want to leave our home."

Rabbi Rosenzweig, long schooled in listening to the problems of his flock, said nothing. Rising from his old leather chair, he went to the samovar and poured two cups of tea.

"I want my boys to have a college education. I work overtime three days a week but the money won't stretch that far. Many times I feel I have failed them. In some ways I've lost Mac and Larry anyway. They are out to make money, but I don't want to lose Duvidl. Not now."

The rabbi put a spoon full of varenja (jam) into each cup of tea, nodding his head constantly as he listened, and after a pause said, "Slow down. Nothing is new. I have known your family since you came from Russia. I was there when Danny was born; I heard you say the death prayer for your own wife. Keep your boys with you and close to you. Try to understand Duvidl. It is always hardest for the youngest one. If Duvidl wants to go out to the big wide world, let him. Don't stop him but always keep the door open. Wherever Danny goes, whatever he does, he will always come back."

That night Danny heard his father praying from the Book of Psalms, chanting the old familiar Hebrew "Hear my prayer, oh Lord and let me cry unto thee. . . ."

After the shock had worn off, young Danny was determined more than ever to stand on his own feet, to do something, anything or everything.

He had developed definite views of life and money, Jewishness and his own future. There were nights when he tried to organize his philosophy. But he felt the first thing he, as a human being, had to do was to earn money. A person, he reasoned, must be independent at the age of fourteen, even without knowing a profession. If one earns money, the outlook on life will automatically be more cheerful. One lives and should help others live. One can cut out his feelings of inferiority when one does not have to ask others for favors.

At fourteen Danny was an individualist. The teen-age Danny Kaye had many problems, not only about material things like money, the gas bill and his father's health but also about religious and philosophical questions.

Why has God divided people into Jews and Catholics? Protestants and Buddhists? Why has He allowed people to be separated instead of united? Why does He permit wars and poverty? Why the jealousies among the denominations and races?

Danny decided the rich were never jealous, only the poor. There should be a way out, so that the Kominsky men would never be poor again. If he had money, he speculated, he would not only be independent but his father would have the things he needed. The family would not live in the Brownsville tenement district; would not count forebodingly the days until the coming of the landlord.

Jobs were scarce, but Danny finally secured employment as a messenger boy for a dentist, Dr. Samuel Fine. The fourteen-year-old liked the tools of dentistry, the antiseptically clean office with its spotless white linens and porcelain bowls. The idea of lessening people's pains appealed to him, and Clara's desire for him to be a doctor kept swimming through his mind. It was a proud Friday when Danny thrust his few coins into Jakob's hand and bowed his head for the evening prayer.

As fourteen-year-olds go, Danny was too inquisitive and too ambitious. Often, to the annoyance of Dr. Fine, Danny hung around by the hour watching the skillful dentist at work, peering into the open mouths of suffering patients and asking endless medical and dental questions. Often, as Danny raced in and out of the office, he did not notice the bright-eyed, petite, teen-age dentist's daughter in the reception room.

It was really creativeness that brought an end to Danny's job as Dr. Fine's errand-boy. One day the doctor found David making a sort of needlepoint design on a piece of wood with a dental drill. David was fired on the spot.

Combined factors intensified the natural restlessness of the teenager. Money problems, the loss of his mother, the routine of a dull high school curriculum made Danny desperate for excitement, new experience, new faces, new ideas, new vistas. He says of this period: "I found my yearning for adventure more powerful than my zest for learning, so I departed abruptly for Florida with another boy. We started out with $1.50 and returned with $7.00!"

Danny and his friend, Louis Eisen, had crashed into Florida's resort places and, like gypsy troubadours, entertained anyone who would listen to them. Danny sang with Louis' guitar accompaniment any nonsense that came into his head. The people were pleasant, the weather warm, and the boys came back with some money, more than they had taken with them. All in all, the Florida trip was a satisfactory adventure.

Danny did not return to high school. But what job could he find now? He had no high school diploma, no qualifications, and the grown men who stood ahead of him in the employment lines were husbands and fathers with much more appealing cases than his.

"And times were tough in those days of the Depression," he said many years later. "I remember when I was seventeen I had only one wish. I wanted to buy an apartment house in Brooklyn, collect the rent myself—just so I could say 'Thank you' to the tenants, whether they could pay that month or not."

His only talent was the ability to make people laugh, and laughter was a scarce commodity in the Brooklyn tenement buildings. One day Danny joined the local "social club" which put on theatricals. He formed a harmony team with his traveling companion, Louis Eisen. Encouraged by the enthusiasm of the entertainment-starved local Brooklynites, Danny and Louis took their act to a small radio station, WBBC. It seemed as if, at last, the pair was going to make the grade. But a program needs a sponsor, a rare benefactor during the Depression era. The great idea folded and became a mere memory.

Danny was not starving, but he wasn't eating very well either. He knew he needed a substantial, long-term job. Even if it did not pay a great deal, a weekly pay check would help the family and might make it possible for him to go back to high school and later to college for a medical degree.

So Danny cinched up his belt and explored the mysteries of chocolate syrups, carbonated water, banana splits and dirty dishes.

"For a time I worked as a soda jerk," shudders Danny, "a job which I loathed and from which I was soon, shall we say, relieved. Then I worked for the long period of ten months as an automobile appraiser."

This endeavor finished Danny in the business world. He wandered up and down the long rows of cars, making recommendations and appraisals until he had lost the staggering total of forty thousand dollars for the insurance company. Danny says, "I was shadowed for months by two Pinkerton detectives hired by the company to establish my sabotage scheme. After a while the dicks and I got quite chummy. In fact, when we all got tired of loafing around, those nice guys used to take me to the movies."

Danny spent many uncomfortable hours facing hearings and accusations at the company office. No one could believe that anyone was so naïve, so inexperienced with money matters, so much a dreamer as to make such a series of costly mistakes. The officials were sure his innocence was an act.

Years later Danny received a letter from the president of the insurance company: "I saw your act at the Riviera Club and enjoyed it very much. Back when you cost us that forty thousand dollars I thought you were either a thief or a nitwit. It never occurred to me you were a comedian and just didn't possess a mathematical mind."

Danny continues, "For weeks after I was fired from the insurance job, in my dreams I saw columns of figures, per cent marks, dollar signs and decimal points. I'd wake up in a sweat and swear to myself that never again would I get involved with business. Even if I had to starve, I would be an entertainer."

He went from door to door, from secretary to secretary, from agent to agent. It was evident he had talent, ambition and enormous energy, but he was unpolished, untrained and had no definite or organized act to show the agents who sat behind their littered desks.

Each agent asked him the same sort of questions: "What can you do?"

"I'm an entertainer."

"What kind of entertainer? Can you sing?"

"Well, no. I'm not exactly a singer. To be honest I can't read a note."

"Are you a dancer?"

"Well, not exactly," Danny would grin and shift in his chair. "You see, I've never had a dancing lesson in my life."

"Are you a comedian?" was the next exasperated question.

"I guess I can't say I am. I've never told a joke on a stage. As a matter of fact, I've never been on a stage—outside of high school, that is."

Then all the agents said the same thing: "Come back in five years," and the interviews were finished.

Sometimes Danny was thrust into the pit of discouragement, and during these depressed periods he often slept until noon in order to shorten the hopeless days of job hunting and rejections. His father never uttered a word of criticism and admonished Larry and Mac, "Leave Duvidl alone. He will find himself one day."

Danny wanted to please people, wanted to be wanted, yearned for even a second-rate chance to show what he could do with his songs. But his auditions were poor, since it was painfully obvious that he lacked a style of his own, a hallmark of his personality.

To his father, Danny bitterly commented, "If I were drowning, those people would throw me a glass of water!" And Pop Kominsky wondered what he could do to help.

"The rest of the family did not know it," says Danny, "but every week or so my father would come into my bedroom and put five or ten bucks under my pillow. There was never a comment from my brothers that I should be working, but they both had jobs, and I know what they must have been thinking."

Viewing the situation as "hopeless but not desperate," he moved into the summer camps and resort hotels in New York's Catskill Mountains called "Borscht Circuit." For four summers he combined the jobs of waiter, singer, juvenile lead, character actor, villain, comic and all-round fool. "In this capacity I amused the paying guests by often falling into the swimming pool—fully clothed, straw hat and all."

In answer to his father's inquiry, "What do you really do in these hotels?" Danny answered, "I'm helping the hotel manager to prevent the bored guests from moving out on rainy days."

"How do you do that?" his father wanted to know.

"It isn't easy," he laughed. "We play games, entertain, and, when the going is rough, Louis and I chase each other through the halls with meat cleavers and make a final graceful lunge into the fish pond."

Danny did anything for a laugh at these resort places, but it was all worthwhile if that laugh came from his audience.

In the language of the entertainment world, Danny was a "toomler," a fellow who keeps the hotel's guests from getting bored with their bridge playing, dieting and nature viewing. The occupational hazard of being a toomler is an empty stomach during the winter months, when the resorts are closed. And despite Kaye's efforts to save money during the season and to land theatrical winter work in New York City, each spring found him counting both his vanishing reserve of money and the days until the hotels would open their doors to the leisured class and to his unleisured antics.

Danny's first job as part of the entertainment staff on the Borscht Circuit was at White Roe Lake in New York State. The year was 1933; Danny was twenty years old and learning his trade the hard way. He appeared in a play a week, entertained at breakfast, lunch and dinner and rehearsed the next week's program until the small hours of the morning. But Danny was getting the feel of people, learning the tricks of turning a sophisticated crowd into a grinning group and enjoying his experiments in the delicate art of producing laughter.

Since Danny had stumbled and fumbled into show business without ever attending a drama, theatrical or dancing school, he stood off stage intently analyzing the other acts. Now the role of the clown became increasingly interesting to him. He watched the vaudevillians with their slapstick humor and noted that slipping pants, pie throwing and awkward falls were sure fire for laughter.

On one occasion he was on the same bill with Eddie Cantor and learned from Eddie that audiences love the comedian who has fun entertaining.

Danny, like Douglas Fairbanks, Sr., Buster Keaton and, later, Burt Lancaster and Yul Brynner, became intrigued with the great art of acrobatics and continued to train his muscles in the neighborhood gymnasium.

During his first year as a performer the thing that mattered most was the laughter of audiences. Again and again he said to himself, "People are laughing—at me." It was the greatest thing that ever happened to him.

Although twenty-one by now, Danny had not fallen in love. There had been a little Catholic girl who wore her hair in long braids, and who was not permitted to play with him on Sunday, and the little Jewish girl, Muriel, who moved with her family to Manhattan's First Avenue. But the romances were never deep or long-lived. Danny's romantic life flickered in the breeze of greater problems and was usually blown out by the strong winds of reality.

Danny's world had been a man's world of the dead-end kids in Brooklyn. Now, suddenly, as a greenhorn performer, he found himself surrounded by women. Many of them were really beautiful; some, alluring; most of them sophisticated show people. Almost all were much older than Danny. He accepted them as associates rather than girl friends.

In the Catskills one of the acts was performed by a typical family group. The mother, Mrs. Brown, had aged from years of travel and saw in Danny a kind of son she had never possessed. She grew fond of him and spread her wings, giving advice and explaining the ropes of the trade.

The night the Brown family closed at the hotel, Mrs. Brown called Danny to her dressing room. She handed him a glass of brandy. Slugging down a jolt herself, she said: "Danny my boy, get out of this lousy work. You would never guess it, but I was trained to be a Shakespearean actress. One of the most important lines the great bard ever wrote was, 'This above all—to thine own self be true; and it must follow, as the night the day, thou canst not then be false to any man.' "

The quote was stronger than the brandy. For several years Danny had been thinking about his family, first. If the wise man Shakespeare was right, he had to follow his own star. He knew then and there he would not leave the thing he wanted most: to make people laugh.

Two weeks later the acts had disbanded for the summer. The cool September evenings in the altitude of the Catskills were sending the resort guests back to their homes in New York, Philadelphia, Pittsburgh and other eastern cities. Danny was once again unemployed. The same story for four long years. On again-off again—never a full-time job. And once again he must move back to Brownsville to live with his father. As he packed his battered suitcase, folded his too-tight coat, he realized how much he dreaded returning. He wanted to stand on his own feet.

By now the Depression had hit the world a crippling blow and was grinding its fist into the abdomen of America.

Pop Kominsky was no longer a young man. Older workers felt the insecurities of the Depression days and nights. Fortunately, although the working conditions of the garment workers were abominable, Jakob's factory had not, as yet, been closed.

Waiting for his dad on a late October Friday night, Danny remembered his vivid childhood impressions of the garment industry. Pop was still working at the same place, treadling the same sewing machine and he, Danny Kaye, was still basically unemployed in spite of his brief summer jobs as a toomler. Pop Kominsky was still paid by the piece and not by the hour, and the payment for his labor was even lower than before.

Danny, tired of waiting in the crisp October air, decided to take the elevator up to meet his father and to say hello to some of his old friends, perhaps even Mr. Silverstein, the manager.

The crowded building harbored six factories, one on a floor, and on the remaining five floors was a conglomerate mixture of distributing agencies dealing in a wide variety of salable items such as oranges, leather belts, plastic jewelry, millinery, cheap perfumes and secondhand magazines. Thousands of people were the human cargo on the grumbling elevator day after day.

When Danny entered the big working room where his father was putting away his work, he watched the antlike workers busily scuttling between the tall toppling bales of woolens, cambrics, cottons and unopened boxes of thread. No new equipment had been added to the factory since Danny first remembered it. Each cutting table was still dimly lighted by a single, naked, fly-specked light bulb. The cutters, using heavy shears for woolens and cottons and razor-edged knives for silks and taffetas, were the most important people in the business. Supervisors watched their process of production. But Jakob had never learned the art of cutting expensive materials.

Danny had always been proud when the workers said his dad was the fastest man behind the sewing machines in the entire factory. "Sewing corsets is very difficult and it is amazing how many pieces he can turn out in a day."

From the cutting and sewing room, Danny used to peek into the fitting section. He saw the many bleak girl-employees fitting corsets and dresses on the headless asbestos dummies. He watched with interest as they folded the materials, made the fashionable draped skirts of that period.

But the air was always like a Turkish bath. The escaping steam from the broken radiators mingled acridly with the billows of moisture from dozens of pressing irons. The factory was oppressively hot even during the coldest days of winter but was unendurable in summer. Men were stripped to their waists and perspiration showed through the women's thin blouses. The smell of garlic, fish, onions, cabbage and sauerkraut was difficult to bear. The sweatshop was an intermingling of body odors.

There were the newcomers from Naples and Sicily, and the women who told in Yiddish of the cold in Siberia and the tortures of Galicia. There were the young girls working to support their families and dreaming of the time when they could save enough for a dowry. All were underpaid. The turnover was great, but Jakob sat behind his machine with his five Russian and Polish

Jewish co-workers, and staying on uncomplainingly, sewing his days away.

Jakob Kominsky glanced up and with a smile spotted his favorite son in the doorway: "Hello, I'm almost ready to leave. Be with you in five minutes." Danny waited amid the machines and tables, shook hands with his father's co-workers, who brightened when they recognized the man, now an entertainer, whom they had known as a small boy. They asked him the usual stereotyped questions—if he were now on the road to his second million; would he give them free passes for his first Broadway show; and how did it feel to be a star. There were the usual commonplaces of "My, how you have grown!" and "I remember you when you were just so high."

Danny was joking with his father's old friends when Mr. Silverstein came up to greet him. "I still think you should join our company," Mr. Silverstein said. "Jobs are not easy to get nowadays. Don't be carried away by dreams of Broadway and the movies. After all, you have to come from the old country to be another Joseph Schildkraut."

Danny smiled. "I thank you once again for your offer, Mr. Silverstein, but I do not want to be a Schildkraut—just Danny Kaye."

On the subway, Pop Kominsky was engrossed in reading *Forward,* the Yiddish newspaper. Danny's mind flashed once again to the scene, a half-dozen years ago, when Mr. Silverstein had made his first offer.

Mr. Silverstein, the brother-in-law of the big boss, took Danny inside the narrow cubicle which he called his office. "Now, how do you like it here? Isn't this a wonderful business? Two hundred people work here. Wouldn't you like to own a place like this sometime? What about starting young? I'll teach you. We like young Americans and your father would be proud of you, too. See all these young girls."

Danny smiled, stupefied, nodded his head and answered, "Thank you for your kindness, Mr. Silverstein. I'll have to talk it over with Dad."

On the same subway home Danny recounted his conversation with Mr. Silverstein. But Pop Kominsky refused to comment. "This is Sabbath. We do not talk business on a jonteff."

That night Danny had nightmares. He dreamed he was in the factory elevator with thirty of the factory girls packed around him like sardines. He felt small and hemmed in, frightened. Just as the elevator reached the third floor, it began to fall. He heard the shrieking and knew the never-ending plunge into nothingness. Jolted out of his dream, he found himself weak and bathed in perspiration.

Saturday night at the dinner table he announced Mr. Silverstein's offer and could not keep from noticing that Larry and Mac exchanged glances over their soup bowls. Pop Kominsky stopped eating. "Over my dead body. Not as long as I'm your father. I have promised your mother that no one of you three boys will ever work in any sweatshop. I am a poor Jew who can't send you to college, but you boys must find a way to become doctors, lawyers or businessmen."

It was a strong and emotional outburst for the usually calm Pop Kominsky. There was no laughter in his voice nor did he punctuate the statement with his usual funny stories.

This was the moment, Danny thought, for which Larry and Mac had been waiting. They had finished their soup when Mac said, "I don't know why he shouldn't, Pop. The rest of us are working." Larry nodded agreement. "Now listen, if you can work there— year after year, why can't Scrawny? It won't hurt him, and will help all of us."

Pop Kominsky waited a second before saying, in a very soft voice, "We are not very much of a family any more without your mother. You two older boys are Americanized. You make your own money and soon you'll be married. You are not home very much. Both of you live your own lives. All I have left is Duvidl, and he and I will work this out together."

While they silently finished their meal, Pop Kominsky, sensing the tenseness of the situation, surprised everyone by suddenly announcing, "I'm in the mood to see a good movie. May I treat all of you?"

Larry took the bait. "It's a wonderful idea. They are playing a Harold Lloyd picture on Flatbush Avenue. I think it's called something like *Why Worry?*"

Kaye-San

DURING DANNY'S FIFTH SEASON AS A TOOMLER, FATE STEPPED IN. Dave Harvey and Kathleen Young, a dance duo, decided they needed a third performer. "With a little training, we can teach Danny where to put his feet," said Kathleen, and so Danny Kaye became a dancer for the first time in his career. The dance group was given the magnificent title, "The Three Terpsichoreans."

Opening night was in Utica, New York. Before a small and unenthusiastic audience which was only mildly interested in watching straight dancing, the group presented a bolero. It was far above the ability of Danny, the novice dancer with a short and superficial training. But with a show-must-go-on attitude, Danny behaved like an old hand at the game and executed the intricate maneuvers with more abandon than finesse. "I wanted to get through the act as fast as possible," he said later. "I knew if we didn't bore the audience too long they wouldn't mind, because the strip teasers were the next performers."

As the music quickened and the steps became increasingly short and fast, Danny was to twirl to the girl and romantically kiss her hand. Twirl he did, but the gyration ended in a wobble. He caught himself, fell off balance again—and fell flat on the floor.

The audience sat up, broke into laughter and applauded with satisfaction. Dave Harvey whispered, "They love it—don't get up."

Danny raised his face from the floor and said in a false whisper that could be heard the length and width of the auditorium, "I can't get up—I've split my pants!"

The theater reverberated with laughter and applause. That night a professional comic had been born. Vaudeville theaters and burlesque shows hired The Terpsichoreans. But they insisted that any classic dance had to be spiced by Danny Kaye's clowning. "The audiences don't give a hoot about long-haired music," one of the producers told them.

The first large city to hire the trio was Detroit. No newspaper reviewed them, because the act was the usual burlesque-vaudeville clowning.

"After one matinee," tells Danny, "The Terpsichoreans were approached by A. B. Marcus, the owner and manager of a traveling road show. He came backstage and said to Dave, 'How would you and Kathleen like to go to China?' My fellow performers were delighted with the idea until they suddenly realized Marcus was not including me. He didn't think I was funny. The three of us talked it over for hours that evening, but they were adamant. We were a team and we all would go to the Far East—or none. I tried to urge them to go without me. Up to this day it has meant a lot to know such loyalty.

"Dave took over the negotiations and Mr. Marcus ruefully agreed that the three of us could go to the Orient.

"While I was working for Mr. Marcus, I always called him by his last name. It was only long later that I got up the nerve to call him 'Abe.' I discovered my new boss had been running a cleaning establishment in New England a few years before and found himself stuck with a lot of stage costumes because a theatrical unit traveling through town couldn't pay its bills. Marcus decided the only thing he could do to get his money back was to fill the costumes with people—and that's how he went into show business.

"We three hams became members of Marcus's La Vie Paree, a troupe of about seventy-five people. I received forty dollars a week. We worked our way across the continent of America by playing every theater and outhouse. Forty-one night stands. On February 8, 1934, we sailed for China, Siam, Japan and all points East."

The tour stopped in the Philippines and then went on to China, Singapore, and finally Japan. The troupe's reception in the land of cherry blossoms was not one of enthusiasm. They encountered a great deal of trouble with the Japanese musicians' union, none of whom could speak a word of English but all of whom could swing out like Louis Armstrong.

"I was afraid of my premiere in Tokyo," says Danny. "I knew nothing of Japan or the Japanese. I came out on the stage and suddenly it seemed to me the whole audience was rushing at me, shouting and making gestures. They later turned out to be a body of labor agitators who objected to Americans coming to Japan and getting jobs. The audience was trying to protest the interruption, but I couldn't understand a word and thought they were after my blood. I left the stage in a hurry!"

The demonstrators were apprehended, but the visiting artists from the United States had constant trouble with the Nipponese authorities. All cameras were confiscated, and they discovered when they applied for extensions of their visitors' visas that careful dossiers had been kept on every member of the troupe. This was seven years before Pearl Harbor.

Danny tells of his jail experience in Tokyo. "The management of the theater committed some minor infraction of the law, and our entire cast was sentenced to serve thirty days in jail. Naturally, I was quite upset. But instead of tossing us into the Japanese version of the Tombs, they put our pictures into jail instead and let the show go on."

In spite of all the unpleasantness and difficulties, Danny fell in love with the Orient. Japan and China taught him more than he had hoped for, and the ancient arts and cultures of these countries were both his drama school and university training.

Nightly, he reached out over the footlights to the impassive faces beyond in a tremendous effort to make them smile, to elicit a chuckle, to give some gaiety and joy. It was quite a task, for the Japanese audience is polite. It never betrays its emotions or interrupts to applaud or laugh. The audiences were friendly and kind, but Danny never knew what thoughts and reactions were going on behind the expressionless, attentive faces. Each performance he was scared, and after each act he racked his brains for better and funnier ways of doing things.

Because of the language barrier, Danny told his stories in pantomime, made faces to emphasize emotions and launched into scat-singing which sounded almost Oriental in its gibberish.

Years later, on a set in Hollywood, Kaye greeted a visiting Japanese actor with a long, fast tirade of gibberish interspersed with an occasional Japanese word. The visitor stepped back a pace and said in broken English to his escort, "I know he was speaking Japanese, but he said it so fast, I didn't catch a single word."

Danny Kaye received his baptism of fire in the shadow of Buddha, in the face of the eternal values of Oriental art. No young actor could have had a greater break. Danny did not know at the time that his career as a great entertainer was being forged in front of the Oriental theater-goers who did not understand a single word, much less a single song, Danny sang.

The boss and manager, A. B. Marcus, little realized, and little cared, what the trip through the Orient meant to Danny Kaye. Marcus was concerned with the box-office results and the sold-out houses, with making travel arrangements and taking care of the endless red tape of visitors' visas and customs inspections. He lost a gold mine by overlooking Danny's rapidly developing talent.

To him, Danny was merely one of many acts, not good, not bad, just mediocre, but he had to admit "the Orientals like Danny Kaye because he doesn't rely on English to put his act over, uses a lot of pantomime and sign language. Oh, he's a smart fellow all right, but I still don't think he's funny and in my estimation he will never be a funny-man."

With money matters and travel details uppermost in his mind, it never occurred to Marcus to question whether the Oriental audiences were packing the theaters because they actually liked the show, or if they were thronging in merely to watch the seldom-seen New Yorkers go through their fast Western paces. Who cared as long as the seats were filled every night?

Danny did. He liked the Japanese, the Burmese, the Malayans, the Chinese. They were people, perhaps bewildered by his art, but then, Danny kept asking himself, what did he really know about his "art," anyway?

Many a travel-weary night he spent in an unfamiliar and unheated Asiatic hotel room doubting his life and ability as an entertainer, pondering his future and trying to picture his next step when the tour ended.

"Don't worry," he consoled himself; "something will show up. Mr. Marcus can be matched, but I wonder why he doesn't like me? Other people seem to think I'm funny. Why doesn't he?"

Then Danny would shrug his shoulders, resolve to do better and to learn from Asia all there was to gain. He stayed away from the social gatherings of the troupe, preferring to investigate the alleys and narrow streets, the tiny shops and unusual foods. He wanted to know the Orientals as human beings so that he could reach their minds and hearts when he was on the stage. He watched carefully to see what gestures made the shopkeeper smile and what tomfoolery evoked laughter from the children in the streets. He began to sense that humor is universal; that people the world over smile and laugh at the same things; that a funny face could make a Japanese boy giggle just as it had years ago amused the older boys on the playground back at P.S. 149.

Often he shared his confusions and discontent with his friends, The Terpsichoreans, over tiny cups of sake. The two listened sympathetically through long evenings, but Dave Harvey and Kathleen Young were equally unsure of a sure-fire formula for success. The dance team had long before decided it was wisest to do their routines as Marcus directed and avoid the question of Oriental approval. But they listened attentively to Danny's questions and often offered helpful suggestions and supplied much needed encouragement.

Travel through the Orient was not without its own dramatic excitement. Two hours before the curtains were to go up in Osaka, Danny was sitting in his hotel room when a great typhoon struck the city without warning. With more curiosity than wisdom he rushed to the window to watch the titanic struggle of buildings against the storm. In the street below him a boy was futilely bicycling for his life, fighting the overpowering pressure of the gale. Danny opened the window in an attempt to shout a suggestion that the boy come into the hotel. Out of nowhere a brick came flying, striking the American greenhorn entertainer on the head. Danny never saw what happened next. To this day he does not what happened to the boy in the street below.

But with a large bump on his head and four aspirins in his stomach, he performed that same night amid the debris of a ruined city filled with injured Japanese. The theater lights had been knocked out, but the determined Danny spotted himself with a flashlight in each hand and kept his audience calm by singing every song he knew and creating a couple on the spur of the moment.

It was that night when Danny overheard a group of Japanese refer to him as Kaye-San, a term of great warmth and endearment which made him a member of the Japanese family. This compliment made up for Marcus's lack of approbation. Danny felt emotionally rejuvenated. With new interest he studied the Japanese prints; he practiced the exquisite finger movements he had watched in the Siamese Temple dances, and then, with a few Japanese words to help him, he used his tapering fingers to tell his stories, to express emotions, to create humor in thin air.

The Japanese were fully aware of the artistry of his dancing hands, were reminded of their own drama, and felt a common bond with this young American entertainer.

The fact that Danny Kaye was learning to use his hands as a tool of his art was no mere happenstance, for since his early school days, when his fists had dangled, large and limp, out of his brother's coat, they had been a source of annoyance. They seemed to flop, to get in the way, to be too long, and too flexible. Only a few months before Kaye left on tour a talent scout for the Shubert Theater in New York had told him paternally, "Young man, you will never get anywhere in the entertainment world until you keep those cockeyed fingers under control."

Today, twenty years later, when critics and reviewers praise his hands and compare them with those of Eleonore Duse, he is unimpressed. "I remember when my hands were my handicap. Now everyone suddenly admires my hands—even ballet dancers and famous surgeons have complimentary comments to make. But I have been conscious of them all my life, and they still seem like two large chunks of meat dangling from my wrists."

At the end of the tour Marcus refused to renew Danny's contract. "He can't sing. He can't dance! His jokes are terrible!"

So Danny was unemployed again. On the long voyage to San Francisco he floated in the thin atmosphere of dreams, hopes and illusions, propped up only by solid desires, solid memories and even more solid ambitions. As the ship sailed through the Golden Gate, the lights of the city winked at him skeptically. They seemed to tell him he had to try all over again. He was faced with nothing but a future of hunting more agents, more producers, directors and summer-stock theaters. The American city that stands at the gateway to the Orient impressed upon him the bitter fact that no one in the United States knew or cared about his success abroad.

Without sending a wire, he boarded the first train for Brooklyn —and home. When Danny opened the door to the old Kominsky apartment, Pop looked up from his newspaper, rose to his feet, embraced Danny with a smile and the words, "Good to have you home, Danny. There's some milk in the icebox."

VI

Ping-Pong on a Rhinoceros Hide

IT IS NOT STRANGE THAT THE NEXT FIVE YEARS WERE THE ROUGHest in Danny's career. After all, he was barely twenty-two, had seen half of the world, was ambitious, inexperienced, impatient and unable to understand why America was not ready to recognize his overflowing talent.

Broadway was not easy to crack, and young Danny Kaye realized the theater-goers had their own ideals of manhood; they expected husky, full-blooded, self-reliant, hard-living and hard-loving men. Danny did not fit these shoes. He, better than anyone else, knew that behind his earnest façade of self-assertion was still a youngster, frightened, groping in the dark and angered not to be given full credit for his ability.

He was no actor, in the first place—not in the traditional sense. Actually he disliked repeating the same show night after night. He hated to mouth the same lines; he liked changes, improvisations, to make quips on the spur of the moment or to sing just plain funny things, nonsense that would entertain a crowd.

"You are your own worst enemy," one of the Broadway agents told him. "You are too young to have your way. Wait ten years and you will have a chance to do what you think is right in a performance. But most people like you don't even last ten years in show business."

"The so-and-so—" thought Danny Kaye.

Still, the agent was not wrong altogether. Danny was a nonconformist and proved a problem to producers and directors of full-length shows. They did not particularly like his jokes or his singing—and he bore no resemblance to Rudolf Valentino, either.

"Should I quit and study medicine?" he asked himself many times. "With what? I have no money, and Pop can't help me," was the honest answer he gave himself. "Take a job—any job, and work yourself through college?"

It was not in the cards. There were too many years to make up. He had not even finished high school. Impossible. More determined than ever, he said once, "I'm going to show you, Pop, and my brothers, that I will make the grade in show business."

Danny has never forgotten that his father, in those desperate moments, encouraged him to go ahead with his trade, not to quit, and to work harder in the entertainment world. That was the answer. His father had instinctive and untutored touches of wisdom and patience. A God-fearing man, he often silently prayed for his son. "David was meant to be a rebel," he confided to Larry. "My boy must find what will make him happy always—not just for the present."

"Pop taught me the art of living—the most important thing a man can possess," Danny says gratefully.

Danny lost weight because of his anxieties. His temper was short; his voice rasped. He was an unhappy youngster overly plagued with dreams and underequipped with patience. He was a poor escort for young women and enjoyed his own company at a Brooklyn baseball game more than wasting his time on superficial girls who could not grasp the turmoil going on inside him.

All he could do was to try once more and still once again. He hounded agents and was rewarded only by sporadic one-night stands, stand-ins, substitutions, cancellations, and short-run appearances. The forty dollars a week he had earned in Japan began to seem like big money. The private parties that sometimes engaged him often offered as little as five or ten dollars. Clubs paid from ten to twenty-five, but the latter pay checks were few and far between.

It seemed as if the world of make-believe was terribly disorganized, revoltingly unremunerative, frighteningly inaccessible to a beginning entertainer.

If the impatient Danny Kaye could have adequately analyzed himself in those days, he might have recognized that he had not yet produced a program which made him outstanding. In addition, he was new, young, and no one, not even the agents, knew him. After six months Danny realized work did not exist for him in New York. He could tour, be a toomler again, "play the outhouses and whistle stops"—New York's night clubs did not have room for him, and certainly not Broadway.

So he was ready to join the kerosene circuit, the town-hall vaudeville shows, the resort places which paid for food, upkeep and the smallest of the small salaries. He did a few radio shows, again worked on the Borscht Circuit, appeared as a vaudevillian on one-night stands in eight states, enjoyed several guest appearances for Benay Venuta and Walter O'Keefe.

During one of the many lulls when Danny was pacing from agent to agent, he was literally dragged into a cluttered office. A cigar-chewing theatrical "flesh-peddler," today no longer in business, slammed his pencil on the desk.

"Say, you, I don't know what your name is but I'm sick and tired of seeing you hanging around my office bothering my secretary. Got a job for you, I think. Some new outfit from Hollywood is shooting shorts out on Long Island. They just called from Astoria wanting half a dozen tall guys. Here is the address. Get yourself out there and see what you can do—but leave all financial arrangements to me."

Danny was almost petrified, but he took the address and headed immediately for Long Island.

"Perhaps this is it—the break I've been waiting for all these years," he thought. And he visualized the huge and slick motion picture studios, the massive cranes and batteries of modern photographic equipment. When he arrived in Astoria, no one had ever heard of the movie company, or its address, but he finally found the wide open spaces, not yet built up as residential areas, where a primitive sign on a broken-down brown wood fence indicated that films were made.

Indeed he immediately saw a few actors dressed as westerners, leading a couple of bony horses and practicing twirling their revolvers and lariats. Under the war paint of one Indian, Danny recognized the familiar face of another toomler from the summer circuit.

"Where is the casting office?" Danny asked.

"In this crazy knocked-out joint, there isn't any casting office, but the guy fixing the broken camera signed me up. They call him Art. Art Miller."

Art looked up from his work and beamed at Danny.

"You are just the person I've been looking for. I need a tall actor to play the lover. You will do. All the people they sent me were too short or too old or too fat or too something. See my secretary over there. She will give you the script. Go learn your lines, and see the costume department for your clothes and the make-up man. We are shooting in half an hour."

Danny was aghast, but asked no questions and did as he was told. He was now in the movies. He grabbed the script from the secretary and hastily glanced through it. There wasn't a funny line in it, or a song. It was an oversentimental straight lover-role and from Danny's standpoint the best thing about his part was that the entire film lasted only eleven minutes.

Danny found himself a shady corner, and, as the make-up man slapped on grease paint, set about to memorize the corny lines. The day was humid and he could feel the make-up slipping like heavy petroleum grease.

His tight black frock coat pinched his shoulders together and he was uncomfortably aware that the striped trousers were too short. The rehearsal didn't go badly. The heroine, a college girl from Boston, was petite and helpful. When Danny missed a line she skillfully covered up or cue'd him. But the worst moment came when the cameras began to roll. It was as if he were brainwashed. Every speech evaporated from his mind. He muffed his lines constantly. He looked at Art instead of the heroine, and suddenly it seemed as if every prop made a point of dancing into his path.

Art Miller was not only the casting director of the company but was also his own producer, director, script-writer and distributor. He wrung his hands with impatience. Every retake cost money and

Danny became the most expensive actor on the lot. One short scene had to be retaken twelve times.

Danny's tensions grew. He never had a chance to characterize his role, nor was he suited for the part. The incessant repetitions of the same lines seemed to hinder more than to help.

After two days of agony the short was completed. Art relieved Danny of his position as a "star" and relegated him to the rank of an obscure and inactive extra, a member of the male chorus.

And thus it seemed that Danny's career in movies was doomed to permanent failure. Art Miller's production dreams were equally doomed and his Long Island production never saw the inside of a major movie house.

Again Danny camped in the managers' outer offices on Broadway, stooged for his old friend, Nick Long, and played an eight weeks' engagement with Abe Lyman. Each new engagement was brief and unsatisfactory.

For a time he toured with Sally Rand, the famous strip-tease dancer, and held her coat one night when she was arrested. Miss Rand, while playing an engagement before a packed house of men in Cincinnati, was bothered by a large blue fly. In an effort to ward off the buzzing attack, she removed her right arm from the place on her body she was supposed to cover, leaving her nude for a second. The audience heartily approved, but the police and judge did not concur. The show was closed locally, and Danny was awarded the new job of holding Sally's fans to assure that she was properly covered—within the limits of Danny's astute decisions, of course.

When Sally's tour came to an abrupt end, Danny gladly grabbed the London engagement arranged by Britain's famous impresario, Henry Sherek, who was scouting for cabaret talent in the United States. Sherek remembers, "I had read reviews and watched Nick Long perform in Philadelphia. I wasn't too impressed with him, but I liked the lanky, pale-faced, red-haired buffoon who was the stooge in the act. He kept me laughing from the minute he leapt on the stage to the second he fell into the wings. After the show I went backstage to book him for the Dorchester House, but this man, Danny Kaye, insisted he was under contract to Nick and it was a case of take both or none. I agreed, provided Kaye would sing two solo numbers, 'Dinah' and 'Minnie the Moocher.' I booked the stooge for fifty dollars a week."

Again Danny had a job, but again it was not in the United States. Of course he felt great hopes for a success in Britain and loved everything about the trip over. He practiced his English accent on the stewards, ordered his milk at the bar in a Scottish brogue, and confused the barber by insisting he was a Welshman born in Brooklyn whose real name was Kominsky. He took his morning and afternoon laps on the promenade deck, talking to himself and making little half-finished flips with his long hands until there was some talk about his sanity. But Danny was planning. He was mentally being a great hit in London.

And then came London, frigid and foggy London, and with it came the same fears Danny had known before. The jokes he tried out on the sales clerks did little more than cause raised eyebrows. He was constantly cold and clammy from the unheated room of his hotel coupled with the icy feeling that ran through his veins. He knew he was only a supporting actor and that it was hard for a number two stooge to become a number one star.

Danny was not only bad; he was terrible.

This adventure was such a resounding flop that Danny still shudders when he thinks of it. Henry Sherek, who had brought Danny to London, simply stated, "My judgment was wrong. Danny Kaye was a complete failure."

Dick Richards of the London *Sunday Pictoral* said, "Danny Kaye's impact on the sophisticated Dorchester House crowd was like that of a ping-pong ball on a rhinoceros's hide. The truth was that he was as near a flop as makes no difference."

Looking back with the perspective of almost twenty years, one can analyze that all the odds were against the young Danny Kaye. First, he opened on the worst possible night, the eve of the Munich crisis, when no one in London felt like laughing. Second, his humor was American, not British, and the stiff tuxedo crowd resented the fast, flippant young entertainer who was only a stooge, the number two man of the act.

"I died the death," was Danny's only comment.

The kindest remark he heard backstage was when someone said, superciliously, "After all, you're not even twenty-five years old."

So Danny and Nick returned to New York with the sincere hope that no one on the western shores of the Atlantic had heard of the fiasco. He refused to talk about London, even to Pop Kominsky.

Finally Danny came to a conclusion. He felt he had not paid enough attention to the way he sang and that he did not present the right songs. They were not right for the audience, these run-of-the-mill ditties or vacuous hit songs, and they were not the right media for his own personality. "I found that out the hard way," he said later.

One night Danny went to a Brooklyn movie. Bing Crosby sang. Of course Crosby has been the idol for most young hopefuls. He has style; he tells a full story in every song; he is relaxed and he sings as if he were crooning to each separate person listening. Danny that night lost his romantic notions, neglected the girl he escorted and began to analyze. Could anyone sing as "right" as Crosby? Could he? He didn't have Bing's voice, had a completely different personality, different background, different schooling— but Bing's ease, relaxed approach and unostentatiousness kept the crowds spellbound. It was the right formula. Crosby was no Adonis either, no hard-hitting, hard-loving, hard-living type of actor or singer.

A few years ago when Danny Kaye and Bing Crosby made *White Christmas* together in Hollywood, the busy press agents behind the film let the publicity machine go full blast to exploit the fact that Danny as a youngster had worshiped Bing Crosby and considered Der Bingle as one of his great teachers.

Danny Kaye never denies that Bing Crosby made a deep impression on him in his earlier years. "Almost everybody in the world thinks of Bing Crosby as a close personal friend," said Danny. Deep in his subconscious Danny wanted to achieve the same relation with his audiences, and he knew Crosby held the secret of being loved by countless millions.

With the new goals in mind of higher standards of performance, more adaptability to audiences, new songs and routines Danny increased emphasis on freshness and originality. He and his programs were maturing.

Then in the spring of 1939 he met Nat Lichtman, whom he knew from the Borscht Circuit.

"How has your life been going, Danny?"

"Not so good, but I have worked out some new routines I'd like to have you see."

"Would love to. I'm on my way to see Max Liebman at the Keystone Theater on Fifty-second Streeet. He is casting for his new show, *Sunday Night Revue*. Why don't you come along?"

Danny, having nothing else better to do, joined him.

There, seated at the piano with Max Liebman, was a trim, attractive brunette who looked vaguely familiar. Glancing up from the keyboard, she gave Danny a shy smile and said: "I know you, but I bet you don't remember me."

She was the woman destined to change Danny's entire career and life.

VII

Sylvia

HER NAME WAS SYLVIA FINE. SHE LOOKED, AND STILL DOES, LIKE a school girl. At first Danny could not place her.

That day of the tryouts on Fifty-second Street Sylvia had a secret. She was wrapped in the family fur coat, shared by her mother and sister, and wore it with their air of a *grande dame* to hide her fears in front of all the new theatrical faces. With her small pointed chin, her elfin figure topped by long black hair, she tried her best to awaken an inner confidence in her own ability. Sylvia had come to Broadway to try to sell her music to Max Liebman.

The girl at the piano had majored in music at Brooklyn College, worked for a music publishing house, had written several songs that were never published and taught piano lessons to private pupils. Students were too scarce to make teaching pay, so she took a job selling soup in a Manhattan department store.

One of her earliest songs impressed Max Liebman very much. It was a political satire, written when Hitler was threatening Czechoslovakia, entitled "Down on Downing Street":

> Sing a song of Blackshirts
> A pocketful of lies—
> Don'tcha know they've got their eyes
> On other pies.

She gave up writing political satire as fast as she could, because "I did not want to rewrite them every night. The situation changed so fast."

Sylvia Fine, an attractive, intelligent young woman, seemed to know what she wanted. She remembers the day she first met Danny Kaye, the grown-up David Kominsky:

"I first saw Danny when he was fourteen, working in my father's dental office in Brooklyn. I remember how he used to sprint through the office and never noticed me. I had a crush on him, but he never knew it.

"I thought he was hilarious the first time I ever saw him, and I haven't changed my opinion yet. He wasn't the most attractive man I'd ever met—in fact, he was rather ridiculous, with his long hair, high collar and tight suit that pinched into wrinkles at the waist. But when he walked across the room he seemed to dance, and his every movement had a flash and a flair to it. What's this guy got for me, I thought—except everything! I was mad about him.

"It is as clear as if it were yesterday. I sat doubtfully in that dusty little theater on Fifty-second Streeet, not knowing a soul and hoping Mr. Liebman could use some of my tunes—and then in came David Daniel Kominsky, tall, grinning and telling some silly story in a Japanese dialect. My heart did a flip, my hands became wet and cold and I stammered out 'I know you.' "

Danny was in no romantic mood. He was out to find a job—a job in New York, or he would have to travel again to the many small towns in America which hired vaudevillians, magicians, monkey acts, contortionists—and Danny Kaye. He was an intent job-hunter.

Danny Kaye was no newcomer to Max Liebman. Only a week before the Viennese-born producer had been scouting for entertainers at a fifth-rate Greenwich Village night club. He had laughed at Danny's antics and made a mental note that perhaps he could use him later on.

Seeing the young hopeful at the rehearsal, Liebman decided he could squeeze him into the *Sunday Night Revue* and hired him on the spot. At the same time he hired Sylvia as his pianist and song writer.

In spite of the earnestness of this young group, the clever music which Sylvia composed and the long hours of rehearsals, *Sunday Night Revue* folded after one night. But it was the beginning for Sylvia and Danny.

Max Liebman, a man with enormously intuitive casting abilities who in later years became an able television producer for NBC, liked Danny's talent and thought Sylvia's music showed a fresh new approach that he could use. Of course, he could not pay much in those years, and when his *Sunday Night Revue* closed, he had new plans for the two.

Liebman began his career as a sketch-writer, and for five years wrote, produced and directed vaudeville acts. In 1932 he began his long association with Camp Tamiment, a Jewish, labor-union-sponsored resort camp, working there for fifteen seasons as social director. Every week he produced and directed a completely new musical revue.

"I was first attracted to Danny as a personality," says the producer. "He commands attention even before he opens his mouth. Of course, in those days Danny seriously believed he was a great singer. Today he is, but not then. I saw the manifestations of his talent in the raw and knew by instinct he would make a great comedian. In this embryonic state I saw his potentialities. In every scene he was a comedian, and his sense of timing and rhythm was highly effective.

"Since Danny insisted he wanted to be a singer and had a voice range that was rare for a comedian, I let him sing Irish and Yiddish folk songs at first, but we soon changed the pace into comedy. He found himself, and great popularity with the crowds. I was amazed at his vocal variety of speech and song—wide extremes from soft to loud, from slow to fast."

And thus began a business partnership that lasted for four years and gave Max Liebman a ten per cent cut out of all Kaye's income. But more than a successful deal in terms of dollars and cents, this was the start of a long, lasting friendship for the three—Sylvia, Danny and Max. They all had great plans and hopes, and when Liebman urged the two to join his *Straw Hat Revue,* also at Camp Tamiment in the Pocono Mountains of Pennsylvania, both readily agreed.

"My pay for playing the piano was fifty dollars a week," recalls Sylvia. "In those days that was pretty good money, but more than that, I was having fun writing songs and dreaming up monkey business. I was intrigued with Danny, but thought he was a bit fresh and forward.

"Personally, I was terrified. I had written some tunes and lyrics for student plays at Brooklyn College, but the idea of composing as a serious career never entered my head. I felt I was not good enough to be successful, and when I realized I was to write all the music for the summer revue, I was in a panic."

The weather was warm and breeze-cooled, the mountainsides green and lush, but hard work took precedence over romance. The two young artists spent the hours rehearsing, planning, creating, composing, singing and laughing. Miss Fine was delighted that she had found someone who could present the hysterical nonsense of her lyrics. "There was no question that Danny had talent, but the problem was that he had too much of it. Trying to crystallize a little of it in a five-minute number was like trying to reproduce the effect of Niagara Falls in a test tube."

Through the long days of contact Sylvia knew she was in love with the funny-man who was working so hard with her. "Of course, I didn't let him know my secret. I'm no fool. Life those days amounted to forced labor. Danny has the sort of antic versatility which consumes months of my best efforts for a few minutes of his performance time. I soon realized he wasn't just a baby I was holding, and at times I felt I was an idiot to be responsible for inventing, devising or just plain whipping up the words with which he, the comedian, was supposed to devastate his audiences.

"His techniques for getting laughs were not accidental. He worked at them constantly, trying to improve. I took him under my wing. He finally reciprocated by taking me in his arms.

"Very often we talked of marriage, first tentatively and half joking, then more and more seriously. Sometimes I agreed with Danny that we should wait until he was professionally secure and we had some money in his pockets, but in my own heart I really didn't feel that money mattered because we were in love.

"And, besides, I was convinced we had the makings of success.

He had what I considered a spectacular performing talent, and I was delighted to channel all my creative ability into writing and thinking only for him.

"My parents approved of my seeing Danny—until they suspected we were in love. Then their enthusiasm waned, for there had never been anyone 'theatrical' in the family, and to compound the problem, I was practically engaged to marry a promising young lawyer. But I think that I unconsciously knew very soon after I met Danny that we belonged together."

In the meantime the rollicking show was a huge success. In the fall the Shuberts took it to Broadway for a ten-weeks' engagement starring Imogene Coca, with Danny doing ten numbers.

A New York paper gave Danny his first good notice, one sentence written by the ebullient and sophisticated John Mason Brown: "Last night Danny Kaye worked hard and well in any number of capacities."

Sylvia fared much better at the hands of the critics, for her toe-tapping melodies and absurd lyrics caught the fancy of the audiences. There was, for instance, "Anatole of Paris," in which Danny was a male modiste with blue hair, whose "twisted eugenics" were the result of a "family of inbred schizophrenics," and who designed preposterous women's hats because, he confided, he hated the female sex. The chanson went on to relate that Anatole's mother was frightened by a "runaway saloon" and he was "forced to be a hobo because she plays the oboe, and the oboe, it is clearly understood, is an ill wind that nobody blows good."

The music was original and sparkling, and so was Danny Kaye. From "Anatole," he rushed wickedly into the frenzied "Wolf of Wall Street," a character too busy cornering the pumpernickel market to get married, and then in sequence became a blibber-blabber radio singer, a dialect waiter and the "Masked Gondolier," alias "Danny Davenport of the United States Secret Service." "The Great Chandelier," a charming travesty on a long line of phony continental operettas, was whirled off by Danny to the delight of an operetta-weary Broadway.

When the show closed, there was a general consensus among those who had seen the performance that "Kaye is okay."

Fatigued by the work and disappointed that the engagement had not run longer, Danny went to Florida for a rest. Perhaps a Miami night club would bridge the out-of-work period.

It may have been the palm-fringed coast and the tropical beauty —or perhaps it was his restlessness. It could have come from the loneliness of being away from someone with whom he had worked so closely for the past months, but more likely it was the recognition of love that did it. But whatever the motivation, one night Danny picked up the phone and called Sylvia: "Come down here and let's get married."

Startled by his own suggestion, he slammed the receiver on the hook before Sylvia had an opportunity to answer him.

Sylvia did not call back, but wrote a long, warm airmail special-delivery letter, telling Danny she considered them engaged, but asking for time and the consideration of her family, who would not approve of an elopement. She signed the letter and added a P.S.: "Danny, dear, please stay out of the sun."

Only a week later Sylvia fell ill, and the doctor obligingly prescribed Florida's salubrious climate for her convalescence.

Sylvia tells of her confused days during January of 1940 when she joined Danny in Florida. "I couldn't afford to fly, so I went by train, sat up all night and arrived in the Sunshine State with the crumpled, rumpled feeling that is unique to thirty-six sleepless hours in a coach. I was waging a fierce battle with doubts, too, for I didn't want to marry without my parents' consent. I had been carefully reared to respect my obligations to my father and mother. Then, too, Danny had been halfway around the world and was a well-seasoned traveler, while I had never been farther away from New York than a few short trips in Pennsylvania. I was a little frightened and terribly homesick.

"So, for three days in Florida, I just sat on that uncomfortable edge of indecision—and thought. Finally I concluded that if I asked my parents, there would be objections, discussions and arguments. I didn't want all those complications, so we eloped and were secretly married."

It happened on January 30, 1940, in Fort Lauderdale, Florida. Max Liebman joined them and was their best man before the justice of the peace.

The day of their marriage they had either seventy—or minus ten dollars between them. Sylvia had thirty, but Danny isn't sure whether he had—or owed—forty.

The two young people married with the full knowledge they had opposing qualities, but felt as long as they respected each other's differences there was insurance for a happy and exciting life together.

The home-coming was not without apprehensions. Sylvia was faced with introducing her unemployed husband to her secure and successful family. To say that the Fines were surprised is a mild understatement. Mrs. Fine insisted they be married a second time, this time with Sylvia in a white gown and long train with lilies-of-the-valley, Danny in a tuxedo, a drove of guests to observe and a fitting reception to fete the couple. On February 22, 1940, the Kayes had a second ceremony, "enough to last two lifetimes."

Danny recalls the reception and his discomfort at meeting so many new faces.

"I remember," he tells, "when my father-in-law drew Sylvia and me in the corner and asked the question, 'Sylvia, just where did you meet Danny?'

" 'I met him formally at a rehearsal for the *Sunday Night Revue*,' Sylvia answered truthfully.

" 'But did you know,' Mr. Fine continued, 'that your husband lived across the street from us for twelve years and used to run errands for me?'

" 'Yes, Dad,' said Sylvia shyly, 'and I think I loved him then.' I could have just hugged her for that statement."

From the pomp and ceremony of their Brooklyn wedding, the now twice-married Kayes frantically dashed to their room at a small Manhattan hotel, tore into their theatrical attire and raced to make their date at an insignificant night club in the Village. Despite the torn purple curtains and the dust on the piano top, the two performed like Jupiter and Juno in the arena of the gods.

Next morning Mr. and Mrs. Kaye climbed aboard a Fifth Avenue bus and went apartment-hunting. Finally they subleased from "a friend of a friend" a two-and-a-half-room penthouse on Fifty-second Street near the East River. The apartment included a terrace, approximately the size of a postage stamp, a miniature kitchen barely large enough for tiny Sylvia and bean-pole Danny and a bedroom which was filled to squeezed capacity by one double bed. Any trip through the apartment had to be carefully maneuvered in single file.

Marriage made only one change in Danny Kaye's professional life: he worked harder than ever. "I don't want Sylvia to go back to giving piano lessons and I don't want her in the soup again. I simply have to find a job."

It seemed unbelievable that the *Straw Hat Revue* did not provide another step on the ladder upwards, for, after all, Danny had made Broadway. But search as he did, there were no shows being cast with a spot for his particular type of wit and humor.

Danny grew increasingly tense. He and Sylvia had far less than seventy dollars between them now, and their meals were reduced to copious amounts of spaghetti and an occasional welcome dinner at the Fines' home. Even Sylvia's new songs, tailored to Danny's singular mother-wit, failed to raise the gloom of unemployment. Often the two walked long hours through Central Park and discussed possibilities. Often Danny would attempt to brush off his deep concern by leaping to the top of a rock and giving vent to some nonsense, but the mood of gaiety was too shallow and unreal to last. They were broke and out of work—and they faced it grimly.

"It wasn't any fun, watching Danny worry so much," says Sylvia, "but those were valuable days in many ways, for we grew close together and learned to share each other's worries as well as laughter."

VIII

Her Head on My Shoulders

ⓧⓧ

ONE NIGHT, AS DANNY WAS POKING LISTLESSLY AT A LONG WHITE string of spaghetti, the phone rang. On the other end of the line Harry Bestry, a Broadway agent, proudly yelled, "Danny, you're in. I've booked you at a night club. La Martinique! Yeh, the one here in town . . . and they'll pay two hundred fifty a week. Terrific, huh?"

"Sure is. Thanks a million." And Danny hung up. He was delighted, but he was afraid. La Martinique was a sophisticated mid-town night club in a sophisticated metropolis. People paid large sums to go there and expected to receive their money's worth. It was an entirely different proposition from being a toomler making bored guests laugh, and it would be even more difficult to arouse these blasé Manhattanites than it had been in London. The Dorchester . . . the very thought of the nightmare of failure in that elite night club turned Danny cold with fear and set butterflies the size of seagulls flapping their wings inside him.

For a split second Danny was tempted to call Harry back, to tell him to try something else, but Sylvia's smiling face was the encouragement he needed. They rehearsed until well past two that night, going over songs, routines and creating a new ditty. Sylvia patted him good night with a motherly, "You'll do fine, Danny—just fine."

"Yes, Sylvia. Fine," he said smilingly.

A week later Danny, dressed in a new tuxedo which he had

75

bought with the last of their money, strode on to the stage of La Martinique.

The night club was a typical cellar bistro, very elite, very crowded, very smoky and very noisy. Languid women with saccharin smiles whispered to their escorts. Life-weary men lit their cigarettes and motioned the waiter for "another round."

Danny sang his very wittiest numbers, mimed his funniest characters and danced his wildest routines. But nothing amused the crowd or raised it from its doldrums of boredom. He was thanked with a desultory flutter of applause. The show was a flop —a complete and absolute flop.

Danny again suffered from what he calls his "Dorchester stomach": the sick feeling of failure, the desire to run, the temptation to cry. He went directly to Dario Borzani, the owner of the club, and pleaded to be released from his contract, immediately and before the next show.

Dario refused, arguing that the next audience would be different, that too much money had been spent on advertising to lose it now, and, more important, that there was no replacement for the next show.

The next hour in Danny's dressing room was like the corner of a boxing ring when the favorite has been knocked down in the previous round. Dario stood in the center of the room saying the equivalent of "Get in there and fight, Danny." Eddie Dukoff, the night club's publicity manager, paced back and forth with an optimist's grin on his face, "You'll hit next show, Danny. That was just a bad bunch of stuffed shirts last time. You see; next show'll be fine."

Sylvia, who had accompanied Danny, was quick to analyze the problems. "You were a little too fast on the Anatole number, Danny. Remember, this is a night club, not a theater. People were talking, and didn't catch your words. And, Danny, your timing was way off. You've got to relax. Here—" and taking him to the piano, they made rapid adjustments, changed some of the business, and for the last ten minutes before the midnight show, Sylvia insisted that Danny lie down and sat silently rubbing his forehead.

True to prediction, the midnight audience was completely different. The older crowd was replaced by a group of eager college youngsters. And, while youth is critical it is also responsive to newness. And Danny Kaye was new. He was vibrant and different. His moods changed in the snap of a cigarette lighter and he had the sort of quick humor that bedazzled and bewitched the imagination of the young people. They turned on their full and noisy approval. They screamed, yelled, pounded on the table, repeatedly applauded him back until the madcap had sung every song he knew.

Finally, face red and wet with perspiration, he turned to the beaming Sylvia with a shrug that said "What now? What else can we give them?" Sylvia shook her head. "I don't know." Danny eased to the band. "Play a conga," he said; "any conga—but play." The band began its one-and-two-and-three-ump rhythm. Danny, without rehearsal, with no particular idea in his head, improvised an extravagant conga, complete with a jaunty sequence of nonsense syllables. The audience joined in by tapping on glasses and stomping the floor. Faster and faster through the laughing crowd and back to the bandstand wove the wiggling, breathless Danny. He got down on his knees and pleaded with the drummer to stop. The crowd was convulsed. He rose to his feet and feigned four more faltering steps . . . one-two-and-three-UMP fell Danny—flat on the floor. Two hefty waiters also improvised by carrying the limp comedian from the stage.

This was the premiere of his now famous conga number, but it was also the first night of a long series of successful shows at La Martinique. Whatever Danny touched that night and the following nights made entertainment history.

He would launch into a silent burlesque of those "la-de-da" dancers, as he calls them, who drift through waltzes and tangos with utter grace and boredom. What was the reaction? Howls of laughter and applause at the phlegmatic way he executed a twirl.

His greatest single song success was "Stanislavsky," which made fun of the great Soviet art geniuses of the Moscow Theatre whose ballet methods, according to Sylvia's lyrics and Danny's pantomime, consisted of teaching Russia's drama students to

> Be a tree, be a sled,
> Be a purple spool of thread, etc., etc.

These absurdly funny words had popped into Sylvia's imaginative and busy brain while driving to Brooklyn at two o'clock one morning.

Time said of Kaye's "Stanislavsky": "Kaye was an immediate hit, not only because he was funny singing in Russian dialect, but also because he puckishly suggested that he, too, could be a tree, a sled or anything his comic imagination wanted."

Ed Sullivan, New York's ace Broadway columnist wrote: "He can do anything and do it well. He can sing, dance, squeeze the last laugh out of a situation and he's boyish enough and attractive enough to play romantic leads."

At long last the breaks were coming to Danny and Sylvia. Danny's salary had, almost overnight, jumped from nothing to two hundred fifty dollars a week. "We had our checks cashed, took our allowances and put the rest in the bank. We only took enough out to pay for our daily expenses," reminisces Danny.

Sylvia has a more specific remembrance of this period of their newly found income: "I watched Danny sign the tabs in restaurants, charge little things, and sometimes he'd ask me for a dollar to tip a doorman. I was terribly afraid I had married a man who was irresponsible about money.

"One evening while we were eating I told him about a lovely garnet necklace I had seen in a Greenwich Village shop, and added that some day, if we ever had any money, I would like very much to own it.

" 'Just a minute,' said Danny, and he ran upstairs. A minute later he came back with a pair of old summer shoes. He took out the shoe-trees and dumped out all the silver and a few bills he had been saving to buy me a present. The next day he proudly walked in not only with the necklace but a beautiful matching ring as well. I was so touched I couldn't say a thing. I just stood there and cried."

Success in no way brought leisure for the ambitious Kayes. Danny became a fireball. Sylvia's songs were obviously right for both his abilities and the audiences. He drove her mercilessly. Sylvia describes this new and rather difficult creative period: "From the beginning of our work together, if he sang with a certain improvised beat I did not get at once, he would be furious with impatience. Often I was hurt. But, on the other hand, he would often surprise me with the patience of a saint in some way I never expected."

Their waking hours were spent either in doing shows at La Martinique or in developing new acts. At this moment of his career, Danny remembered the hard years of struggle and professional humiliation. It seemed as if he were running away from his own past, determined never to go back, never to stand still but to leap as many rungs on the ladder of success as he could in the shortest possible time.

La Martinique flourished, and the Kayes basked in the flattering limelight. Soon only a twenty-dollar tip to the head waiter could produce an unreserved table for the midnight show. "I saw Kaye last night" became the fashionable thing to say. There were many new and salty songs and acts added to Danny's repertoire, but Sylvia always stayed close to the piano to keep control over Danny and the sensitive impromptu atmosphere of their creations. Each new routine was welcomed by a demonstrative crowd, and many of the old numbers were already on their way to becoming Danny Kaye classics.

This marked the beginning of the trip up Broadway. The next offer came as a complete surprise, an unsolicited invitation. No longer did Mohammed have to wait for the mountain; Broadway came to Danny.

Moss Hart, at the suggestion of Max Gordon, went to La Martinique, watched Danny in a sixty-minute show, and immediately wrote a part for him in Kurt Weill's *Lady in the Dark,* starring Gertrude Lawrence. Moss Hart and Danny Kaye clicked from their first meeting.

Although Danny had only a very small part in the play and was on stage for only a few minutes, he was now in big-league show business. This was New York theater at its renowned best, and he was rubbing elbows with experienced stars.

In the role of a silly circus photographer he was to jump from a wooden horse and sing an Ira Gershwin tune called "Tschaikowsky," a song that contained a list of some fifty unpronounceable Russian composers' names:

> There's Malichevsky, Rubinstein,
>   Arensky and Tschaikowsky,
> Sapelnikoff, Dimitrieff, Tscherepnin,
>   Kryjanowsky,
> Godowsky, Arteiboucheff, Moniuszko,
>   Akimenko,
> Solovieff, Prokofieff, Tiomkin,
>   Korestchenko, *
> Etc., etc., etc.

Danny learned the words in one afternoon, and on the opening night he rattled off the fifty Russian names in the record time of thirty-eight seconds, all in sing-song, easy-to-understand enunciation—that is, easy for anyone who is familiar with the names of Russian composers. He finished the Tschaikowsky song and climbed awkwardly back on his wooden horse. The house came down in applause and laughter and Danny grinned happily from his perch. He was on top of the world.

For a moment Danny forgot he was not the star of the show. The wonderful music of laughter and applause was pounding up at him from over the footlights. He gave an encore, and another.

"I was still bowing and smiling when the awful realization hit me! The great Gertrude Lawrence was on stage waiting to sing a number called 'Jenny.' And I knew that when a star is waiting, the worst crime in show business is to delay her entrance. I bowed all right—but I wanted to bow out. I was well aware greater men than little ham me had been fired for hogging the show. The audience may have liked me, but I was close to being a great flop with the management."

Danny had won the approval of the crowd, but at the moment he did not know how to stop the victory celebration.

"Finally Gertrude Lawrence saved me with showmanship I will never forget. She walked majestically to center stage, threw me a wondrous and gracious smile and then sang 'Jenny' as I have never heard her sing before. She used every trick known to show business and kept the audience in the palm of her hand.

Gertrude Lawrence was a great trouper. She wasn't upset by my diverting the audience; she merely met my success by winning greater triumph from those people who sat out front. That night she brought the house down!"

In spite of the friendliness between the two performers, the unwanted competition between the two great songs coming one on the heels of the other was not a happy situation and placed "a strain on our nerves."

Danny philosophizes with amusement that there are many rungs on the ladder of success where one can stub his toe. "One night," he reminisces, "while I was singing 'Tschaikowsky,' the audience's attention wandered for the first time. Glancing over my shoulder, I saw Miss Lawrence nonchalantly waving a red scarf. It was a good-natured theater 'incident,' and in turn I plotted my equally good-natured revenge. While she was singing, she was startled by an unexpected laugh because I, sitting astride my wooden beast, was doing a little mugging in the background. The lovely Miss Lawrence turned around and raised an arched eyebrow at me. I received the subtle reprimand with a slight bow. And after that we called it quits."

Gertrude Lawrence and Danny Kaye never discussed the incident, but with the warmth and charm that were so much a part of the great actress, Miss Lawrence summed up her reaction to the silent professional duel between them: "When Danny was halfway through his number, I knew I was up against it. My song had to be good, as good as I could possibly make it if I was going to meet the challenge of Danny's ability and personality. It was an intoxicating feeling. There is nothing more fun than meeting an audience when they are feeling on top of the world—and that Danny Kaye had certainly put them there.

"Off the stage we were great friends. After the 'incident' I gave him an earring as a souvenir and a token of assurance that I held no grudge. And now the rascal pesters me every time we meet by asking for the other one!"

Danny never received the other earring. The career of the great Gertrude Lawrence ended in her untimely death.

Both Danny and Sylvia knew, however, that the competition was likely to become unwholesome, if not ever fatal; so they decided to "call it quits." Danny resigned from the cast.

Eddie Dukoff, the publicity manager of La Martinique, was ready to capitalize on Danny Kaye's enormous success with Gertrude Lawrence. The termination of the *Lady in the Dark* contract was a profitable one, and the two Kayes were no longer worried about work. Any night club would sign them immediately, but Danny remained loyal to La Martinique and Eddie Dukoff, who later became his business manager.

Danny was now the man from Manhattan, no longer the Brooklyn kid. He tried to be sophisticated in manner, in quips, and sometimes deliberately made puns which sounded artificial. Success was too new; he could not always cope with it.

Danny's return engagement at La Martinique topped everything in night club entertainment history. His salary doubled, tripled, and then the café gave him a percentage of the gross. Private police were hired to control the waiting line of customers. The twenty-dollar tip to the head waiter was raised to fifty for a seat near the stage to see the funny-man. Danny was a riot.

The day the management offered him a percentage of the gross, Danny bought a long, black, chrome-bedecked Cadillac and drove proudly around his old Brooklyn neighborhood. But no one commented on the car. Neither his father nor brothers seemed impressed.

Stopping at the drugstore where he once had worked as a soda jerk he was greeted by the same owner, but one of the old neighbors who saw Danny's fancy new car deliberately told an anecdote to the coffee drinkers at the fountain: "I saw a very funny cartoon the other day. The picture showed two silk-hatted boys from Wall Street driving in a fancy automobile. One is pointing to an old couple picking up sticks along the roadside and he says to his friend, 'And just to show you how far I've come, there are my parents.' "

Pop Kominsky, still living in their old-fashioned home, was fundamentally proud of his actor son, but at the same time saw that flattering applause and overnight success had intoxicated his Duvidl. He worried what vanity could do to his son; he worried about the money Danny was spending on elegant sports clothes and extravagant foods.

Old man Kominsky wanted Danny to calm down before the

fireball burned himself out like a straw fire. He feared the success could not last and he had certain qualms about Danny's and Sylvia's marriage. Danny was running too fast.

"Nu? Nu?" he asked Danny in Yiddish. "What is it you are waiting for? Why don't you have children? Does Sylvia want no children? Everyone in the family and the neighbors on the street wonder why you love every child you see—and have none yourself."

Danny smiled a little evasively and answered, "Pop, give us time, please. I had it tough enough for years—and don't blame Sylvia. I just have started to go places. One day I will have enough money, Pop, so that you can retire."

"I don't want to retire, and I am not impressed by your fancy car. Perhaps I'm only a *schlemiel* but I want you to be honest with yourself."

That night Danny Kaye surprised his audience by being serious. He expatiated on success, kindness, human warmth and values. Sullivan's next column read: "Last night Danny came out on the floor and went into a serious line of talk. He was elegant and he was sincere. Suddenly Danny emerged from the extremely literate philosophy he was expounding and went into a completely insane routine. The transition was so swift, the high comedy touch so expert, that your reporter rolled under the table. I've never seen a star so completely fracture an audience."

How did Danny manage to "fracture" his audience? It is true that he sang, danced, mimed, rattled off Sylvia's bravuras with perfect precision, but Danny's key was hidden in what he calls his "radar sense."

"I can tell within seconds after I step out on the stage what that particular audience is like and what it expects of me. I can sense immediately whether the majority is composed of people who would like my more esoteric intellectual type of songs like 'Pavlova' or 'Stanislavsky' or whether it's an audience for hot licks. I don't know why or how I know this, but I do. Maybe it's a sixth sense or, more likely, the result of many years of experience."

Perhaps the greatest key to his first year of success lies in Danny's love for his audience, his sincere desire to please and his unstinting efforts to please.

Life was good to the Kayes. They had moved to a huge apartment on Central Park South, down the street from the Plaza Hotel. There were more rooms than they could use—but there were also many visitors. Agents flocked to confer with Mr. Kaye. His surname, instead of Danny, was now used by most of the covetous agents who ached to sign him up on exclusive, long-term contracts. Sylvia always sat in during these business conferences and usually tactfully and firmly said "No." She was attentively watching over the future career of her husband. This had been a year of success—would it last? They had to play their hands carefully—Broadway is a jungle where very few remain in the top branches for a long period, where most entertainers spend more time waiting and rehearsing than playing before the footlights.

It was a happy year for the two.

Danny's greatest desire was to give Sylvia full recognition, to give her the tribute she so richly deserved for helping to obtain his first real success. He wished he knew how. He knew that without her he would perhaps still be toomling on the Borscht Circuit. Danny insisted his success was her doing, the result of her talents as a writer, her criticisms and exactness, and her persistence in predicting his potentialities. Sylvia was proud—terribly proud—but she continued to work, and to work hard, ever creating and planning new scat songs for her husband to weave with his genius into a hit routine. During those years Sylvia told an inquisitive reporter, "To be funny, especially if you are a perfectionist, is just plain darned hard work. And the hard work starts from the moment I pick up a pencil and face a leering piece of blank paper. Then ensues a period of anywhere from two to eight weeks, during which time I chew and swallow eighteen pencils, twenty-nine cups of black coffee, argue with my collaborator, Max Liebman, and am very careful not to let Danny see a single word. This last stems from the fact that Danny hates everything we write—which makes it pretty discouraging to discuss material with him. Essentially a fine actor with an exquisite sense of comedy and what I think is a phenomenal sense of timing, the written word is nothing to him. He has to take the words in his mouth, eyes and hands. He must play with them, bend them, stretch them and cajole them, and—most important—bounce them against an audience, before he can truly evaluate them. It's a great thrill for a writer, who must necessarily determine what is funny by intellectual and mechanical means, to see someone arriving at the same conclusions—and even top it, by sheer and unerring instinct."

The millions who have enjoyed Danny's humor and have laughed with him must conclude that being married to a comedian is a very wonderful state of affairs, but the woman behind the man has, in the past, verified that it is not all a rosy and easy life: "I guess it must be the stimulation he needs from an audience that makes it so difficult to rehearse with Danny alone. Mechanically there is absolutely no trouble. With his quick memory and perfect musical ear, he not only knows a number in no time at all, but is a great help to me. I forget my own lyrics. My own lyrics slip out from under me and I am stuck. Not Danny: he remembers every word, every chord; and after a pardonable husbandly dissertation on my inefficiency, we go on from there. But, strangely enough, there's one place where his memory fails him—and drives me to distraction. He'll improvise hundreds of swell pieces of business—and the next day remember only two or three. That, if I may coin a phrase, is murder. It means I have to try to remember them and re-describe them to him—and if you've ever seen a cat trying to bark like a dog, you'll know exactly what I go through.

"But in the final analysis," concluded Sylvia, "Danny is on his own. He's a natural. He supplies his own gestures, intonations and builds a characterization that is right for him. I'm just along for the ride."

Danny smiled at this modest statement, for he knew that it was Sylvia who suggested the changes, insisted on hours of rehearsal, and came out of their work more exhausted than he. It was Sylvia who prodded him into the immense passion for perfection which in turn made him demand more and more from her. It was a successful union and blending of abilities. The two were caught together in the cycle of ambitions, hard work, success and future dreams.

While Danny and Sylvia were hanging onto the tail of a comet, the man who had helped so much on their ascent was experiencing the horrible feeling of falling.

Dario Borzani made a fortune for Danny and himself, but lost his golden egg—La Martinique—when the famous legs of a French lady succeeded Danny Kaye. Mr. Borzani—a debonair, middle-aged man—was used to gaining and losing fortunes. He tried to re-hire Danny Kaye many times, but failed, for Mr. Kaye in later years was too involved and harbored different plans.

"Oh, if Danny would only come with me again," he told anyone who was willing to commiserate—the Kayes or Eddie Dukoff, the entertainment columnists or the agents. "It's all Mistinguette's fault. I heard she was playing in Montreal to a packed house. I hoped she would bring in the crowds, as Danny had done. I decided to sneak out to do some detective work. I found that evidently she was a sensation because all the nearby clubs and pubs were deserted. Her agent told me she was all women put into one, a combination of Gipsy Rose Lee, Marlene Dietrich, Mona Lisa and Josephine Baker. The agent talked fast and I fell into the trap. I booked her for La Martinique.

"Don't ask me what happened then. Danny Kaye brought the people to swamp my place, but Mistinguette organized their disappearance. The day after her opening the critics were crawling down our backs because we had, as they claimed, produced a pair of antique legs. Of course, the gal was closer to a hundred than to forty, but she still looked good. Her face had been pulled up almost a dozen times; perhaps the Canadian folk stormed the place to see her—but for Manhattan, she was a real bird."

Danny looked sad when he heard the story—"And then what did you do?"

Dario continued, "You ask me what I did? I went to Mistinguette. I finally dropped on one knee and pleaded with her to cancel the contract. 'Madam,' I said, 'let us be reasonable. Don't you think you are feeling ill?' She looked at me with fury. She kicked a high-heel mule off her foot. She flipped her chiffon robe and screamed at me, 'My public demands me.'

"And that, Danny, is how La Martinique folded—and after you made it such a success."

"Not I, Dario," replied Danny immediately. "It was Sylvia. Her songs, her words, her encouragement, her insistence. After all, she is the head on my shoulders."

IX

Pure Nonsense Can Be Funny

WHAT MADE DANNY CLICK DURING THIS PERIOD? WHY WAS AND is the Kaye humor different from the entertainers of this century?

Basically he possesses two major qualities. One, the humility, the anti-pompousness, the *sympatico* which Americans admire and which has also endeared him abroad. Second, the skill to catch a mood and sketch a scene with delicate movements and ridiculous wit. These two abilities produce an amalgam of pure nonsense and utter sophistication.

The Kaye humor is never unkind. If anyone is hurt by his jabs, it is himself. His repertoire is without mother-in-law stories, race-prejudice stories, and off-color tales. He does not use poverty, ignorance, deformities or depravities as a springboard to laughter. If he puts in a quiet barb, it is against arrogance, such as the pseudo-elegance of an authoritarian waiter or the falseness of a Wall Street tycoon. And all the world laughs with appreciation as he relieves their minds and hearts.

On his stage shows, Danny learned ways of avoiding the clichés of amusement. While once he had been willing to fall into swimming pools for a laugh, he now learned to appeal to the minds and hearts of his audiences. He did not wish to be a clown, to be laughed at, but an interpreter to be laughed with.

Sylvia was his aide. She recognized that Danny had a "nimble brain and even more nimble tongue." By using each, he could create his own niche in the alcove of humor. And as he has grown, Danny has discovered other skills he can use: the art of the dance; the perfection of his voice; the casual techniques of making the audience at home with him.

Danny keeps back nothing. He uses every muscle of his face, every gesture of his body. The years spent from the Borscht Circuit to the Orient and to England were dedicated to the development of a style of his own. The successes on Broadway were giving him confidence that his formula was right. He could never be a sad-looking Buster Keaton, a jazzy Eddie Cantor, or a maltreated Bob Hope. He had to be a versatile Danny Kaye who used his mind, his body, his brain, his personality, his warmth, his voice, his memory, his fast talk, his ability to pour out the gibberish, and his talent for ingratiating people.

He learned, slowly and not easily, the subtle art of closing the gap between the paying audience and the paid performer. He learned that seriousness and sincerity are not contrary to, but often a part of, humor, and always the contrast upon which laughter plays.

Danny had gone through three phases of his professional development. During his first fumbling days he was pushed by ambition and embryonic talent. He experimented but his songs and acts were recitations. They were not a part of himself. He put them out, rather than wearing them. Sylvia appeared in the second phase when the acts were so carefully tailored that they became a part of his personality. But it was not long before Danny began to fear that he would become "canned," too glib and unthinking.

The last phase was intensified when Danny accepted an offer to be a guest star at the Paramount Theater on Broadway, doing five performances a day. He wondered if the fatigue and one show after another would destroy his verve and spontaneity. It was another challenge.

The audience at the Paramount bore no similarity to the night club crowd at La Martinique or the legitimate theater enthusiasts who flocked to see *Lady in the Dark*.

During the years while Danny struggled for recognition, the world had its own great and tragic chaos: World War II. Hitler had invaded almost all Europe, and on the other side of the world

Japan had seized the opportunity to strike America. All the world was mobilized. Broadway was not blacked out as were London and Berlin, but the once carefree street looked like a parade ground for the army, navy and marines. Movie houses were jammed to overflowing. Boys who would never otherwise have visited New York now thronged the Great White Way for a final fling before being shipped out to the European theater of war.

They stood in long lines to see this "nitwit," the funny-man who was making fun of Hitler, the menace, and could imitate anyone from a newborn baby to Colonel Blimp, and who had a striking resemblance to at least one officer in each of their companies.

The redhead who had found his satisfactions in the rarefied atmospheres of swank clubs and musicals now sensed the new thrill of winning over the galleries and peanut heavens filled with just plain people, soldiers with their girls, mothers with their children, and old couples out on the town for a night's entertainment.

Charlie Chaplin once defined laughter as " a shock which brings home to people the sanity of a situation which they think is insane." Danny filled the bill. He chided war and its stupidity. He made fun of the frailties of people, but always with kindly good taste which left his audiences in a hopeful and amused frame of mind.

"What kind of entertainer were you at the Paramount?" he was asked.

"I was a comedian. But there is a great distinction among types of comedians, entertainers and actors. When someone asks me with whom I like to compare myself and who my favorite comedian is, I have first to ask the question: 'What kind of comedian?' No two are alike. Bob Hope is the best storyteller, Jack Benny the best situation comedian and Charlie Chaplin the best pantomimic. Entertainers are a highly specialized breed of people. They don't merely make you laugh. They make you think or even cry, but, more important, you forget your troubles. That was what I tried to do at the Paramount. In short, I tried to entertain, and there is more to entertainment than laughter. You have to do more than tell jokes to keep people interested in your act for thirty minutes or an hour and a half."

And Danny gave more than jokes. He gave all his talent in its full range to his audiences. They, in turn, sensed his honesty and gave their warm applause.

Danny was receiving the staggering amount of $20,000 a week for his work.

Some of his reviewers, while praising his exhausting performances, realized there was a huge and effective publicity machine grinding out a successful Danny Kaye. They hinted somewhat snidely that $20,000 coming from many men in the armed forces and going to one man who should also be in uniform was an ironical situation. This young man, they whispered, should be in the audience with the rest, not on the stage.

One remark, in particular, irked a sour critic. Danny had just bounced on the stage with his set opening line, "Gee, I'm glad to be back on Broadway," when there was a tremendous blast from a nearby brick building which was being demolished. The theater rocked. Danny grinned impishly, "Never mind the cannon salute, fellas. Just tell them I'm glad to be back." The abusive critic, who was out to scalp Danny, remarked that there was nothing funny about cannons to the young men who were going out to face them. Danny, he continued, was tactless and unfeeling.

However, Danny grew with his one-man show, and both civilians and military personnel enjoyed the endless laughter he spread among them. From his work there emerged a new kind of entertainment.

To analyze his antics means, in a way, to psychoanalyze Mr. Kaye. His "nimble tongue and nimble wit," the utter confusion of his actions, the excessive tempo, the sheer zaniness, the satire and the improvisations gave audiences very real reasons for holding their sides in laughter.

Al Smith had once said, "The American people never carry an umbrella. They prepare to walk in eternal sunshine." And so it was that Danny felt it was far better to poke fun at the demons of war, the Hitlers and the Tojos, to minimize war's bestialities by characterizing human idiosyncrasies.

Danny pelted his audiences with words as rapid and staccato as machine-gun bullets, shouted his bantering nonsense, impersonated anyone who popped into his head, and sang in a reasonable facsimile of half a dozen languages.

Kaye is a talented and rare individual who combines the spirit of jazz, swing, bebop, fast double-talk, pantomime, mimicry and scat singing with a large dash of human sincerity and personal concern. His talent ran so fast, so wild, so untamed, and apparently so unstudied that the audience, at the end of each performance, oozed on to the street in a state of exhaustion.

It is very difficult for a young man from such an impoverished background as Danny's to avoid getting a swollen head. From her place at the piano or by his side, Sylvia tried to keep his feet on the ground and to guide his path in reality. At times it seemed that her husband had lost some of his boyish charm, had gone wild with success, was too sure and sometimes too pat.

On the positive side, Danny had not forgotten his Brooklyn family.

"Yes," he told a co-worker at the Paramount, "I am making money, and I hope it is enough so that Pop can retire and consider his problems a thing of the past."

Pop Kominsky was now aging rapidly, and Danny insisted that his father spend the winters in the sunshine of Florida. There old Mr. Kominsky fraternized with Mr. Kubelsky, the father of another famous entertainer, who spoke often and lovingly of his son, Jack Benny. As the fathers were friends, in later years so were the sons. Danny and Jack pride themselves on a genuine, deep friendship.

But while Pop Kominsky "toomled" in the sun of Miami Beach, Danny was busier than ever at the Paramount in New York.

New Yorkers saw, for the first time, Danny Kaye at popular prices—popular, indeed, for not even standing room was available. The thousands who had not the fifty dollars tip for La Martinique waited patiently in line to see the funny-man who received so much flattering space in the columns of the newspapers.

The critics all agreed Danny Kaye was a funny-man, a funny-man fully capable of making Buster Keaton giggle or the chairman of a senatorial committee break out in a guffaw. For the most part the reviews were glowing.

Danny was plumbing the greatest secret a performer can ever perceive: the art of turning the huge, cold, impersonal stage into his own private and amusing living room, creating the impression that every member of the large audience is an invited and wanted guest visiting him.

He had no set pattern to accomplish his ends. Often he was not certain of the variations he would insert, but he sensed correctly what each audience expected and wanted. Coming from the wings, Danny took over with aggressive charm, persistence and know-how, seemed to find the center of the stage half blindly, and from its glaring spotlight made sure the entire audience felt rapport and performed with him. "They all wanted to get into the act," was Danny's key to a happy and delighted audience, his most successful formula at the Paramount in the early 1940's and still his trade secret fifteen years later.

His audiences are always lured into singing silly songs, ranging from his famous "Minnie the Moocher" to Indian war-songs; from South African ugh-ugh absurdities to his ever varying versions of Frère Jacques.

In the middle of a straight speech he may suddenly become a five-year-old who has just visited the zoo, and what Kaye can do with a word like "hippopotami" is a fearful and wonderful thing. Or he asks for a "seductive" spotlight and slides artfully into a sly imitation of a certain singer named Frank Sinatra.

He does anything with an audience short of luring them to turn on the theater fire hoses. Danny has learned that everyone likes to participate, rather than merely to react. The audience evolves into helpers, producers of fun instead of passive, disinterested consumers of tidbits of humor tossed at them like fish to a tank full of seals.

After every show Danny's dressing room resembled a general merchandise store. Complete strangers showered him with a motley assortment of gifts: cakes, butter, candy, a diamond wedding ring, jars of canned fruit, autographed pictures, costumes, hand-knitted socks, shirts, two dogs and a tiny hamster. Danny was grateful, for he knew each and every gesture came from a heart brightened a bit by his efforts.

The five daily rounds of applause, the sizable weekly pay check and the good reviews in the papers did not slow down the ambitious Danny. He and Sylvia continued to labor over new ideas during show breaks. There were few opportunities to see other

Broadway shows, and only once in a while did they catch glimpses of their families.

His closing program was scheduled for only thirty minutes, but the audience kept him on the stage for ninety-one, during which time he presented his best acts. During one number he unexpectedly doubled up with spontaneous laughter. "You won't believe it," he told the audience, "but a little girl in the third row is looking at me through binoculars." Who could escape such gracious informal sharing of a joke? New York couldn't, and rose to its feet singing "Auld Lang Syne" as the last curtain fell.

X

Okaye

DANNY'S ROLE IN WORLD WAR II REMAINS CONTROVERSIAL. DURING a period of war hysteria there will always be just and unjust accusations. Danny tried to enlist in the army as soon as war was declared because he felt he must do his duty and in a sense repay the great advantages his immigrant family had received in the United States.

After his rejection because of a temperamental sacroiliac, an injury incurred by an unfortunate leap off a stage, he tried to join other branches of the service, each time to be turned down. Frustrated, Danny dedicated his career to entertaining wounded veterans, making large contributions to war bond drives, assisting the Red Cross and helping in any way he could through his talents as an entertainer.

His long hours at army camps were duly publicized, but the skeptical public pointed a finger of scorn at this healthy-looking young man who wore civilian clothing. They pooh-poohed the reports of physical disability as sheer press-agentry. Danny seethed. He wanted desperately to help destroy the mass-murderer of the Jewish race, the man who had started World War II. Whispered remarks—"Danny is avoiding war service"; "Danny is making millions of dollars while millions of people die"—added to his anger.

It was a sobering period for the successful entertainer, in many respects a sort of turning point. He had drunk deeply from the wine of success and had been intoxicated by the money and its power. He had tossed dollars around like confetti and satisfied his whims by living extravagantly. Now, most of all, he wanted to do his part.

"If I show that I feel guilty about being a civilian, people say it is all a publicity stunt for my show. If I hide my feelings, the same people say I am brazen and heartless," he said bitterly.

But he mustered together all his energies, talents and spare time and offered them on any occasion to any cause that would help in the global emergency. During six months he sold over a billion dollars in war bonds, including the one million dollars he collected by auctioning off Jack Benny's fiddle in Gimbel's basement in New York. He appeared at veterans' hospitals and army camps and never refused an invitation to entertain for the troops.

One night in 1942 Danny was called to Washington. The occasion was a giant war-bond rally at which every member of the Cabinet was present, with both President and Mrs. Roosevelt as guests of honor. It was the American equivalent of a command performance.

Both Sylvia and Danny felt honored to meet the president. Sylvia pleaded with Danny to keep his performance dignified with the reminder, "It is not every day one performs for the president."

Danny nodded. He had not the slightest idea what he would do, how much time would be allotted to him, or what mood was befitting the Washington hierarchy that grim war night. He dimly planned to try some of his songs, some of the imitations of his version of Prussian–Teutonic–Wagnerian–Hitlerian tongue-twisting Dutch. That, he knew, would bring a laugh.

Because the audience warmed up to Danny from the first moment on, he became daring and insisted on audience participation. Why not? They were just people, and this was a democracy. Responding to his suggestions, the Cabinet members, senators and the president sang with him like any Broadway audience. Then pixie mischief leapt on his back. He barked like a dog, sang a rhyme, and said, "You, come on, follow me!" and the audience barked—sang, barked, laughed and barked again.

Someone in the audience guffawed madly and could not stop his laughter. Danny wondered what to do. Who was he? The man who still laughed. "Don't you know?" a stage hand later told him. "He was a senator, a Republican, and he was so amused because you are the first man in history who could get an American president to bark like a dog."

These were great days for a performer and anxious days for any patriotic American. Danny threw himself even deeper into war work on the home front.

Ed Sullivan recalls from those days when Danny phoned him, "Suppose I do a comedy for Lily Pons in an aria. Let Lily sing, opera-style, and we'll get André Kostelanetz to lead a ninety-piece band. Against that background, whatever I do will be funny!"

"That was one of the great moments in Madison Square Garden history," comments the unsmiling television M.C. "They tore the roof off the place."

The occasion was the Army Emergency Relief show. Danny stole the act.

He worked so insistently during this period he was twice forced into the hospital. "I've seldom seen such vitality," said one doctor. "Mr. Kaye drives himself as if pursued by a demon. His energy must come from an internal dynamo. Then, occasionally, he just wears out. He comes to us in a state of complete nervous exhaustion, makes a few wisecracks and falls into bed like a dead man. But it is only a matter of a few days of rest before he is leaping around the room like old Doug Fairbanks used to do, and we send him out before he tears the hospital up with his vigor."

After the engagement at the Paramount Theater, an even bigger offer was made to Danny and Sylvia. Vinton Freedly asked the comedian to star in Cole Porter's *Let's Face It*. Dorothy and Herbert Field had helped Cole Porter, but Sylvia was commissioned to write the songs for all of Danny's special numbers.

Danny liked the idea of the show because it was a war parody, but there was a problem of finding time to plan and rehearse among his other duties. Sylvia liked the idea, but she too was busy with war work which left her with a dried-up feeling, an exhaustion which made words fly out of her mind and melodies stick like a broken record.

After a number of unsuccessful beginnings, Sylvia and her faithful collaborator, Max Liebman, went into retreat, once again in the quiet of the Pocono Mountains. Danny joined them as often as he could get away from war-tense New York.

"I was progressing very slowly," Sylvia recalls, "when one night I remembered a silly bit of improvisation Danny had once done at a dinner party. Our host, a doctor, was called away to perform a very delicate emergency operation. My medicine-happy husband begged to be allowed to accompany him. When they returned someone asked Danny how the operation went, and he answered them by going into an elaborate pantomime, punctuated by scat and a few intelligible words.

"This memory started an idea. It was the first year after our entrance into the war. Every man—and every woman—had the draft uppermost in his mind. The draft, medical examinations, doctors. . . .

"In approved movie style, I woke Danny up with a loud, 'I've got it!' and scrambled out of bed to wake up poor Max with a phone call."

This was the birth of "Melody in 4F," otherwise known as "Local Draft Board Makes Good," a zany bit of comedy destined to establish Danny once again as a Broadway great, and Sylvia as a song writer of originality and distinction.

In the act, Danny caricatured a draftee from the time he receives his questionnaire, through his sessions with the army doctor, the dentist, his trials and troubles with the drill sergeant to his final success and honors in maneuvers. It required pantomime, triple-time and quadruple-time scat-singing with an occasional recognizable word.

The growth of "Melody in 4F" was laborious. Sylvia, tiny and attractive, her black hair caught up by a scarf, sat coercing the piano to talk in much the way an author pounds his typewriter to make it say what he wants.

Max, cigar in mouth, hung over Sylvia's shoulder, humming an offkey theme while Sylvia attempted to catch it in notes. Occasionally he would pound on the piano, then wipe his brow and stride up and down the practice room. Danny worked by fits and starts, sometimes sitting relaxed listening to the two argue over an idea, but more often gyrating through a bit of business to try it out. And slowly but surely evolved the song and the sketch, "Melody in 4F."

Sylvia analyzes their cooperative work this way: "It is hard to say who contributed what to such a number as the one which finally emerged. There are less than two actual words to each eight bars of music. If you think I know what all that gibberish is in between, you are wrong. I can't even say it, much less write it. That is where the cooperation of Danny himself is invaluable to the creation of a number."

Sylvia and Max suffered and sweated over this song, but it was Danny who had to pay the final price of cycloning through the rapid tempo of his own nonsensical double-talk. As usual, Danny disliked rehearsing without the stimulation of an audience, and, as usual, he remembered and captured each phrase, each musical situation as soon as it came off the keys. Many times the two musicians refused to believe the next day they had created the scene as Danny repeated it to them.

"It's really a series of hot licks that worked its way from New Orleans in a Dixieland tempo to the rapid-fire propensities of my poor tongue. It is a miracle to me, however, that the tricks of my tongue should be regarded by so many people as my most important asset. I most certainly do not want to base my career on one ability."

Then followed five long weeks of New York rehearsals. The producer, Mr. Freedly, watched with apprehension. Danny Kaye was not the brilliant performer he had counted on. Kaye was stiff, anxious, overworked his role, labored at the songs. "I'm losing my shirt if Danny doesn't click," Freedly said to one of his assistants. The entertainer, overhearing the comment, added, "Mr. Freedly, if I don't click we will *all* walk *naked* down Broadway."

Danny worked harder, but each rehearsal seemed worse than the previous one. The dress rehearsal in Boston was as tight as a violin string. It seemed as if one false move and Danny would snap. At five o'clock on the evening of the opening the worried producer could stand it no longer. After a preface of unconvincing pep talk, Mr. Freedly asked Danny to understand that, in the event his scat songs were not the anticipated success, they would have to be deleted from the show. He went on to mention the fact that he could not afford empty houses. "This is not *Lady in the Dark*. We have no Gertrude Lawrence in the show."

Mr. Freedly's attitude further deflated the worried Mr. Kaye. "I knew Danny needed reassurance," says Sylvia. "Max and I tried to be blithe, to cheer him up, but it was like trying to change the course of the Columbia River. Danny was in the channel of worry, gloom and despair."

Danny tells his reactions this way: "Every time I closed my eyes I saw myself standing nude on an empty stage before an empty house. When I thought of my opening lines, they vanished from my mind. The usual fluttering butterflies in my stomach were all wearing big lead shoes on their feet. Sylvia helped the most by reminding me that the opening night was a sellout. I tried to console myself that I would be protected by a thousand pairs of eyes, and vowed to give them all I had in the best way I knew."

In what seemed like an aeon's time the house-lights dimmed, the curtain rose, and *Let's Face It* was launched. Danny made a slow beginning, faltering and going stiffly through his first acts. But the audience laughed, and laughter was the anodyne for his fears. As always, Danny played many roles, starting as a statue in a war-memorial group, moving into a Dracula in a boathouse and coming to a near climax with a song about fairy-tale tomatoes. Each new scene was easier, better and more Kayeish than the previous one. Danny's qualms were melting under the warmth of the applause and laughter.

Danny, reminiscing about his opening night, tells with touches of nostalgia: "I was afraid of a number called 'Fairy Tales for Grown-ups,' a comedy monologue about the three bears, spoken in a baby voice. The first time I came out on the stage and spoke the lines to an empty theater I began to think, 'Isn't this silly—an adult standing up here and talking this childish nonsense.' I broke into a blush, and I just couldn't go on.

"On opening night I was scared stiff to start the number, but after I had said, 'Once there were three bears,' in a silly voice, the audience laughed. I picked up and went on, putting in all sorts of motions and expressions according to audience reaction."

"Melody in 4F" was probably the best song Sylvia had written up to this time, and Danny was fearful he had not done it justice.

Still perturbed after the curtain, he ran backstage and, amidst all the cheering and applause, blurted out, "Syl, I loused up your song—didn't I?"

Well-wishers closed in, clapping him on the back and offering congratulations, but not before Sylvia had turned on her heel with a condemning "You sure *did* louse it up!"

A wise woman would not have made such a statement and at such a time, but Sylvia was very young and personally ambitious.

As for the success of the song, Sylvia and Danny could not have been more incorrect. The audience was delighted, and the show was a smash hit on Broadway for sixteen months. At each performance Danny brought down the house with his fierce pantomime, his jabberwocky patter, Sylvia's songs and his clowning.

"Melody in 4F" was the show-stopper. In ninety seconds of double-talk and expressive gestures, Danny ticked off the life of a draftee, told in his "own riddle-de-biddle de reep." It was new, it was fast, and it was funny. It poked fun at an uppermost concern of every adult.

The USO and other organizations brought wounded soldiers by the busload to see the show. They laughed and Danny, still tingling from the stinging remarks of caustic critics, was visibly pleased when one New York newspaper reported that he was making an "immeasurable contribution to the war effort."

Meantime, however, Pop Kominsky's hopes that Danny would calm down, perhaps even start a family, were far from realized. His son's tensions increased. He was still possessed by his ambitions and fearful of his professional enemies. A critic, he discovered, has all the tenderness and restraint of a caged rattlesnake, but when he strikes he shows the same deadly precision.

Danny's stage work and his war entertainment enforced an eighteen-hour-a-day schedule, and he became the prototype of the nervous wreck he portrayed night after night on the stage. His tensions resulted in his eating very little and sleeping even less. He walked with fast, bouncy steps and drummed incessantly on the table or chair arm. He sped like a madman through dressing and make-up and literally catapulted himself onto the stage. His constant race against time acted as adrenalin which geared him up to the frenzied pitch he felt necessary for a good performance.

Stage managers and doormen were kept in a constant state of alarm. They were very fond of Danny for his generosity, kindness, his concern for their families and personal problems, but they were near insanity because of Danny's split-second appearance to dress for each performance. Each one feared there would be one terrible time when he would not split the second accurately enough, would be tied up in New York's mad traffic, or could not get his trousers on by the time his cue was called.

But Danny's stupendous success accorded him a prestige so that he could get by with some peculiarities. The nerve-racked call-boys noticed he was conspicuously absent during each second act and arrived only in time to race directly onto the stage. Where did Danny go? No one knew until the stage manager, near an apoplectic attack, started an investigation.

His discovery made his blood curdle. Danny left the theater between acts, stepped across the alley to the neighboring theater where *Beat the Band* was playing. The play contained a scene in which a Don Juan hero said a suave farewell to a flock of chorus girls as he left by train. Mr. Kaye, on his way to earning more than $100,000 a year, had the illustrious, unseen and unpaid role of standing in the wings and, at the proper cue, yelling at the top of his lungs "Allllll—aaaa—board!"

Then Danny turned, sprinted out the door, across the alley and onto the stage of his own show, just in time for his entrance in the second part of *Let's Face It.*

Geared-up and keyed-up, he sang his best songs.

"Why are you doing it?" asked the exasperated producer.

"It is fun for me," was Danny's only explanation.

On hearing this, Vinton Freedly commented, "It's harmless. Some actors take dope, others drink. As long as he is there on time, let him have his fun."

Danny gave Sylvia a more explicit reason for the crazy "all aboard" stunt. "It helps me to reduce the tensions under which I work. Actually I am more relaxed when I get away and am doing something. Before each performance I often have a sort of manic-depressive mood. I snap at my friends. To get out from under these malevolent influences, I sing, or dance, or stir up horseplay—anything to keep occupied. I find myself whistling like mad, and the more nervous I get the more I whistle. It was more fun to shout 'all aboard' than to whistle all the time."

Anyone watching Mr. Kaye realizes he burns up more energy during the thirty minutes before a performance than most actors do during an entire show.

His energies seem to come from a bottomless well. He seldom smokes, never takes a drink before a performance and is generally in such excellent physical condition that he is fresh and sometimes eager to attend private parties with Sylvia after his shows, and often entertains there for a few more hours.

Popular as a guest, Danny takes over if a party goes sour and, with a few gestures or imitations, replaces the doldrums with gaiety. "Entertaining people means bringing happiness—even if for only a short time—and certainly entertainment need not be confined to a hard wooden stage."

Much depends on his moods. He can be the lion of the party, or he can be its best listener. He can be chatty and intimate or aloof and silent. When he gets bored, he is a fast man to walk away.

Dr. Irving Somach, the well-known New York physician, remembers when he once saw Danny give a complete performance of Chaplin's *The Great Dictator* at a party. "Do you know," he says, "he made us laugh, of course; but more than that, he convinced us all that we had never seen the picture. Danny has an abnormally developed mechanism. I've never looked into the matter formally, but some part of a comedian's brain must be overdeveloped. Comedians see more, hear more and remember more than an average person. In Danny's case that part of his brain must be the size of a watermelon and as retentive as photographic film."

At another party the host asked Danny what he thought of the performance he does twice a day. Was the audience a nebulous dark blob of unknown enthusiasts, a group of frightening critics, a mass of individual faces?

Danny did not consider the question long, hinting that perhaps he had analyzed his feelings before. He startled the party with an unusual and impressive simile: "I see a performance as a mass of molten gold. You can shape it into whatever form you think best."

It was an odd description, and the guests wanted to know more details.

"I like to mold my act into many shapes, depending on the mood, the show, the country I'm in. Sometimes I mold a long, delicate necklace, or short, wide earrings, or intricate bits of fili-gree. I see the necklace as the overall effect of a long performance, the earrings as solid mass of applause, appreciation and laughter as the result of my performance. I visualize the filigree as cunning bits of business woven in and out of the performance."

Week after week of successful performances and glowing reports passed, but Danny did not learn to relax. Financially life was fab-ulous, but he continued to run . . . run . . . run. Sylvia received sizable royalties for her music, but she too was caught in the vortex of ambition.

Their close friends shook their heads and handed out unheeded advice. Would Danny eventually fall? Or would he fill in the thin-ning lines of a new generation of laugh-makers. The royal line of comedians appeared to be dwindling. Where were the heirs appar-ent? Vaudeville was virtually gone from Broadway, burlesque was dead, and radio had kidnaped the major comedians from the Great White Way.

One night Danny received a visitor in his dressing room—none other than A. B. Marcus of the Vie Paree group, the man who had unwillingly taken him to the Orient and who never thought the young vaudevillian was funny.

"How did you enjoy the show?" queried Danny hesitantly.

"Well, it was grand, wonderful, a smash hit—but, Danny, I still do not think you are funny."

The two men laughed.

But John Mason Brown, the critic who had once written a single line which damned with faint praise, now called Danny "unrivaled along Broadway," and continued, "It is art of a high and rare and most exceptional kind. It makes some of us wonder if Danny Kaye's first name should not have been 'O.' "

"Just glad he didn't say Dee," quipped Danny.

XI

Sam Goldwyn's Office Box

THE STORY OF DANNY'S ASCENT FROM A FIFTY-DOLLAR-A-WEEK tumult-maker to a motion picture star has often been told. Each memorable anecdote has been blown up for Danny's publicity: the stories of his unhappy youth; his failures in his early professional years; his flop at London's Dorchester House; his pleas for recognition; the long working hours and Sylvia's vast contribution to his success. But Danny was not in Hollywood, yet.

There, the laughter was different. The stooges, court jesters, situation comics and slapstick manipulators were, quite literally, a dime a dozen. Their humor was hard; it was biting; it cut with a lash of bitterness and was not considered funny unless someone was hurt by it.

The Hollywood studios were and are impregnable fortresses surrounded by iron gates and guarded by a sturdy string of studio police. Hopefuls come and go; tourists are readily turned away, and passes are as valued as much as tickets to the Rose Bowl Game on New Year's Day.

For the Kayes there was no motion picture contract in sight. In reply to the questions from reporters, Sylvia developed a pat phrase to hide behind. "We will go to Hollywood when we are ready. But it is not the time yet."

Early in 1944, *Let's Face It* was playing to demonstrative audiences night after night on Broadway. When the first Hollywood offer came, it was not expected by either artist.

There exist, today, two versions of the manner in which Danny Kaye was plucked from New York and settled before the cameras of palm-fringed Hollywood. The first, a product of the liberal thinking of studio press agents, makes good fan-magazine reading, but does not quite come up to the real truth.

The story goes that Danny Kaye kept the great Sam Goldwyn waiting for the better part of an hour while he played a joke over the phone: "See here, dis is da hangout of Marblehead Moe . . . and I'm warning ya, lay off callin' here or I'll get da mob to take ya for a ride—unnerstand? I got da wires tapped and I know where y'are."

With this tirade Mr. Kaye slammed down the receiver. It was the eighth time the phone had rung that morning, and Danny had not been able to finish the potato pancakes he was trying to prepare for breakfast.

He returned to the kitchen, where Sylvia had taken over. While pouring his orange juice, she asked innocently, "That poor soul will never call us again. Who was it, darling?"

"Your mother," answered Danny, reheating his coffee from the silver pot.

Sylvia's mouth flew open. "Mother!" she stammered. "You— you—this time you've gone too far. Phone immediately and apologize. You must have scared the wits out of the poor woman."

"I won't either," grumbled Danny stubbornly. "That would take all the fun out of it." But a glance at Sylvia's firmly set mouth and the fire leaping from her dark eyes told him it was the better part of valor to phone and explain. It took some time to soothe the ruffled feathers at the other end of the line, and when he felt he had succeeded, he turned the phone over to Sylvia.

The entire conversation with Mrs. Fine took quite a time, and that is why Mr. Goldwyn had to wait for many impatient minutes.

Mr. Goldwyn is the last man in the world to be kept waiting. In similar circumstances he generally wires, cables, fumes or phones the White House for help. But the Kayes' line was busy.

Sam Goldwyn had placed a call from Hollywood to the Kayes

in New York to offer David Kominsky a five-year contract to make four motion pictures at $100,000 each. At long last the busy signal was cleared, and Danny heard the voice of the great man.

Although this version is in keeping with the pixie quality of Danny Kaye's general behavior, its truth is as far away as Sylvia's washing machine was from the sound tracks of the Goldwyn studios.

Abe Lastvogel of the William Morris Agency had urged Mr. Goldwyn to hear Mr. Kaye on Broadway, to consider an "option" and give him a screen test.

Goldwyn complied, listened to the spontaneous antics of the combustible comedian, returned to California with a new personality in mind, but also with some reservations. It appeared obvious that Danny's forte was improvisation. Could he stand the discipline of rehearsals and steady lines? He was certainly personable, clean-cut and tall, but on closer observation, he was also leading with a very long nose which would be a problem to photograph. He appeared to be intelligent. Could he cooperate?

But in the top drawer of his desk Mr. Goldwyn had a script, *Up in Arms,* which needed a Danny Kaye personality and Hollywood needed a new face. The producer made contact with Kaye and offered him a contract. The publicity wheels ground out their joyful words of superlatives on the West Coast while Eddie Dukoff worked madly to promote "his boy" in the east.

Danny was besieged with congratulations, admonitions, advice and horror stories about Hollywood. His friends in the legitimate theater, realizing the tremendous stimulation Danny received from his audiences, wondered if he could perform without hundreds of eyes focused on him and laughter pushing at him from a darkened theater.

Gertrude Lawrence later admitted that Noel Coward and Moss Hart had joined her in warning Danny to stay away from Hollywood. They felt he was not ready for the shift. Miss Lawrence told Danny bluntly, "You can't stop a camera in Hollywood! You, dear boy, will miss the applause."

Pop Kominsky was excited. He disliked the thoughts of having Danny so far away, but he had grown accustomed to his son's many absences.

Danny Kaye was a little staggered by this sudden happening. The events of the past years, both to himself and to other entertainers, seemed to indicate that there were few actors who could stay permanently on Broadway, and certainly he could not vie with the notable Metropolitan opera stars who were now being hired for musicals and operettas. A try at success before the motion picture cameras seemed a likely move.

Sylvia was even more certain.

"We argued night and day over the advantages and disadvantages," says Sylvia. "There were many times when I had to bolster Danny's nerves. There were times when he would retire behind the thought that it was wiser to keep the success he had than to explore a new medium of expression for his talent."

A few months later Sylvia and Danny arrived in California, and, after fighting the battle of the studio guards, were admitted into Sam Goldwyn's outer office.

"What is Goldwyn *really* like?" Danny whispered to the receptionist.

"He's terrific," was the answer.

Moss Hart, Jack Benny, everyone "in the know" had told him the same thing. "Goldwyn is a fantastic character with unlimited energies and boundless ideas. He is a master-mind—and he's terrific."

When the young couple was ushered into the producer's plush office, Sylvia, with the assurance so typical of her, gave the dapper Goldwyn her hand with the air of one used to meeting Hollywood moguls, as if she considered him just another successful European who had found his way to fortune in America. Danny was shy and retiring, almost ill at ease.

The producer's opening remark was, "I won't pay you a cent more!"

Danny grinned. "But you haven't paid me a cent yet."

For a moment Goldwyn was stopped. He looked at Danny, sized up the well-dressed Mrs. Kaye and smiled. He liked Danny from the start.

Goldwyn settled himself at his desk and began pushing buttons on his intercom system. He issued instructions for screen tests, for costumes, for make-up, for script conferences. The short meeting was concluded with the command that Sylvia and Max Liebman begin at once to write songs that were "funnier than ever."

During the following days the Kayes tried to feel their way into their new community. If New York was a jungle of agents and aspirants who daily added one more ulcer, Hollywood was a world geared more rapidly than the eastern subway system. Three fast martinis for lunch, then a dash to an European sports car. Three fast Scotches at dinner and a mad whirl to a party where it was always difficult to recognize the women since they seldom had the same color of hair twice.

Actors in Hollywood, they soon discovered, do not live like other people and certainly do not live with them. They successfully hide in mansions, protected from prying eyes of the tourists by private police and intricate systems of electric eyes. They entertain their guests and publicity agents around their oddly shaped pools and stay in a state intoxicated by their own dreams.

The two kids from Brooklyn realized after a short time that they were not in the class with Clark Gable, Bing Crosby, Bob Hope and the rest. As a matter of fact, they were virtually unknown.

Danny, impressed with the reputation of the great Goldwyn, awed by his obvious originality and aggressiveness, was also amazed that this man was willing to gamble millions on a nobody, unrecognized off Broadway.

While he worried and tried to discover Hollywood on his own, Sylvia was engrossed in more practical matters. She conferred with Abe Lastvogel on business details and began mapping the stratagem of dealing with Sam Goldwyn, a man who is used to having his own way and accustomed to winning arguments.

Life inside the studios was a world of its own. Armies of laborers, propmen, make-up men, craftsmen, directors, women, women, and more women. There were the agents' contractors, caterers, sound men, assistants and assistants to the assistants.

On their nights out, the Kayes found restaurants crowded with loud people, men wearing padded coats and women with low cut dresses. Many wore dark glasses.

The land of make-believe. The dream factory, but it was a factory.

In Hollywood, some of the rudeness of metropolitan New York

is replaced by an artificial enthusiasm which is worn like a royal badge. No one, however, commits himself to anything, for the lawyers and the legal departments are the real bosses even though their names are not known.

People talked nothing but movies—and the weather. Big names were tossed about even by those who knew them only from the screen. Gossip was rampant, being concocted from whole cloth over the bar or at the dinner table.

Sylvia complained to Danny that Hollywood ran faster than New York, for the Glitter City always rushes, while New York makes the dash only twice a day—going and coming from work on the subway. In Hollywood everyone always has an appointment with someone "important." But when Sylvia and Danny met an appointment they were, two times out of three, kept waiting. The delays were the result of a tie-up on the freeway, an accident on Sunset Boulevard, a retake on a screen test or a preview.

Danny analyzed what he saw. Narrowing his blue eyes, he searched the people he met and sometimes tried to imitate them with the thought his caricatures might some day make an audience laugh. "Everyone here," he said, "seems to be a fame addict. Little do they seem to realize that more actors land in the garbage cans of defeat than on the ladder of success." Many bit actors with whom he talked were gamblers at heart, working for only a few weeks and eating their dreams of grandeur the rest of the year.

A certain amount of fear began to assail the Kayes. Goldwyn had not signed the contract.

Danny hung around the sets watching the shooting of a "colossal" picture. On one side, quite out of camera range, was a large table which made an ordinary drugstore look like a cosmetic counter. There was a fantastic array of pills of every color, green, blue, pink, and a delicate mauve, Benzedrine tablets to keep you awake, Dexedrine to give pep, vitamins for strength, cold pills to ward off the sniffles, Emperin, cideine and Bufferin for headaches and hangovers, histamines and antihistamines, and sleeping pills for the aftermath of a nerve-racking day.

"We were pikers when we did 'Melody in 4F,' " said Danny to Sylvia in a whisper. Sylvia threw her husband a frightened smile. She sensed what might be in store for him.

Then came the day when Goldwyn cleared all pending matters, signed the contract with Danny Kaye, and made the final clearance for the initial screen test.

Everything went wrong—totally, completely, discouragingly wrong. Danny's screen tests were hideous. His nose photographed somewhere between that of Cyrano de Bergerac and the proboscis of an anteater. He seemed to be all angles, topped off by a wad of unruly hair.

Goldwyn was in a rage, and Danny wallowed in despair. He was not photogenic, not handsome, projected no Romeo charm and was as funny as a wet tea-bag. The fact that Goldwyn liked Kaye made no difference.

Frances Goldwyn, who shared the worries of her husband, describes these days: "In that first screen test Danny's face was all angles and his nose so long and thin it was almost like Pinocchio's. More tests were made; then more. Each day new make-up and different lightings were tried. And none was good.

"Meanwhile the script had had its final editing, the sets had been built, the cast engaged, down to the last Goldwyn girl. Meanwhile, too, everyone around the studio you most respect and trust had, at first hesitantly, then insistently, urged Sam to take the loss in pride and money and call the picture off—to forget Danny Kaye.

"How well I remember that hot summer morning. I had been up half the night before listening to Sam argue with himself that there must be some way to make Danny possible to photograph. Then I drove him to the studio and we went alone into the projection room to have one more look at those endless Kaye tests.

"Perhaps three had been run off when Sammy let out a kind of yelp, reached for the studio phone and asked for the hairdresser. I've often wondered what he thought when I heard Sam announce over the wire, 'I've got it! I've got it! Expect Kaye in ten minutes. He's having his hair dyed blond.'

"Without that inspiration and the peroxide bottle, who knows— would Kaye be a picture star today?"

If the Goldwyns were facing a crisis with their new star, Danny was ready to leave Hollywood, to run back to the other side of the continent, where he had been happy.

Sylvia maintained her calmness and assurance during the trying days. She was sure Danny would make the screen—with or without Sam Goldwyn—and so stated to any and all who would listen to her. She efficiently managed their house, which they rented on a monthly basis in Beverly Hills, played travel agent, packed and unpacked, and organized their life of commuting between New York appearances and Hollywood struggles.

Sam Goldwyn altered Danny's early motion picture career and nearly changed Kaye's face as well. It is Dr. Somach who is to be thanked because Danny Kaye possesses today the same nose his mother gave him. In spite of all Goldwyn's advice that Kaye's troublesome nose be changed by plastic surgery, Dr. Somach steadfastly opposed the operation. Dr. Somach tells of the day when a nervous and upset Danny Kaye called at his office.

"Irving," Danny said, "I want you to help me."

"What's the matter?" asked the doctor.

"I need plastic surgery on my nose. It is not straight and it is too big. I'm a movie star now, and I am supposed to win the girl in every picture."

"You are crazy," said the doctor. "You need your nose just as much as Chaplin needs his mustache, but I will tell you what I'll do. Personally I strongly disapprove of this operation, but I will ask the greatest plastic surgeon in America, Dr. Gustave Aufricht, to watch one of your Broadway performances, and if he says the operation is necessary, I'm with you."

Danny agreed on such a consultation.

Two days later Dr. Aufricht found two tickets in his mail and attended a Kaye performance. Danny, knowing he was in the house, played to the seat in which the prominent surgeon was supposed to be sitting. Either unfortunately or fortunately, the tickets had been mixed, and the doctor was sitting in another seat.

After the show, the doctor took a plaster impression of the Kaye nose. And the next day the two doctors met with Mr. and Mrs. Kaye for a consultation.

The eminent Dr. Aufricht opened and closed the session with a brief speech delivered in his heavy Viennese accent: "Mr. Kaye, you know I'm a very expensive doctor, and I know you are a star with ample money to pay me for my work. I also realize it would be excellent publicity for me to perform an operation on you, a noted performer. But, Mr. Kaye, all the money you possess could not induce me to do plastic surgery on you. It is an operation you do not need."

Dr. Somach concludes his story, "Just recently Danny came to the house to spend an evening with me. When he entered the front door, he gave me a resounding kiss on the forehead. Naturally I was astonished. 'What was that for?' I asked. 'The beginning of a new gag?'

" 'That,' said Kaye, 'was for the operation you did not let me have.' "

Back in Hollywood, Sam Goldwyn accepted Danny with his own nose. After all, nothing in the contract stipulated a change in the new star's face. The blond hair, new techniques in make-up, and different camera angles were showing Danny on the screen as the appealingly handsome young man he is. Even Goldwyn had to admit the entire situation worked out satisfactorily.

After two months of working with Sam Goldwyn, Danny felt the producer was a funnier character than he, the supposedly funny-man, could ever be. He gave out a constant flow of be-fuddled language that earned a never-ending supply of mirth.

Sam Goldwyn was all the columnists, authors and gossipers said of him—and more. His career began as a Polish immigrant boy who ran away from Warsaw at the age of seven, spent a few years in England, left his relatives there and came to the United States. At the age of eighteen he sold fifteen thousand pairs of gloves a year for a factory in Gloversville, New York, and thus became their ace salesman.

In 1913, with his brother-in-law, Jesse Lasky, Sam invaded the motion-picture industry. Between them they had a lump sum of $26,500. Known as one of the bossiest men in Hollywood, Sam was also respected as the "maker of stars."

Now Mr. Goldwyn sat behind his massive oak desk ready to launch a new star—Danny Kaye.

The executive offices of the great Sam Goldwyn reflected the splendor of the Hollywood Napoleon. All four walls were lined from ceiling to floor with pictures of the men and women he had "made" in the past. His expansive desk-top was cleared, as no work could ever come from that desk, with the exception of the folders containing the latest script which lay in front of him. An array of secretaries, "yes men" and subservients surrounded him. The Kayes waited patiently while Mr. Goldwyn spoke with New York, Paris, London, as if it were the most natural thing to do between breakfast and lunch.

Danny was impressed with Sam Goldwyn's astute operations and the high standards he held for his productions. He also felt he must give his fair share to the contemplated venture. As he wrote Pop Kominsky, "Dad, if they let me do what I think I can, I will surprise even Mr. Goldwyn. Sylvia has some great new ideas, and we are prepared to work as hard as we can."

In reply, Mr. Kominsky answered briefly, "Just remain the same guy you've always been and you'll make good. I don't mind settling in California myself."

At times it was difficult for the Kayes to accept the eccentricities of Hollywood—its actor worship, the false gold and glitter. They accepted invitations to parties in order to get acquainted, but Danny begrudged the hours because he had to get up early in the mornings to be at the studio or on the plane back to New York. He took a dim view of the publicity stunts in which actors were thrown into the swimming pools. "I used to be paid for getting wet," he whispered once to Sylvia as the host dragged a dripping blonde out of the water.

Sylvia knew that the two, in their small rented house, would have to reduce their social life to a handful of friends who mattered on a professional or human level. They were still on the fringe of the film world, and, as such, could not boast of so much as an evening with the Boss, the incredible Goldwyn.

They often talked about the moon-faced producer who seemed to command a battalion of staff members, each one regimented like a Prussian army officer, with the duty to get things done in the fashion the General demanded. Underneath it all, however, Sam Goldwyn was noticeably kind and gracious to his co-workers.

The Kayes enjoyed the motion-picture helmsman from their first meeting with him. They were amused at his upside-down speech and impressed by his forcefulness, although Sylvia sensed there could be trouble with this active, aggressive and determined boss who demanded his own way, a privilege for which he was willing to pay fabulous sums. A generous man, but a perfectionist, his genius had given birth to many of the world's greatest pictures— *All Quiet on the Western Front, Little Foxes, Wuthering Heights, The Best Years of Our Lives, The Pride of the Yankees, Dead End, Dodsworth* and *Arrowsmith.* His next project was *Up in Arms,* starring Danny Kaye and Dinah Shore, with scores and librettos by Sylvia Fine and Max Liebman.

It is interesting to surmise whether or not Danny was unconsciously drawn to Sam Goldwyn as a kind of father figure. Both Mr. Goldwyn and Jakob Kominsky had come to the United States from eastern Europe; both were rooted in their Jewish past and had experienced the suffering of their impoverished families. Both spoke Russian and Yiddish and both had found new lives in the same country. However, there was the one great difference, Sam Goldwyn soared ahead into success in Hollywood while Jakob Kominsky sewed and slaved to keep his family together.

Goldwyn has been accused of ruthlessness by people who envy his power, plush life and accomplishments. Pop Kominsky was never a man to push his way into the limelight.

While Danny recognized Sam Goldwyn's dynamic powers, he was also surprised by the paternal attitude of the tycoon of the movie world. There was a bond of understanding. Danny behaved as if he knew the secret of Goldwyn, who had risen from the poor man's ghetto in Poland to the golden ghetto of the movie island of Hollywood.

Later, when Danny knew Goldwyn much better, he said of him, "Sam would have bought Shakespeare, had he been alive, and reserved the right to mispronounce his name. He argues a man into a coma or a disorder resembling the bends. His victim signs anything. His voice breaks men down like a rubber hose. Goldwyn is the only man I know who can throw a seven with one die."

There were times when Danny did not see eye to eye with Goldwyn, but there was never a time in their long relationship when Danny did not speak of the man with deep respect, for Mr. Goldwyn contributed much to Danny Kaye's career.

Once, in a group discussing the determined character of Goldwyn, who never took no for an answer, a director commented, "When we were filming *Up in Arms* there was a scene which I considered impossible to shoot the way Mr. Goldwyn suggested. I said I could not do it—it was impossible.

"Goldwyn looked at me with a pitying expression and said, 'I'll give you my answer in only two words: Im POSSIBLE, try it.' I did— it was really possible."

Danny enjoyed all the stories about his new boss, particularly those involving his mispronunciations and words which he assembled with the finesse of a chef tossing a Caesar salad.

While Danny Kaye was the champion of tongue-twisters, Goldwyn was the inventor of muddled metaphors and mangled maxims. Some were so funny that Sylvia and Danny collected them just as others collect stamps or autographs. In the Kaye list of Goldwyn's Golden Garbles are nouns, verbs and adjectives murdered by his mispronunciations and misplacements.

Said the incredible Goldwyn:

"Gentlemen, include me out!"

"A verbal contract isn't worth the paper it's written on."

"The trouble with this business is the dearth of bad pictures."

"We can get all the Indians we need at the reservoir."

Max Liebman, who had been contracted to collaborate on the musical score and lyrics for the first two Danny Kaye pictures, tells an anecdote about Goldwyn. "I had been out in Hollywood for ten weeks when, one day, as we were playing one of our tunes, Don Hartman, the producer, turned to Sylvia with the comment that it sounded almost as good as Gilbert and Sullivan.

" 'Who are Gilbert and Sullivan?' inquired Sam.

" 'They are the greatest lyricists and composers in history,' explained the patient Hartman.

" 'Well, then,' exclaimed Goldwyn with a snap in his eyes, 'why don't we hire them?' "

Although Goldwyn demanded long working hours and meticulous preparations, he often had time to play golf with Danny. Goldwyn never carried money with him, on the basis that "bills make bulges and ruin my jackets, and coins cut my pockets and make noises"; so Danny footed the bills until he decided to imitate the great Goldwyn and also golfed unimpeded by filthy lucre—and Sylvia was left with the chits.

The producer was a series of surprises. "Do you know," said

Danny to Sylvia, "that man never forgets a line of the script, a tiny bit of business, the exact position of a prop—but the guy can't remember his own address or phone number."

Although a sincere friendship was built between producer and star, membership was not shared by Sylvia, who felt it was her duty to hover over every detail of her husband's career and to see that he received every possible break. At the studio Goldwyn was the recognized, unchallenged and unquestioned master, but Sylvia, young and inexperienced in the ways of the film city, had her own decided ideas how each scene should be shot, what Danny should do and where he should stand to have the best advantage. If too many cooks spoil the broth, too many bosses on a Hollywood set create a complete holocaust. An outsider, be she a song writer or wife, is not wanted, appreciated or long endured, and Sylvia ran headlong into a stone wall in the physical form of Sam Goldwyn, who always wished, and often said, that she should stay off the set.

A typical incident occurred one day when Sylvia burst upon Goldwyn with a bright creative idea to be injected in the script. The producer objected, saying the scene was not for Danny. Sylvia stubbornly insisted, raising the ire of Goldwyn, whose voice became high pitched as he shook his finger under her nose.

"Young lady, that same idea came up fifteen years ago, and I rejected it. The picture was a hit!"

Sylvia, with the feminine propensity for the last word, flung back, "Well, if you had used the idea fifteen years ago, it might have been an even better picture!"

That evening, as Sylvia confessed the conflict to Danny, she ended her story with another Goldwynism for their list. "And then," she giggled, "he asked if I would cohabit with him. Of course he meant cooperate."

Every day of production meant a new worry. Their burning ambition was to be a success in terms of the entire United States and the world. Danny could make Broadway laugh, but he wondered if the little audiences in the mountain country of Tennessee, the isolated communities of Arizona's deserts, the folk who went to the movies when the films were run on Wednesdays, Fridays and Saturdays in Alaska, New Caledonia or Timbuktu would think the moving reproduction of himself worth their time and money.

Hollywood is confusing for any newcomer. Much that is written about the Glamour City is correct—the eccentricities of the movie colony, the high-pressure production, the vast labor that goes into working for a single master called Box Office.

Danny, who loves Hollywood today, was at first homesick, a little nauseated by what he saw, and ready to leave. He quickly had enough of the naked palm trees, sun-ripened oranges, crazy sports cars, blue suède shoes, sun glasses and the phony baloney called Hollywood. It took him years to sift through the mobs of people and find comfortable friends in California.

Perhaps Sylvia knew better than he what the difficulties were. She managed his affairs, watched his money and health, and was a tyrant when Danny was not given full opportunity to do his best. She was painfully aware there were people in the gossip center who were digging at her and criticizing Danny for weakness. "People said he was a puppet," she admits, "and sometimes he was not secure enough to know it wasn't true."

Although it was obvious that Sylvia had lost her first round with Goldwyn, she wasn't licked yet in this city, where a genial Polish immigrant ruled as the industry's Napoleon. She changed her stratagem and took her attacks to stage managers, electricians, editors, writers, make-up experts, band leaders, film cutters and sound experts. Small points became major planks in a platform for "Make Kaye the Best," and, while her objective was certainly admirable, her techniques did not enhance her popularity with her co-workers.

Fortunately Danny's warm personality provided the oil on the oft-troubled waters.

Dinah Shore, the co-star, comments, "Danny, I'm sure, had his troubles, but believe me, ours were worse. Each one of us—actor, technician, or stage hand—had a rough time keeping serious enough to get the scenes shot. Danny was a constant act of hilarious nonsense, and keeping a straight face was impossible."

Between scenes Danny entertained the crowd on the set. Everyone enjoyed working with him, although many of his scenes had to be taken over and many of his songs resung. Danny had the patience of Job and the good humor of a May morning.

"He can charm the birds from the trees and make blasé stars jump through hoops," said one of Goldwyn's publicity girls admiringly. Her reverence for Danny stems back to the time when she first started to work for Goldwyn. Just out of college, Ann was shy and frightened, awed by the imposing reputations of the stars, confused by the sets and overwhelmed by the equipment. During a scene she watched Danny with fascination and, when the shooting was completed, retired to a remote corner to be out of the way.

Danny noticed her and sought her out. "What's your name and what do you do in this circus?" he asked.

Ann told him her story.

"That's fine," he said. "You'll enjoy your work in publicity. If there is anything I can do to help, let me know."

The next day Ann was assigned to do a write-up involving details of Danny's costumes. She cautiously approached Mr. Kaye's secretary in the dressing room. Suddenly Danny's tousled hair appeared around the edge of the door. "Ann, come in. I'll give you the information." Danny seated her comfortably in a chair and leisurely gave her an hour of his time.

Ann left his dressing room with a story that was so complete and personalized by Danny himself that it was picked up by all the news services, giving her the first big break in the highly competitive publicity world.

And so it was that Danny, worried but beloved, and Sylvia, ambitious and unpopular, labored through their first weeks and months in Hollywood. There are times, perhaps, when Danny, the usually sensitive man, failed to realize the trauma Sylvia was facing. He was busy and preoccupied, even resistant to the trail his wife was breaking for him.

It is not easy to know one is disliked, but Sylvia put Danny's success above her own comfort and assumed her multiple jobs as wife, manager, director and song-writer.

It was a tremendous task she had undertaken, a tremendous responsibility. Sometimes she wondered if she were really appreciated. Goldwyn seemed not to need her; Danny was absorbed in his work and had several times asked her to keep out of discussions. He seemed to believe these film bosses would not listen to new ideas and suggestions coming from newcomers.

Sylvia was not happy with the screen script. She felt the weak plot would make a bad picture and was well aware Danny could not afford to be a flop in his first movie.

But revisions are costly. The situation was miserable, for, in spite of her constant and irritating protests, Sylvia was unable to negotiate a change in the script.

Up in Arms was based on Owen Davis's play, *Nervous Wreck*. Well directed by Elliot Nugent, Danny played his usual many-faceted role, each with its own carefully maladjusted personality. The story wove around a hospital elevator operator who is jerked into the army, a hypochondriac who suffered a hundred imaginary aches and pains, was tossed mercilessly onto a troop transport ship and assigned the major task of keeping the colonel from discovering the army nurse stowed on board.

As the army nurse, Dinah Shore, the girl from Tennessee, warbled enchantingly, making full use of the dusty, throaty quality she has learned from the Negro mammies in the South. Despite her small role, her contribution was as great as it was musically fine. Dana Andrews, then new on the screen, and the late Louis Calhern stayed in the background, placing the major portion of the burden on the shoulders of Danny Kaye.

The film footage rambles through the all too familiar and not very exciting phase of hide-and-seek, and ends with the inevitable love affair between the nurse and her pill-taking suitor.

The role was not new for Danny, and neither was his performance. In an enlarged treatment of "Melody in 4F," he blustered, gawked, grimaced, perspired, and generally threw himself into a fit. He capitalized on scat-singing, rapid-fire words, insane antics and the dynamic satire that had devastated Broadway.

In terms of good common Hollywood camera sense, only a desperate or slightly crazed producer would have gambled on such a wild farce—especially with an inexperienced screen actor. But Goldwyn was willing to take the chance, although he knew full well that a firecracker on Broadway when put on celluloid could flop with the flatness of a three-day-dead mackerel.

He had Danny under contract for four more pictures, paying $100,000 for the first three and $150,000 for the last. The canny Goldwyn knew no one could write any better songs for his new star than Sylvia had done for this picture.

Sylvia's "Lobby Song" did for *Up in Arms* what "Tschaikowsky" accomplished for *Lady in the Dark*. In telling the story of an imaginary motion picture, Danny sang with unbelievable agility and, gradually increasing his tempo, came close to breaking the jet speed record.

"How can anyone write such nonsense?" someone asked Sylvia. Sylvia thought a moment. "Trying to tell anyone how such a number is written is even more confusing than writing it. Each step in the continuity starts with an idea. Then comes a problem of appropriate words and music. Next comes working it out with Danny, who fills in his own bits of business, his dialects and gestures, his own interpretation of the music."

Weeks passed with long hours of works, nerves, tensions, arguments, until the film was ready for its premier showing. Sylvia and Danny dashed for the papers with the same anxiety they had felt on other opening nights.

Danny's reviews were good. Bosley Crowther of the *New York Times* commented: "He is unquestionably a rich and rare comedian with a wonderful sense for the bizarre. He has youth, good-looks and vitality—and a warmth which even radiates from the screen." However, the reviewer went on to ask, "How long can Danny Kaye last at this pace?" and was openly critical in his comment, "Give Danny back his natural hair and not the mop of yellow taffy which is so flagrant in *Up in Arms* and . . . provide him with a better and more imaginative script."

When the reviews of the nation's critics were assembled, it was clear that Danny had won plaudits. Sam Goldwyn was panned for a poor story, and Sylvia and Max Liebman cursorily recognized for their songs. Danny pulled the show through to make it another Sam Goldwyn hit which the producer recognized with one of his famed malapropisms, "The office-box was terrific."

When asked, "How can you explain Danny Kaye's film success?" Sam Goldwyn had the answer: "He is real and natural, which makes him the kind of fellow any girl in the second balcony knows. His honesty is real. His humor is real. He has sex appeal. There is a tender, warm and vulnerable quality about Danny that touches the audiences—and they want to touch back."

Fifteen days after the release of the picture Danny knew he had accomplished more than he had in the previous fifteen years. The United States had met him and accepted his humor, and soon the world would be familiar with his hot songs, dancing feet, waving arms. Danny Kaye was now on his way to becoming a household word, the topic of conversation in conservative parlors, noisy beer-halls and over the bridge table.

Sam Goldwyn, although pleased, was in no hurry to start the next picture. The script for *Wonder Man* was not ready, and it was the consensus of opinion that the public should not be drugged by the new overwhelming personality of Mr. Kaye.

During this intensive working period, Danny had given less than his usual time to bolster the morale of the armed forces. During the lull he began to fulfill past invitations at canteens and army hospitals. Goldwyn's publicity boys were delighted by his efforts. To have a new face who was willing and even eager to put himself before the public would help their promotion campaigns greatly, would build toward his next picture, would assure his and their success.

So, while the skeptics once again called Danny overambitious and publicity-minded, he went out of his way to help others.

Danny unhesitatingly accepted the invitation of the armed forces to entertain the troops in the Pacific theater. He knew his familiar role of the flat-footed, neurotic soldier would bring chuckles to the lonely, fatigued men in the outpost areas. The idea of being close to the front pleased Danny in every respect.

The Army insisted that he wear a uniform on his trip to Asia. He was briefed by Army officials and given instructions he could not share even with Sylvia.

Sylvia, hiding anxieties that Danny would be away from her and in danger zones, buckled down to do her part by writing new songs which would appeal to the fighting men.

Accompanying Danny was his accompanist, Jack Snyder, and Leo "the Lip" Durocher, manager of the Brooklyn Dodgers. Durocher was a welcome part of the act, telling baseball yarns for an hour and submitting amiably to the usual heckling that comes to anyone connected with the Dodgers. The show concluded with the two Brooklynites doing an old-time vaudeville shuffle-off-to-Buffalo routine, wearing the standard straw hats and blazers.

As an encore Danny often approached the entertainment-hungry audience with a serious, "I will now do Hamlet for you," and before the soldiers had a chance to groan, began his soliloquy, "To bunt or not to bunt, that is the question."

The USO tour covered 32,000 miles of the South Pacific area. They entertained before hangar doors, in the narrow lanes between hospital cots, among the sprawling palm trees on desert islands and racked up a total of ninety-eight shows before 275,000 service-men. The largest single group on this tour was 43,000 soldiers on Okinawa just after a typhoon had leveled the stage, necessitating the quick improvisation of a new platform from packing boxes.

Danny risked his life on several occasions and often took unnecessary risks. His activities have now become history to be exploited by press agents. It was Sylvia who shuddered when she told her family, "Danny worries me. He has to see everything. He takes chances he shouldn't just to satisfy his curiosity and to show the men in the foxholes that he is there with them."

In spite of strict instructions to stay away from fighting areas, Danny insisted on being close to the soldiers. He asked for no special privileges and seemed to find a distinct happiness in the front lines with the camaraderie of the fighting men who were grateful for any bit of laughter and a touch of home.

Leo and Danny became good friends during the days and nights of difficult travel, uninspiring Army rations, mosquitoes, heat, bathless days and sleepless nights. The baseball wizard tells, as his pet story, of the time when a tough sergeant, fed up with Hollywood stars, started to give Danny a bad time. Durocher stepped in with his notorious ability to tell off offenders. "Listen, three-stripes," he barked, "one more crack outa you and I'll belt you into the Three I League on the first bounce."

Danny, with this characteristic talent, used the scene for the rest of the tour. Needless to say, it was a tremendous hit with the soldiers, who were very familiar with similar top sergeants.

"Operation Kaye" was a great success. Danny was rewarded by the sincere appreciation of high-ranking Army personnel in Washington.

In Hollywood, Sam Goldwyn was pleased with the publicity

Danny was making for himself. Happy with the reactions to *Up in Arms,* the producer had bought a new script for the next Danny Kaye picture, *Wonder Man,* as well as hired his next leading lady, Virginia Bruce.

"But, Danny," said Mr. Goldwyn, "I have other plans too. One day I want to film the life of Hans Christian Andersen. And I dream of doing *Porgy and Bess.* Danny, we are going to do many things together."

XII

I'm a Wife-Made Man

IT HAD BEEN A GOOD MARRIAGE. THE YEARS SINCE THEIR TWO weddings were short but also hectic. Danny, who sometimes seemed to Sylvia like a tower of jelly during their first professional days, was now a full-sized, strong-willed and dominant man.

Some people said he could not have gone so far without Sylvia. But Sylvia remained in the dark, unpopular among his colleagues and unapplauded for her role in Danny's life. A motion picture star belongs to his public. He must be fresh—the star, the matinee idol. The woman he calls his wife has to learn to play second fiddle.

Sylvia recognized the problem. Her talent had been a springboard to her husband's career and she was more than willing to give her best, but it was often hard to keep in the background. She discovered that when people were exceptionally nice to her, it was because they wanted something from Danny. Her music was only good as a prop for Danny. The attentions were all for Danny.

Among the glamorous women stars and starlets, the long tall blondes, the slim redheads with their protruding bosoms, the petite dark-haired Sylvia must have often felt lost. On the dance floor with Danny, it was difficult for her to see to whom he waved—and he waved and greeted many people as he waltzed.

Danny did not notice. He was busy making pictures, being a star, planning his next rehearsal, dreaming of things to come.

Sylvia worked as hard, if not harder, than Danny. She wrote

his songs, watched his finances, and worried for him. She had to learn the art of patience, which was not easy for a dynamo in her late twenties. Rehearsals of a single song meant as many as twenty or thirty tries with Sylvia giving criticism, making suggestions, singing encouragement, and issuing threats.

When Sylvia first met Danny as an adult, she pictured him as the youngster from a Brooklyn background. In those days he did not look like an actor or musician—just a long lean kid who was polite, well mannered and had eyes that twinkled with amusement. The affinity between them was inexplicable, but it was there. That was what had mattered.

Perhaps her life had gone by too fast. Their love, marriage, the night club tours, Broadway, the lights, the planes, the money, the dreams which were now fulfilled in Hollywood. In many ways, life and living were secondary to the whirl of ambition and success, fears and joys. The days were composed primarily of work, and recreation was still work because it involved being nice to people "who mattered." The years had been better than she hoped for.

While Sylvia adored the man of her choice, she was still not happy with her own career. She was a woman hanging on the rim of a flying saucer.

There were many qualities Sylvia admired in Danny: his generosity, deep honesty, good sense of reality, remarkable command of facts. He was even-tempered, which made for happy living, and, because of his volatile disposition, he leaped from one worry to the next while she tended to brood on a single major issue.

Out of professional courtesy, people called her Miss Fine, the artist who wrote Danny's songs and lyrics. There were times when she insisted that she be called Mrs. Kaye, the wife instead of the songwriter. But at the studios she remained Miss Fine.

Her desire became a dichotomy, one to be a recognized person, and the other, to be the well-loved wife of Danny Kaye.

Danny was always gallant. He was frank and often he tried to explain that Hollywood was a whirlpool in which she should protect herself against being hurt by small incidents. His adventures in celluloid had put his feet on the ground and, in many ways, he was now more secure than Sylvia, who was secretly competing with him.

The down-to-earth, business-minded, practical Sylvia was often close to revolt while standing in the shadow of the man she loved, watching him bow at the end of one of her songs. She knew how much of her own talent and heart had gone into his success.

This battle going on in her mind was not obvious to Danny. For once, his radar sense failed. The object on his mental screen was too close and dear to him.

There was no longer an issue of money. Sylvia had made sure that Danny would not, in his generosity, squander their money, and their funds were stashed away in sound investments. But she longed for understanding and even accolades from her husband. There were moments filled with fear and irritations, self-pity and condemnation.

Hollywood, it seemed, had changed her shy fun-loving husband. It had changed Sylvia, too, but she did not realize that the brashness of the cinema world had rubbed off on her. She blamed herself, criticized herself for ambitiousness while, on the inside, the festering desires still grew. There was no one else whom she could blame with a clear conscience.

Hollywood embraced Danny and put his wife on the sidelines. Sam Goldwyn praised her songs but bolstered Danny's ego by the constant prediction that he was a new "star," a "find," a "great guy destined for motion picture eternity."

The next two years in the lives of the Kayes were a whirlwind of success and activities, a whirlpool of personal adjustments and difficulties. "I had a bundle of complexes on my hands," said Sylvia, while Danny confided, "I had my problems with Sylvia. Hollywood does not like the wives of actors."

Many things were new to the Kayes. There was the fabulous Bel Air mansion with its swimming pool and notoriety, for it belonged to the divorced former boxing champion, Slapsie Maxie Rosenbloom. There was the twelve-room apartment on the other side of the continent, overlooking New York's Park Avenue and including a range of treasures from an early eighteenth-century American dining table to Danny's new and inclusive library of books on psychology and psychosomatic illnesses.

Danny, completely disarming because he had no touches of

the *nouveau riche,* answered when complimented on his new home in Hollywood, "Yes, I am enjoying it very much because it is close to my work."

He commuted the 3,000 miles between New York, where he was wanted for personal appearances and radio shows, and Hollywood, where Sam Goldwyn was preparing to go into production on the next Kaye picture, *Wonder Man.* Again Sylvia was to write the songs and lyrics, but had received the implicit instructions that there was to be no more scat-singing. The words of the songs had to be clearly understandable. Sylvia seethed a bit over this new development, for she felt Danny was a master with the scat routine and the ultimatum constituted sabotage of his talent.

The plot of *Wonder Man* was a roller-coaster of speedy events and impersonations. The picture came out as a burlesque of the Jewish Dybbuk, with Danny bursting out all over.

The Dybbuk went back into the mysticism of the Middle Ages, when the soul of a murdered Jew took possession of a living Jew, resulting in violence, disaster and desperation. The film version of this legend, in a modern Brooklyn setting, was a jewel for any comedian, and particularly adapted to Danny, who played the parts of twin brothers, one of whom is an outgoing, exuberant, gay night club entertainer, the other a fearful, solemn, bespectacled bookworm. The night club entertainer is murdered by gangsters and reincarnated into the body of the shy twin.

The cheese-cake Army nurses of *Up in Arms* were replaced in *Wonder Man* by twelve dancing girls "guaranteed to uphold the tradition of travel-folder illustrations of Bali girls issued by the American Express Company." Danny contradicts this statement by saying the girls in the show had "just a few square inches more of clothing than the travel advertisements."

Goldwyn went Hollywood-wild. He paid the new dancer, Vera Ellen, who had never before undergone a screen test, $1,000 a week, and spent more money for advertising and promotion than was spent on Hemingway's *For Whom the Bell Tolls.*

The end result was Danny Kaye with a thin film story wrapped around him. His jokes were good, his songs captivating, and his madness contagious. Perhaps best remembered was his impersonation of an asthmatic gentleman singing "Ochi Tchornya" which someone remarked would have made Moussorgsky rewrite the Idiot's role in *Boris Godunov*.

The idea behind the play was not new, the role was not fresh, but no one in Hollywood could have duplicated the zaniness and half-insanity with which Danny surprised his newly won audiences. Sam Goldwyn was pleased. Sam Goldwyn was happy. Sam Goldwyn had an "office-box hit." Sam Goldwyn wanted to do more pictures with Danny.

The only one who still did not quite realize what had happened was "the grand young man," Danny Kaye.

But he was deeply pleased with John Mason Brown's review, which read: "Danny Kaye is the only legitimate successor to the royal line of clowns," but went on to spank the film for its silliness and weakness of plot.

Underneath, however, Danny was not happy. He wished—how he wished!—he could make his co-workers accept Sylvia. On the set he hid his concerns with his lovable tomfoolery, making impromptu caricatures of Hitler's last speech in perfect "German" by saying not one single understandable word except "Dumm-kopf," aping Mr. Goldwyn's stride, and singing "O sole Mio" in a tiny baby voice.

A few perceptive people were aware that life for Danny was not as gay or easy as it appeared. The late Hungarian, S. Z. Sakall, beloved by millions and affectionately called "Cuddles" by his associates, said confidentially to his friends, "Danny and Sylvia have troubles. Hollywood is a difficult place. Danny is such a nice kid, and she is a strong woman—too strong. People think he is clay in her hands, but it is only because she loves him, wants so much for him, that she never gives him a chance to do things on his own. I think he has a guilty feeling toward her for all she does. She pushes too hard. I fear there is trouble ahead."

Of course Danny was worried. He knew their marriage was in trouble. There had been a constant change since their arguments about his acting and singing, about Sam Goldwyn and her undiplomatic activities on the studio lot, about Hollywood parties and Hollywood life. The tensions increased more by the day, culminating in temperamental outbursts. It was stupid, all of it—his own conduct, her protests and irritations. But calling a quarrel stupid does not erase its existence.

Then came the time when Danny tired of hearing the persistent whispers that his success and career would not have been possible without Sylvia. His ego was hurt. For the past seven years he had been asked to bow in her direction and certainly *under* her direction. It was too much for even the best husband to take.

There is no doubt that Sylvia molded Danny's style and controlled his work. It is likely that Danny often, consciously or unconsciously, revolted against her reins, particularly her untempered frankness, her aggressive behavior on the set, her unwanted discussions with Mr. Goldwyn and her occasional impolite attitude toward directors, technicians and stagehands.

In later years Sylvia frankly admitted her mistakes. "I used to control him from my seat on the piano bench. If I thought he was hitting a number too hard, I would change the octave so it was higher and lighter, and without really knowing it, his sensitive ears would detect the difference and he would ease up and become lighter too."

Perhaps at first Danny did not notice Sylvia's commanding position at the piano bench or her imperative suggestions over the breakfast coffee cup, but gradually he became uneasy—a feeling which led to unhappy pressures of guilt. He fully realized the limelight was all upon him, and Sylvia seldom received the credit due her. After all, he was her creation. His successes had been random and accidental before she created for his special abilities and directed his talents.

Unfortunately Sylvia never let him forget that she had her fingers in all their pies, governed the money, arranged his appointments, created his songs, commanded his successes.

Danny succumbed. He told Hollywood reporters, "Sylvia has a Fine head on my shoulders. Sylvia's words in my mouth have made me what I am today." One part of his brain told him that without Sylvia he was a failure, that he owed all to her, but another part revolted against her domination and demanded a showdown.

Unfortunately showdowns are often ill-tempered, lead to loud voices, badly timed arguments, bumpy interludes—sometimes even in front of other people. But Danny was in rebellion, angry with himself and upset about Sylvia, who still seemed to believe he was a child. Often he could not help thinking she was his mother rather than his wife. But, above all, he had to prove to her and to himself that it was *his* art, *his* know-how that led to his success. Never did he belittle her great contribution to his life: her songs and her advice, the management that had helped him immeasurably. But he could not always compete with her. He felt she was too bossy, and Sylvia felt he was weak, easygoing and often compromising. Danny was horrified by the open discussion of their lives, the public explanations of the factors that had led to the downfall of their relations and, above all, the unfair accusations. Nagging innuendoes around the studio urged Danny to be the star in his own independent right, not a pawn in the hands of an ambitious wife.

There were many people who preferred to bypass Sylvia and to deal directly with the easier-to-handle Danny. There were women who enjoyed Danny without the company of his wife, for Danny was now a star, and, as such, an important man whose recommendation carried weight with such notables as Sam Goldwyn.

Sylvia, painfully aware of what was happening, resented their new "friends," agents, well-wishers, spongers and would-be's who were trying to push her into the background or even completely out of Danny's life. Desperate in her fear of losing the man she loved, she reacted by growing more possessive, more critical and holding on to Danny tighter than ever before.

Danny fought back. He openly avoided her and began to make decisions in the belief that a wrong decision on his own was better than having Sylvia make a right one. He resented Sylvia's ordering luncheon for him without asking his preference. When Sylvia straightened the funny hat he insisted on wearing during rehearsals, he pushed it back awry. Sylvia's comments on a new song he now took with irritation and sarcastic remarks.

At one time their nerves were so bare that Sylvia purposely left the recording room during some disagreements on musical questions and sat in the projection booth. Danny stopped the session, complaining he could still see her in the booth, still directing, sitting on her throne and shaking her head, "No, no, no! That is *wrong!*"

More fatal than the struggle for power was the withering away of mutual respect and the growing irritation which is so undermining in any relationship. The two artists existed with spoken and unspoken alienations which both tried desperately though spasmodically to patch up.

After months of struggle Danny came to a solution—to work alone, to find another accompanist, get out of Hollywood and initiate a coast-to-coast radio show which Sylvia would help to prepare but would have no other part in. He wanted and needed experience on his own to prove his strength.

Sylvia, hurt as she was by this decision, had delightedly found a new outlet for her problems, too. She was going to have a baby.

Hollywood had been stifling, tiring and oppressive. The Kayes' home life was far from pleasant, and Danny was relieved and pleased when C.B.S. hired him for $18,000 per week on a two-year contract. Sylvia's songs were to be included, but the creation of the show itself, sponsored by a brewery, was assigned to Goodman Ace, one of radio's top scriptwriters.

A New York reporter, noting that Danny had started work in Japan for $40 a week, graduated to $100 in the *Straw Hat Revue,* had "resigned" from *Lady in the Dark* at $250 and was now commanding the superlative figure of $18,000, asked the usual question, "To what do you owe your success?" Danny, half resentful and half proud of his frank courage, snapped back, "I am a wife-made man."

Sylvia did not laugh when she read this crack in print, and neither did Danny's public. He felt pangs of remorse for his brashness and lack of good taste.

But Danny was embroiled in preparations for the show, and again he was apprehensive. His past radio experiences had not been happy ones. Much of his fun-making was blocked by the uninspiring wooden fronts and dials of sets which faced the listeners. While people in the studio watching him do a commercial could split their sides while he drank an imaginary bottle of castor oil, the audiences depending on his sounds alone could not even know why the slight pause was funny.

Danny reverted into his pattern of nerves. He knew the script-writers would help in every way possible, and that Sylvia's old songs were bound to go over and her new ones likely to be equally popular, but this venture was to be his trial by fire to prove his own merit.

Sylvia did not let him down. She wrote with new vigor and carefully planned material that would project over the air-waves. The first show was well prepared and minutely rehearsed, but Danny stepped to the microphone missing a live audience and knowing he could flounder under the weight of serious dialogue which was required by parts of the scripts. But a new experience, however worrisome, was better than dragging through the old doldrums and irritations.

The show, ably supported by Lionel Stander, Harry James and Eve Arden, was a hit from the first week on. Quite by accident it produced a gag that became a national craze similar to the "Knock-knock-who's-there?" flurry. It began spontaneously as a Kayeism. The lines ran:

"My sister married an Irishman."

"Oh really?"

"No," quipped Kaye, "O'Riley."

Goodman Ace picked up the gag and continued it the next week:

"We have potatoes for dinner."

"Oh really?"

"No, *au gratin.*"

Hardly a word beginning with the word "Oh" was safe.

Within six months Danny's program had the sixth highest rating in the nation. Sylvia's place at the piano was now filled by Sammy Prager, a good-looking, jovial, rotund musician who had caught Danny's attention during a rehearsal. During a difficult piece, Danny was having a frustrating time with the conductor, who could not catch his whimsical and unorthodox treatment. Prager caught the feel, the humor, the mood—and pulled the tune off the keys. Danny looked up from his toes, which he had been studiously and a bit sullenly surveying, and said, "I want you for my accompanist."

This simple statement was the beginning of what is now an over-ten-year-old friendship. The two men are the closest of friends, inveterate golf partners, indefatigable travelers and partners in the art of humor.

Prager, no newcomer to the entertainment world, had first studied under Carl Friedberg, until he was slapped down by the bitter realization that he would never be a Rubinstein and that at least one square meal a day was necessary for life. In his thirties when he met Kaye, Sammy had an imposing record as a musician, having played with Paul Spechtum, Freddie Rich and Red Nichols and accompanying Bing Crosby, Lily Pons, Kate Smith, Morton Downey, Lanny Ross, Jane Froman and Frank Sinatra. Once he had an invitation to play the piano solo in *Rhapsody in Blue,* under the direction of André Kostelanetz.

Sammy is quite serious about his role in helping Danny. "You know," he says, "it is quite an art to be an accompanist. The major prerequisite is that he must never detract. The performer and the audience must never be aware that there is music in the background. An accompanist must live within himself, find his satisfactions in not being noticed, in knowing inside himself that he is an integral part of the production.

"Many performers do not know one note of music from the next. Danny, although he denies it, can read music, but it should not be his responsibility to follow notes. He should be given room to expand and create on the spot. This is what I try to do for him. I merely follow him around the stage with the personal appreciation and musical ability that I have because he never really knows what he is going to do next. There is always the skeleton of a program, but the embroidery changes from show to show. To accompany Danny is three-fourths intuition."

Danny found a new exhilaration. There was a new friend and co-worker. The radio show was a smash hit which proved that he could do things successfully on his own.

At least Danny now had the assurance that he was running his own show. But, to the outside world, it never looked that way. Sylvia still wrote the new music. The songs were her creation.

Danny's wife was still very much in the picture, but he was feeling a breath of self-assurance. Sylvia worried, for, while the show was a success, she felt the rumblings of trouble ahead. The slippery substance of humor was obvious in the radio studio, but did not always glide over the air. Much of the success of the show lay in the sincere laughter of those who could watch Danny, not a contagious element for those who listened in homes somewhere across the country.

Sylvia did not share Danny's new blush of glory. In her mind poor materials were thrown at her husband, golden opportunities lost in both the film and radio world, because she was not on the spot to direct and help. In addition to her constant output of songs, she added a manuscript to her list of activities and contracted with Doubleday to write an as yet unpublished and unfinished book entitled *Seven Years in a Pressure Cooker,* the story of her married life with Danny Kaye.

In typical style, Danny improvised on radio, and in some inexplicable way projected his pantomime into sound, making it as comic to hear as his Stanislavsky was to watch.

"Good evening. Maybe you overlooked it, but spring [chatter of teeth] began last Monday, March 20th, at 11.36. If you are like Mrs. Hicks and myself [primly] you've been talking about [superciliously] gardening, seeds, and [grimly] fertilizers. . . .

"Yes, whether it is used as a top dressing or side dressing, ammonium sulphate bearing the famous label of United States Steel is rapidly [wildly] becoming the most. . . ."

On listening to the commercial one could visualize the inimitable grimaces, the extreme posturing, the comic expressions, and the commercial would become a panic.

One night Betty Hutton was the guest star, and Sylvia was worried. Perhaps her advanced state of pregnancy had increased her tensions and anxieties, but she voiced the opinion that Danny's script was not brilliant and the rehearsal too short. "He will not be good tonight," she fumed.

Goodman Ace, the writer, retorted bitterly, "Stop worrying! We'll have the orchestra louse up Betty Hutton's number."

"That should satisfy Sylvia's monomaniacal concentration on Danny's career," commented another staff member. And a third added, "She is the least popular stage mother I have ever seen."

Stinging words, but they were said. Max Liebman, a man with insight and keen sense of evaluation, came to Sylvia's rescue again and again. "Whatever the arguments were or are," he stanchly maintains, "Sylvia always makes sense!"

Rightly or wrongly, Sylvia was not appreciated by the radio staff. Remarks that would chill a martini swirled through the air.

The unfriendly atmosphere toward his wife made Danny terribly unhappy. It was difficult enough to be "funny in the dark" and to emulate characters of half a dozen nationalities, two sexes, assorted ages and a corner of the animal kingdom.

The nearer the day came for the arrival of the baby, the more excited Danny grew. He told everyone, "I'm going to have a baby; and boy, am I excited! Got a suggestion for a name?"

Again Danny was commuting between Sam Goldwyn's office, where plans were being made for a third picture, *The Kid from Brooklyn,* and New York, where Sylvia, desiring to be near her family when the child arrived, was waiting impatiently for the important event, predicted to be sometime between Christmas and New Year's Day.

"Personally," cracked Danny to Virginia Mayo, "I expect Santa Claus, in a white coat and with his beard tucked under an antiseptic mask, to step out of the delivery room and say, 'Merry Christmas. It's a baby.' "

"What have you decided to name your kid?" asked Sam Goldwyn one evening.

"I know you want it to be Stanislavsky," replied Danny, "but that's too long a handle for a little baby. Maybe it will be Sam."

Danny's coming fatherhood was the talk of the two coasts and a million admirers. Fan mail included advice on child-rearing and assorted baby gifts. To the often-asked question, "Do you want a boy or a girl?" Danny answered, "When I pass a cute little girl on the street, I want a girl, and when I see those cute kids lugging around fake six-shooters that are bigger than they are, I hope for a boy . . . but mostly I want a baby. When I hear that baby bulletin, it will be absolutely the biggest moment I've ever lived through."

Danny was in a period of being a man of many moods: torn, unified, secure, frightened . . . on the bridge of success and the brink of failure.

In a kind of exhilarated wondering he awaited the baby. It would be the answer to his father's questions and the bond between Sylvia and himself. If his behavior was not quite normal, it was because Danny was not quite himself. His life with Sylvia had not been comfortable for some time, but now he felt himself as an individual on his own, not only the artist but the protector of a family. He was upset and peaceful, gay and depressed at the same time.

Fortunately for his nerves, Danny was busy making his new picture, but unfortunately *The Kid from Brooklyn* was another uneven plot, based on a warmed-up farce, *The Milky Way,* produced with Harold Lloyd in the days of silent pictures.

Danny played the role of a mousy milkman who, by a freak turn of fate, becomes a boxer, gripped by a furious passion to kill the champ. "Not since Charlie Chaplin," said the *New York Times,* "has such a bewildered boxer been seen on the screen."

The boxing match stole the show, providing a setting for Danny's fast footwork and unforgettable facial expressions. He ably demonstrated what not to do in the ring.

Although the idea and the monkey-business were not new, the sage Goldwyn knew that a routine which had made money twenty years before was a formula that could make money again. He was right, and the motion picture audience howled approvingly as Danny, the scatter-footed milkman, swung his arms in wild abandon under the nose of the dirty-mouthed monster who was the world champion boxer. *The Kid from Brooklyn* was another box office success.

A new sort of peace settled around the heart and mind of the busy actor. His relationship with Sylvia was both contented and anticipatory. Usually a listener, he found himself suddenly verbose, suddenly an authority on child growth and development, suddenly consumed with a deep realization of his responsibilities to Sylvia and their unborn child.

"Will you teach your child how to be a star?" asked Louella Parsons, the Hollywood columnist. "That would surely give it a head start by about a million dollars."

Danny tossed her one of his mocking glances. "No," he said. "I'm the one who will need the teaching. I will have to learn how to keep out of his—or her—way; so that the poor kid won't ever be burdened by being the child of Danny Kaye. But, then, Sylvia will manage that. She always does. She is the brains in our family." There, he had said it again!

The presents under the Kayes' Christmas tree did not include a well-wrapped baby, but the New Year of 1946 brought with it a delicate, thoroughly healthy little girl, well equipped with lungs. She was given the name Dena, which, from its Hebrew origin, means "gracious." Danny and Sylvia were both grateful and overjoyed.

XIII

"Danny Walked Out on Me!"

"I WAS RECOVERING FROM PNEUMONIA," TELLS SYLVIA. "I FELT better, but still in bed, when our cook came rushing into my room, breathless and armed with a butcher knife. 'There's an old man, says he's an uncle of Mr. Kaye's. I tried to tell him you can't see him, but he insists. Now don't you be afraid. I'll stand right here.'" and before she could say another word, in hobbled an old man with a matted beard and ragged clothes, muttering rapidly in half-Russian dialect.

"I was terrified. It was obvious that he was a crank or a madman. I couldn't understand most of what he said, but I nodded politely and gauged the distance to the telephone.

"For five minutes this crazy monologue went on. He'd been in Europe, hadn't seen Danny since he was a baby, had walked across the continent. I asked him what he wanted, and he muttered, 'Nothing, nothing—just give me $30,000 and I'll go away.'

"That did it. When he mentioned $30,000, I burst out laughing. It had to be—it was—Danny Kaye, my unpredictable husband."

Sylvia Kaye has a collection of literally dozens of similar yarns, and the term "unpredictable husband" comes close to the truth.

Unexpectedly, Danny decided to terminate his radio show. Sylvia, occupied with the many duties of new motherhood, was too busy to help on a full-time basis, and Danny yearned for a live audience he could see and be close to.

To the complete bewilderment of the advertising agency, he cancelled the last year of his contract. The puzzled agency offered more money, which he flatly refused. The sponsor generously granted the release, with the definite proviso that he would not appear on any other network for the next twelve months.

The sponsor, the agency and the listeners were disappointed, but Danny had not been happy separated from a responsive audience. He made up his mind that radio was not his medium, just as, years later, he evaded television when all the rest of the stars were either acting on the glass screen of the nation's front room or drawing gigantic salaries for the mere statement, "So-and-so Presents."

No one could grasp why Danny declined the enormous income, with the exception of one man—a great comedian who amassed a fortune through radio presentations but finally died of a broken heart because radio and television audiences and sponsors had failed to understand him with the appreciation he yearned for. The late beloved Fred Allen pronounced the prophetic words, "Whether he knows it or not, the comedian is on a treadmill to oblivion. When a radio comedian's program is finally finished, it sinks down Memory Lane into the limbo of yesterday's happy hours. All the comedian has to show for his years of radio work and aggravation is the echo of forgotten laughter."

Danny agreed with Fred's point of view. He made his decision final and decisive. Sylvia, though perhaps not completely understanding his motive, agreed, for Hollywood had a greater range of opportunities to offer and there were constant feelers from other companies interested in making Kaye pictures.

Danny, no longer worried about money, was far more interested in being a good father—a career he accepted with seriousness. Dena brought new happiness into the Kaye home, and for the moment it looked as if their personal differences were resolved.

As a father, Danny was proud and helpful. He accepted the baby's crying with rare good humor, attempted to entertain her with funny faces long before her little eyes could focus, assisted with her bath, changed diapers and brewed her formula, but his joy with Dena was later blighted by a suspicion that his marital problems were not altogether solved. The major issues had only been postponed.

Sylvia, too, though overjoyed by her baby, had her share of forebodings. She was tied down and no longer able to travel with her husband. In spite of help, she felt she should not be separated from Dena, and grimly feared that her grip over Danny's professional life was slipping. Others were gaining important influence and status in his affairs. There was Eddie Dukoff, the amiable business manager; Sammy Prager, the talented and good-natured accompanist and golf partner; Sam Goldwyn, with his endless hours of conferences; and even James Thurber, the author of Danny's latest picture, *The Secret Life of Walter Mitty*. Anyone of these people had a greater part and more influential position in Danny's life than Sylvia now occupied.

Sylvia resigned herself to the fact that she had the responsibility of two children, Dena and Danny. She took her mothering seriously, with the assumption that neither her daughter nor her husband could make a move without her guidance.

And Danny was in revolt again.

The new picture was a godsend for the restless actor. The script was sparky and Thurber's basic idea challenging, but even the stimulation of the new picture did not completely erase the dualism of his feelings: gratitude to Sylvia for all she had done for him, on the one hand, and on the other, a burning wish that she would at least try to understand the turmoil her overprotective attitude instilled in him.

Without a doubt, *The Secret Life of Walter Mitty* was the best role so far and the script the most inspired. Sylvia's touches were in the songs, although her busy days with Dena made it impossible for her to have as much to do with the film as in the past. It is generally conceded that *Walter Mitty* was Danny's best picture, only to be topped later by the Hans Christian Andersen film.

Goldwyn had bought the classic short story from James Thurber, a genial former editor of *The New Yorker,* author of the amusing book *Is Sex Necessary?* and cartoonist known for his drawings of melancholy hounds, frustrated males and lantern-jawed feminine tyrants. The character of Walter Mitty reflected Thurber's pungent belief that humor is a "kind of emotional chaos, told about calmly and quietly in retrospect."

Walter Mitty is a day-dreamer, an ineffectual cipher who works as a proofreader for a pulp magazine and finally triumphs over his domineering wife and humdrum life through escape into his imaginary world. This yarn of a weak man fighting against a strong woman had a special appeal to Danny.

To make a full-length film from the short story, Danny "lived" through seven different sequences of day-dreams, each concluding with the personal victory or valor lacking in the life of the mediocre, pathetic little nobody, Walter Mitty. Several of the heroic dreams were taken from Danny's previous sure-fire successes. There was Anatole, the male milliner from the *Straw Hat Revue* and the ludicrous surgeon's operation scene.

With no nostalgia and little author temperament, Thurber patiently watched his story evolve into something which only vaguely resembled the original narrative and philosophically observed that "Hollywood movies are made by groups of men and— their wives."

This was a crack Sylvia did not relish, although it is doubtful if Thurber was referring directly to her. More likely it was only a Thurber generality. But the shoe seemed to fit Sylvia's foot.

The renowned author often sat on the set, making suggestions, but generally merely encouraging the director and actors, especially Danny, to make any needed revisions. "Presenting a humdrum Walter Mitty in Technicolor with Danny Kaye," he observed, "would be as difficult as presenting the witch scene from *Macbeth* on the center court of Wimbledon Stadium at high noon on a summer day."

In spite of all the changes, the scenario retained the charm of the Thurber touch and whimsy.

There was Walter as Captain Mitty, standing behind the ship's wheel during a perilous typhoon, saying stanchly, "It's the worst typhoon in forty years, but as sure as my name's Captain Mitty, I'll see it through!"

A huge wave battered our hero against the mast, but he struggled bravely to his feet. "Captain, you're hurt," a sailor cried in alarm.

"It is nothing," answered the Captain grimly, "—just a broken arm."

Walter, in another dream, saw himself as the dashing, handsome gambler on a Mississippi river-boat, surrounded by a bevy of beautiful women dressed in the best *Gone With the Wind* tradition. "Cunnel" Wadsworth, a planter from the old South, pushed his last chips on to the table and said imperiously, "I raise you!" "Raise again," said the gallant gambler, forcing the "cunnel" to add the deed to his plantation. The unfortunate Southerner tried to cheat, but Gambler Mitty shrewdly outwitted him. "You Yankee dog," snarled the frustrated planter, whipping out a horse-pistol. Mitty calmly and adroitly flipped the gun from his hand and coolly walked away, leaving his broken opponent speechless.

Millions of movie-goers identified themselves with the dull little proofreader and applauded the success of the picture. Sam Goldwyn was well pleased, and Danny himself enjoyed the filming and the end results more than he had any of the other pictures.

For the first time in his career, Danny as the Southern cardshark was able to use his hands to the greatest advantage. Since the early days when agents had criticized his fingers for being too fast, too agile, he had consciously controlled them. Graceful hands on a man seemed almost effeminate, but shuffling a deck of cards was great fun and he did it well.

Boris Karloff, playing the role of the villainous Southerner in the Mississippi gambler sequence, tells an anecdote which was later picked up by the Hollywood press agents and made into motion picture huckstering.

The scene needed a sleight-of-hand artist who could be shown in a close-up with his hands stacking the deck. Each time the cameras focused on the nimble fingers of the stand-in gambler, he fumbled with stage fright, dropped cards and went to pieces.

From the sidelines, Danny casually walked over, picked up the deck and asked, "Here, let me see if I can do it." The cameras began to roll. Danny stacked the deck so expertly that no retake was necessary—and no one would play cards with him for weeks later.

The reviews on *Walter Mitty* were satisfying. The *New York Times* said that Mr. Kaye showed an "amazing exercise of his acrobatic larynx," and praised the "Symphony for Un-strung Tongues."

Sam Goldwyn called Kaye "another Harold Lloyd." "Another Chaplin," said Arthur Rubinstein, the pianist, while Kaye's good friend, George Jessel, pinned on the label "another Jolson." Danny was unimpressed by comparisons and wanted most of all to be a popular and beloved Danny Kaye, an entertainer with his own personality and methods of creating humor.

In the film the ending was happy, with Walter Mitty finding himself, falling in love with an appreciative girl, and escaping from the clutches of his dominant mother and demanding fiancée.

In real life, however, the ending of the film was not a happy one. Thurber, the author, was displeased with the final product. There were letters of protest exchanged between him and Sam Goldwyn, and Danny was caught in the middle. He refused to take sides.

The night of the gala premiere when the nervous arc-lights crisscrossed the sky, two men were lonely and unhappy. James Thurber was fed up with Hollywood. So was Danny.

While he was fascinated by Dena's constant growth into a real personality, his marriage had somehow lost its deepest meaning. The conflict was rapidly approaching a climax.

Danny was in revolt again, torn between the guilt of ingratitude and the knowledge that marriage could not be based on constant feeling of obligation.

Dena was learning to take her first steps, display her first smile and fumble her first intelligible words, but the inner struggle between the two adults was fearfully close to the surface and threatened to explode.

Sylvia failed to realize that no one can ever possess another, especially a personality as mercurial as her husband's. She loved Danny, but restricted him. She was appreciative but often hurt him. She was ambitious for him, but many times mothered him too much. It is indeed a wise woman who knows how to love the way her husband wants to be loved, not the way she herself wants to love.

Show business deals with emotions. The skeleton, the nerves, the guts of any performance are emotions, the feeling of the entertainer and the reaction of the audience. The creative artist wears his emotions nearer the surface than do the members of other professions. His emotional pendulum swings wider between hope and despair, laughter and tears, joy and anger, peace of mind and restlessness.

Lovers' quarrels and marital disagreements in this setting of emotional upheaval and range of reactions necessarily include a hazardous factor of potential disaster.

Sylvia made sense. But Danny did not want to see it.

Under all the aggressiveness and outer strength in Sylvia's make-up there was a large nodule of insecurity, the scar from being hurt.

Sylvia wanted desperately to understand Danny's craving and need to explore himself, to be alone, to shake off the pattern of misery into which their relationhip had fallen, but there was bitterness inside her. She questioned why he would endanger the success they had built together. She tried to analyze his changed behavior, for he had closed a door between them and retreated into a kind of hostile politeness. She felt a vacuum of loneliness when he was away from home—which was often—and even more when he sat silently brooding.

Danny was on the run, flying to San Francisco, New York, New Orleans and Podunk Center—or pacing rapidly around the eighteen holes of a golf course. A close friend of the family shook his head and commented soberly, "That guy is the fastest walk-away-from you ever saw."

Storm-clouds boiled darkly. Nothing could prevent the hurricane that was to hit the Kaye family.

A magazine calling Danny Kaye "the world's highest-paid buffoon" lay on the stand when Sylvia picked up the phone, called her sister in New York and said five words: "Danny walked out on me."

XIV

"My Second Home"

On september 5, 1947, the news wires carried a short notice informing the public that Mr. and Mrs. Danny Kaye had decided upon a trial separation. Danny and Sylvia deemed it best to live alone in order that time, the healer and soother, would provide a solution to the emotional turbulence that had crested after seven unforgettable years.

What could Danny say to Lou Mandel, his lawyer, to Sam Goldwyn, to Max Liebman, to Irving Somach, to Pop—to all their friends?

The columnists and reporters rubbed their hands in fiendish glee and uncovered their typewriters.

Danny provided no succulent material. His comments were dignified, restrained and sounded honest.

"You must remember that I was born poor in Brooklyn and learned the values of life early. Some people may think Hollywood has made a heel out of me; others may say the town has changed me for the better. They have the right to their own opinions.

"About my split-up with Sylvia, I can only say no outside influence caused the separation. In the course of becoming successful professionally, our marriage relationships got a little lost. So we decided on a temporary situation so we could stand back, look at our marriage objectively and try to figure out a way to make a go of it.

"Don't think I fail to appreciate Sylvia. She was perfectly content to work through me, let me be the big guy. But I didn't want things that way. I believe in people standing on their own feet and retaining their identity. I think to belong to someone truly you must first belong to yourself; to make other people happy you must first be capable of making yourself happy.

"I'm chiefly interested in Sylvia finding personal happiness and keeping her own individuality. If we, as two distinct individuals, can work towards the same goal, I think our marriage has a chance to be saved. If our marriage should end, Sylvia won't work with me. And even if she would, I don't think I would want her to."

And what could Sylvia say? A woman rejected. A woman incapable of holding the man she loves. A woman who "always made sense" who was willing to learn from defeat. Her answer was equally sincere and honest.

"Danny and I talked things over for a week, so I cannot say he walked out on me in a sudden mood. The trouble seemed to snowball into something definite.

"I love Danny, and I always will. But he is nervous and unhappy. It is difficult for him with the baby in the house. Danny loves the baby and he is proud of her. She has his hands. But he is so nervous and tired that her crying worries him. I'm still hoping for a reconciliation.

"I cried all night, and it just doesn't seem possible that he has left."

For Danny and Sylvia their past world had come to an end. "I've never been so deeply hurt before," Sylvia said as she tried to withdraw from the public eye. She hid behind a new calmness and reserve. Life, she knew, had to go on for the sake of her daughter. She was pressed for explanations by her family, but she pleaded with them not to be unfair to Danny.

Pop Kominsky alone was optimistic. "It will all work out," he said. "Don't give up hope. Danny will do what is right." But no one could be sure he meant what he said. "Too much money has caused this rift," he continued.

"Too much poison from the lotus flower of success," said the literati.

"Too many emotions," said Sylvia pensively.

Danny received the bulk of the blame. Some people said his restlessness, his constant search, his recalcitrant moods were the reasons for the rift. But more impartial onlookers close to the Kayes thought the problem was more serious than the usual complexes or mutual tantrums that come and go in squalls in many Hollywood stars' homes.

Sylvia, in the eyes of many, represented a kind of human tragedy that results from lack of recognition. In spite of her often flamboyant, imperious ways, she was, after all, a woman of many talents and many dimensions, of great depth of feelings and sense of responsibility. While the two had started out haphazardly to conquer the fancy of millions, it had reached the point where Sylvia Fine, the musician and craftswoman, was pushed into the background in the role of Mrs. Kaye, the mere wife of the sky-rocketing entertainer. Not only were her contributions overlooked, but her personal identity was often snubbed by the pontifical bosses in Hollywood.

What could Sylvia answer to the traditional queries, "How does it feel to be the wife of Danny Kaye?" Could she tell the truth—that it was lonely, that it was hard work to keep the songs rolling out to make her husband successful, that it wasn't all beer and skittles to stand unnoticed in the wings while he bowed to the applause? It was wrong for the public to heap the laurels at the feet of Danny alone, without even tossing an occasional limp posy to Sylvia. The careless slights had done something to this dainty tiny woman resulting in an understandable bitterness which was not conducive to the wisdom she needed at this time of crisis. The result was a stumbling-fumbling showdown and the agreement to say good-by, at least for the time being.

Many an outsider who knew the Kayes professionally was quick to coin criticism. "Danny Kaye is a bad father, a temperamental husband, an ungrateful ham. He has left his family . . . and for what?" But in the choosing of sides—so inevitable in family feuds—there were those who also rejoiced over the separation, and recited anecdotes of Sylvia's aggressiveness and possessiveness, and to them Danny Kaye was "entirely right" and "better off on his own two feet."

"The world has come to an end for me," Danny repeated again and again. "Suddenly everything looks different." He was miserable, oppressed with guilt and pessimism. But this was the solitude he wanted, a respite from pressures so that he could learn to walk alone; an opportunity to deepen his art and probe his limitations.

Sylvia, maintaining a gleam of hope even through the shock of the separation, soon came to realize that the Hollywood claptrap rang false and that she had been caught in a dense net from which she could not disentangle herself. Work was her anodyne. She plunged into a sea of more lyrics, more tunes, more work and the book about Danny.

Seven Years in a Pressure Cooker was half ready after a few months of intensive labor over a typewriter. Sylvia presented it to her editors, who were quick to reject the first chapters. Her anger, bitterness and despair slithered out between every line. The publishers had asked for a funny book—one that would catch the mood of Danny Kaye's rich glint of deviltry. But Sylvia was in no mood to laugh at her husband or to capture his volatile charm in the printed word. Her open wounds showed themselves on every page. She withdrew the book, repaid the advance and during sleepless nights wondered if she were a failure without her Danny.

Days gathered themselves into weeks, and weeks soon ushered in Christmas and a New Year that was far from happy for either of the Kayes. There was a half-hearted exchange of expensive gifts and emotionless trite salutations for the season . . . and Danny's announcement of his decision to return to London, the city of his greatest failure.

Danny's simultaneous break with both Sylvia and Goldwyn came as no surprise to those who had analyzed the star as the man who had to find himself without the support of those who loved or admired him. His psychiatrist doctor friends were not surprised, but many of the less analytical and thoughtful Hollywood personalities called him downright ungrateful—"as ungrateful to Goldwyn as to his own wife."

This hurt deeply, but Danny had been unhappy as an actor too. Goldwyn was the kind of boss who thought, "I don't get ulcers. I give them." Danny did not want to join the ulcer ward of Hollywood and did not want any more productions in which he was merely a well-paid and well-dressed puppet with no word in the selection of the story, the leading lady, the script or his fellow actors.

To the accusations of ingratitude he gave the answer, "It has been suggested that I am ungrateful toward Sam Goldwyn. I don't look at the matter that way. I consider Sam a great producer and admit he has been wonderful to me. But, however much I like and admire Sam, I have my own career to think about. I don't think Sam gave me my first break out of charity. He took a gamble on me, and the dice came up eleven. We both profited by our relationship.

"Now I want to find out what I can really do on the screen. Warner Brothers offered me a wonderful deal, and I took it. I am to make five pictures for them with the privilege of approving the director, story and leading lady. My contract stipulates that I can have twelve months off between pictures. That will give me the opportunity to make outside films if good ones come along.

"The very fact that Warner's is considering me for Don Quixote is encouraging. I did not make the reported statement that I'd never do another picture for Sam. If he had a good story for me, I'd sign with him tomorrow."

It is no mystery that Danny planned to open on February 2, 1948, at the London Palladium, the entertainers' Grail of all music-halls. He wanted to be away from Sylvia, the states and cities that reminded him of her, and to challenge himself with his past failure.

The inseparable trio—Danny Kaye, Sammy Prager and Eddie Dukoff—spent excited days and weary nights planning for the London opening. They tried to analyze the characteristics of British humor, for, in spite of their basic beliefs in the universality of wit, all three were well aware of the horror stories about a British public which was belligerent and unwilling to accept Hollywood stars.

Mickey Rooney had returned only a few weeks before, bearing the bruises of his rough treatment at the hands of the Londoners because of what they called his "American cockiness" and his style, "inferior to British acts at a fraction of the salary."

One Hollywood star who was leaving London as Danny arrived

issued the warning, "You won't stay long either. It's a darned shame their beer isn't as cold as their audiences!"

Eddie Dukoff, upon whose shoulders fell the stewardship of press-agentry, knew he had a tough problem on his hands and was not surprised by the sarcastic reporters who arrived at their hotel wearing unfriendly attitudes toward loud movie stars and carrying resentments about the Hollywood movie industry, which they called "a dream factory lacking in ideals but over-abounding in the neurosis of money-madness."

Quite to the astonishment of the men of the press, this American artist Danny Kaye was a charming, humble, wide-eyed man who professed no less ideals than they themselves had, a well-read performer who completely disarmed them by admitting he knew very little about England and bombarding them with questions until they found themselves giving answers, instead of asking the usual round of prosaic queries. They left his room promising to help Danny know their country.

Unlike some of the other visiting stars, Danny was not surrounded by press agents, hucksters and publicity palaverers. The reporters found only a lean, relaxed-appearing "chap" who had a bottle of Scotch on the table for their pleasure and called each by name as he offered a drink. They were impressed.

The results were immediate. Danny's initial publicity at the hands of the London press was favorable. When asked about the marital rift, Dukoff replied, "If the two are left alone and there is no outside meddling, they will get together. I am sure of that. But, fellows, can't you leave that sort of stuff out of the papers?" The press obliged.

The Palladium was sold out on opening night. Every seat was filled by Londoners who had seen Danny's motion pictures and flocked to see if this Hollywood star could also perform on the stage. The audience ranged from cynical big-shots in show business to bobby-soxers. There was tension and expectation in the air that Monday night.

Danny, standing shaking in the wings, suddenly heard the master of ceremonies announce his name.

He tried to respond, but found something terrible had happened. Despite his efforts, he was glued to the spot, paralyzed, unable to take a step. Ted Ray, the M.C., was waiting, and out in the darkness of the theater came the roll of welcoming applause. Danny heard the cheers, a few piercing whistles, and Ray repeating, "And here—here is Danny Kaye!"

Still petrified, a hand locked around a rope, Danny had a brief thought of Sylvia before he found himself being literally hurled onto the stage. The production manager had observed the stage-fright paralysis and catapulted him out of the wings.

Danny stumbled to the center of the stage, almost fell, caught his balance and said the first thing that popped into his mind "I am shaking like a leaf!" He was greeted by an appreciative, approving roar of laughter, the emotional stimulant for Danny Kaye.

Whether or not the source came from the adrenalin created by fear, Kaye's burning desire to succeed or the approbation of the thousands of unseen faces, Danny's performance was effluent, overemphatic, erupting like lava from a volcano. He remained on the stage until he was totally worn out and had left eight thousand Londoners with sides aching from laughter.

With incomparable skill he sang his scat songs, told of his trip to England, lamented his fears and thrilled the audience with scintillating wit and a voice of surprisingly good quality. He jockeyed the mood of the British to a point of seldom experienced lunacy. He lured the audience to sing with him, to imitate his voices, noises and ugh-ughs. Without a pause for fresh air or sensible syntax he mimicked the Nazis and the Russians and outsang the fiercest operatic diva.

The audience was completely under his spell. The heartbeat of the performance gathered momentum and Danny careened through his acts faster than a London tube train. In twenty-nine pseudo-languages and a hundred expressive gestures, he convinced the staid Londoners that they were witnessing the genius of the "clown of the century."

Short of calling for fire apparatus or blowing up the theater, there appeared to be no way to break up the show. The audience stood clapping, smiling, laughing, stamping—and refused to go home.

"From that night on," says Danny, "England was my second home. I needed it then, too.

"But I never again want to feel as low as I did that night, either. I was so sick with nervousness I thought I would never be able to go on. If Charley Henry or Val Parnell—I'm still not sure who did it—hadn't pushed me bodily, I swear I never could have made it to the center of the stage. Why, I might be standing there yet, and the stage hands would have to dust me off now and then. 'Poor Kaye!' they'd say—'rooted to the spot!' "

Of all the visitors, critics, admirers who came to his dressing room to lay praise at his feet, there was one man Danny will never forget—a slender, stern-appearing old gentleman with a random mop of Einsteinian hair who looked as if he had stepped off a page of a Dickens novel. Hannen Swaffer, London's most celebrated—and most feared—critic, stood erect against a wall, eyed the exhausted performer and boomed with the solemnity of the chimes of Big Ben, "My boy, I have been going to music-halls for fifty-odd years, and I have never seen a greater personal triumph."

Swaffer stopped abruptly, as if shocked to find himself paying a compliment, and then quickly added, "Of course you didn't make *me* laugh!"

Overnight Danny was a sensation in London. Front pages of the papers lauded him in glittering generalities—with the exception of one hard-bitten and mystified drama critic who wrote, "Mr. Kaye jerks about the stage as if in the grip of a paralytic spasm; all the time making those queer, disturbing noises, as though he were a rabbit in agony . . . or a bull with a toothache."

An unprecedented record, Danny's six-weeks' run at the Palladium was sold out and more than $50,000 had to be returned to disappointed applicants. In Birmingham people with blankets lined up for twenty-six hours in a mile-long line to buy tickets for a future appearance. It was hard to believe that in 1938, when Comedian Kaye first trouped in London, no one noticed him except to demand that he stop "the infernal din."

With each new performance his popularity grew. Legend of enormous and almost embarrassing proportions was growing. Danny, who from 1948 on visited and performed in England every year, suddenly became a sort of cult in austerity-bound and rationed England.

In spite of their own plight, the British were overgenerous to him. Taxi-drivers refused to accept fares from him; there were Danny Kaye fan clubs, Danny Kaye sweaters, Danny Kaye neckties. Two teenagers proudly boasted they had seen the show nine times, and another bobby-soxer crashed Danny's dressing room via the fire escape just to say, "You're wonderful!" The stage door was constantly barraged with the fiercest of all human animals, the autograph hunter. Fans tore his suits, tried to touch his face, to kiss him.

There was a new quality in Danny's performance. He moved away from his basic, rehearsed and well-studied routines. He improvised and embroidered, catching each situation as it came to him. More and more he relaxed under the glare of the footlights, and Sammy Prager, at the piano, followed him intuitively as Danny created on the spot.

"Often Danny used me as a sort of mirror," says Sammy. "He seemed to play to and for me only, for a while, and if he saw me laugh he knew his audience would laugh too."

Danny grew with his audiences in the sunshine of their laughter. Assured of their approval, he often sat on the edge of the stage, feet dangling into the orchestra pit, smoking a cigarette, and chatting—chatting about things that came into his mind, sometimes humorous, sometimes general observations and sometimes even philosophy, such as his remembrances of Sir Harry Lauder, who preached two truths: Be content with yourself and don't try to be anyone else.

To a people like the British, whose deep emotions are normally restrained by traditional reserve, Danny appealed as the great democratic unifier of the classes, a sort of traveling salesman for democracy who sold the idea that laughter is international and that, if people the world over could laugh together, there would never again be a blitz or human destruction by human beings.

Night after night Danny enjoyed laughter, applause and appreciation, but one show proved to be his near nemesis.

In the middle of one of his fastest songs, he realized the audience was wavering. The house was bulging with people and the Marquess of Milford Haven was in the standing-room section (which cost three pounds), but the eyes of the audience had wandered. There was commotion in the orchestra, and people leaned perilously over the balcony rails. Something unique had happened. The louder Danny sang, the less response he drew. With a sense of frantic despair, he worked his way to Sammy Prager and whispered, "What gives?" Sammy, equally aware of the disruption and twice as confused as to its origin, shook his head. Someone or something was stealing the show!

The lightning from flash-bulbs cut the darkness. And there was the grinning Winston Churchill, who had arrived late, posing in best political cheese-cake manner. Danny strode to the footlights, peered over, grinned back and said in a wheedling voice, "Aw come on now; I'm the star of this show—and a guest in this country, besides!"

The great Churchill, well versed in the tricks of public performances, laughed loudly as he relished the switch in the situation. Later he invited Kaye for a private chat.

"Young man," he said sonorously, "it's a good thing you are not a politician. You have a tremendous grip on a crowd and would be a formidable adversary in politics." Danny treasured the comment. Churchill is a man who does not give compliments lightly, especially to a visiting entertainer.

Churchill continued, "I noticed the routine you did when you momentarily turned away from the audience, paused, and then, with proper timing, put the greatest possible emphasis on the next few words. Mr. Kaye, that was well done. Yes, it's a good trick. I first used it myself on a speaking tour of Canada twenty years ago. I picked it up from Otis Skinner when he did the *Merchant of Venice*."

Churchill's visit to Danny's dressing room was reported by all the newspapers, and the legend of the American entertainer continued to expand like a field of mushrooms during a wet spring. A virtual black-market developed. Theater tickets were forged and sold at exorbitant prices, one even landing in the hands of a bewildered diplomat who had traveled all the way from Turkey to see the show. Scalpers asked as high as $50 per ticket.

As the result of Churchill's attention, both the Conservatives and the Laborites issued invitations to Danny for political cocktail parties and after-show sorties. The sage Dukoff wisely protected

Danny by tactfully refusing such overtures, including even those from Lord Strabolgi, the Socialist peer, and Anthony Eden, the future prime minister, on the grounds that this American entertainer could not afford to become entangled in the internal affairs of Britain.

Following close on the heels of Churchill came a visit in Danny's dressing room by the Archbishop of Canterbury, who shook Kaye's hand and said with the dignity so characteristic of the British, "My word but you are a funny man!"

Several days later Danny had occasion to meet the Archbishop again. Kaye, with a Member of Parliament, was getting into a car outside the House of Commons when the dignitary came walking down the sidewalk. Danny was again introduced to him.

"Oh, yes," said the Archbishop, "I remember you well. You are the funny man. Well sir, I used to be quite funny myself." And with that he stepped off the curb in front of the automobile, which had already started to pull away. The driver slammed on the brakes, missing His Grace by only inches.

The Archbishop, visibly shaken, walked back, put his head in the car window and said to Danny, "Young man, this time you very nearly achieved a measure of *real* fame!"

One of the incidents during these days at the London Palladium is told by Sammy Prager, a humorist and wit in his own right. "It was customary at the Palladium for tea and sandwiches and biscuits to be served to Danny between each show, by a young woman named Olive. During the show-break on this particular afternoon there was no Olive and no tea. Danny didn't seem to notice the change in the routine until he was on the stage, and suddenly, right in the middle of a song, he stopped dead, looked at me and said as casually as if we were in his living room, 'Sammy, we didn't have our tea this afternoon.' Then he wistfully added, 'Gee, I'd like some tea.'

"The Londoners loved it. Tea and Englishmen go together like ham and eggs, Marilyn Monroe and curves, and 'either' with 'or.' I'll bet there weren't three people out of the thousands who hadn't had their tea that afternoon, and they were in full sympathy with Danny.

"Danny moaned and groaned a little more and went on with

his act. Suddenly I spotted Olive standing in the wings with her silver tray, teapot and cup ready to serve Danny at the first opportunity. I signaled for her to come on the stage, and she, good sport that she was, gingerly slid out before the footlights and stood waiting quietly just outside the direct beam of the spotlights, but where the entire audience could see her.

"The audience were panicked! And they were delighted. It was obviously spontaneous, and it took Danny several seconds before he caught on. He stopped and savored his refreshments while I tenderly played 'Tea for Two.'

"This little bit of silly business was so in keeping with British psychology and wit that we decided to keep it in the show. Of course, each time Danny went through it the pantomime was a little different, but the basic idea was a great hit, the result of a completely unplanned situation."

The gag of Danny and the tea had an amusing aftermath.

On February 28, 1948, something unexpected happened. King George VI, with the royal family—Queen Elizabeth, Princess Elizabeth, the Duke of Edinburgh and Princess Margaret—came to the Palladium to see Danny Kaye's performance, marking the first time the King had seen a variety show since his coronation. And for the first time the royal family spurned the royal box and watched the show from the front row of stalls—unheard of in the annals of kingly visits to the theater.

Danny, alerted that the royal family had arrived, pranced on the stage and burst into his act in his inimitable, innocent, exuberant style. Suddenly he spotted Sammy, looking very dapper and suave, wearing a new tuxedo he had bought for the occasion. As Sammy tells the rest of the story:

"I felt the least I could do was look my best when the King came to visit; so I had spent some time getting a new suit, new glasses, a manicure and haircut. Danny spotted my newly shorn tresses—and what did he do? He pointed a finger at me and in a shrill voice began intonating that tune and rhythm so familiar with kids, 'Sammy got a haircut. . . . Sammy got a h-a-i-r-c-u-t. . . . Sammy got a H-A-I-R-C-U-T.' The audience picked up the chant, and I could feel the blood rushing to my face until I was sure I looked the color of a Maine lobster. I glanced out into the audience, and could hardly believe my eyes. There was the King singing along with the crowd, 'Sammy got a h-a-i-r-c-u-t.'

"The King seemed to have a marvelous time. It was rewarding to see him so amused. That evening I felt we had done our fair share of welding Anglo-American relations.

"Danny went on spinning his thin, breezy thread of routine and hanging on bits of amusing business that came into his mind. Then, according to plan, Olive appeared on stage, standing slightly behind Danny, with his tea and biscuits. Danny pretended he did not see her. Olive moved closer, but Danny continued his story to the audience.

"Suddenly I heard a loud whisper from the audience, from the first row, in fact—from King George himself. His Majesty was sitting on the edge of his seat, gesturing to Danny. 'Danny, your tea!' "

With his tomfoolery Danny had snared even the King of England. Tea, biscuits and the Kaye warmth were just what the Britishers loved. Danny was their boy.

Olive, accustomed to the British class system, unwittingly put her finger on one of the basic differences between British and American behavior when she said: "Mr. Kaye is a real gentleman. He treats the stage door guard and me with the same consideration he gives the King."

Danny, hearing this comment, was silent for a minute. His laughter was gone. "That's what I like about America. We treat all people as equals." Then he added, almost to himself, "At least we try to—and we should."

During the years that followed, the members of the royal house have been listed among Kaye's admirers. Danny has been honored by invitations to both Buckingham Palace and Clarence House. Princess Margaret was photographed with him in 1956, when she officiated at the premiere of *The Court Jester* at a charity affair. Princess Margaret Rose never misses a new Kaye show, and has visited him backstage and sung duets with him. The petite, charming Princess and the Duke of Edinburgh sat on the floor with Danny, drank champagne and listened to phonograph records until five in the morning, when someone tactfully reminded the

Princess that none of the guests could leave the party until she herself departed.

In 1955 a London reporter, Rex North, claimed that Danny was on such intimate terms with Princess Margaret that he greeted her, "Hello, honey!" Danny was furious and called the accusation a dreadful lie. Princess Margaret reciprocated with a gracious invitation for Danny to visit her at Clarence House again, and thus squelched the unpleasant rumor.

Danny, besieged by reporters for juicy tidbits of impressions or conversations with the royal family, has made it an ironclad rule never to mention any member. "I absolutely refuse to comment. Anything I say might be misconstrued, and I do not want to embarrass anyone—ever." It remains a fact, however, that Danny Kaye has a closer contact with England's nobility than most entertainers.

Then, on a Tuesday, a glittering collection of American and British notables assembled at the Savoy Hotel for an important luncheon. Those at the head table included U.S. Ambassador Lewis Douglas, British Defense Minister Emanuel Shinwell, the Lord Mayor of London and the sheriffs with their chains and badges of office.

Guests included the future Queen Elizabeth and Prince Philip, the Marquess of Milford Haven, who was later the best man at the royal wedding, J. Arthur Rank, the Earl of Listowel and Sir A. P. Herbert—in short, the most illustrious group of leading men and women ever to honor an entertainer.

The Lord Mayor of London, Sir George Aylwen, spoke first, "I'd like to see every meeting of Ministers preceded by a little turn of Danny Kaye. That might even have an effect on Mr. Vishinsky."

The traditional British toastmaster, in scarlet uniform, silenced the throng with a traditional cry, "Mr. Chairman, Your Excellency, His Majesty's ministers, My Lords, Ladies and Gentlemen."

The assembly came to rapt attention. Then, in tones loud enough to jar the crystal chandeliers, the toastmaster shouted, "Pray silence for Danny Kaye!" The prayed-for silence fell, and orator-of-the-day Kaye delivered a brief, almost gagless and not very original message: people are people. But even Danny's most hackneyed platitudes were news in Britain.

The Savoy luncheon served only to reiterate the strange but undeniable fact that Danny Kaye, the comical kid from Brooklyn, had become a national figure in England. It was not merely that he was a popular entertainer, for the British had seen good troupers before. Nor was it so much that Britons laugh at Kaye's antics. It is simply that the British admire the man himself. Kaye is all the things the British love, rolled into one larger-than-life-size package of fresh ebullience and uninhibited charm.

Shrewd Ambassador Douglas came to this official luncheon—his first since the fishing incident that scarred one of his eyes—especially to join in praising Danny Kaye. Said Douglas, "If I were deliberately to set out to do him justice, I would say he has been a better and more effective and persisting ambassador of goodwill from my country to yours than all the accumulated personalities of officialdom."

London's highbrow Sunday *Observer* remarked, "His dressing-room at the Palladium is now as crowded as the anteroom of an eighteenth-century nobleman in the days of patronage."

Life wrote: "In London Kaye got 70,000 fan letters in seven weeks. Later the number exceeded 100,000. Two telephone lines have been set up to handle his calls at the Savoy. The operators keep both busy telling fans Kaye isn't in and cannot visit a store or restaurant."

English anthropologist Geoffrey Gorer appraised the Kaye phenomenon: "In the U.S. he is admired for his entertainment technique. . . . To the British he is exotic, and since he is a foreigner who won't be around tomorrow, they let themselves be carried along by his personality. His appeal is emotional, and his openness and lack of shame are most welcome. He makes love to his audiences."

Mr. Kaye would agree. "Never have I encountered such warmth, such enthusiasm, such emotion," he said. "Here, when I give the audience some emotion, I can feel it coming up from them. It goes back and forth like waves."

The tap dancer who preceded Danny's act at the Palladium said during this period, "If that guy wanted to run for King, he could get elected in a walk."

It came time for the final curtain of the final show at the Palladium. The closing night climaxed all that had gone on before. The crowd would not let him finish. Members of the audience flung themselves into the aisles, kicked their heels on the floor in a demonstration to prevent Danny leaving. When the time grew past twelve when subways and buses cease to run, Danny reminded them of the hour. "We'll walk home," they shouted back.

The farewell show lasted two hours. "Auld Lang Syne" brought tears to Danny's eyes, and the audience hoped he would return again to his "second home."

In his dressing room and at the Savoy a crew of assistants busily packed into fifteen wooden crates the gifts that his adoring public had given him. Danny, a rank sentimentalist, was deeply touched by these gestures of friendship.

The day his ship sailed, two typical British office workers sat in a subway car, reading newspapers. One, a complete stranger, turned to the other and said in a lugubrious tone, "It's a lot different with him gone, isn't it?"

The other man nodded sadly, "Aye, 'tis," he said, and the two went on reading.

The headlines on their papers said: OUR DANNY'S GONE AWAY.

A man with new self-confidence was on his way to the United States. He had confirmation of his ability, believed in his performances and felt in his soul that he had matured.

Danny went home—home to Sylvia and home to Dena.

"One day," says Sylvia, "he just came home."

During the weeks while Danny was gone, Sylvia had time to think too. "I had to learn the hard way to conquer some of my faults. I had to learn that marriage is a woman's job. I am not different from other women. Babying? Trying hard? Never again. I still hold tight to my husband—but with open fingers."

Then there was the low roar of a plane stitching its way across the dark cloth of the night, taking both Danny and Sylvia to London. Sammy Prager and Eddie Dukoff sat two seats ahead. The occasion: a command performance for King George.

The splendor and importance of this unexpected invitation were viewed with mingled emotions by the studio. Warner Brothers was shooting *Happy Times* with Danny as the latest star and projecting plans for another picture, *The Inspector General*. But the cinema moguls waived their objections, wrote off the great loss of money caused by the delay as an "occupational hazard" and hoped the publicity value of the event would balance the budget.

The Kayes flew almost non-stop from Hollywood to London, with only a brief rest as they changed planes at New York's crowded and unimpressive La Guardia airport and arrived in London in a state of near exhaustion after a stormy stomach-in-the-mouth trip across the Atlantic.

A few months before Danny had promised the Londoners he would return. Little did he dream it would be so soon.

The Londoners outdid themselves. The red carpet was not only laid out, it was covered with rose petals as well. A brigade of reporters were waiting at the airport; an army of officials and hosts were gathered in the lobby of the Savoy Hotel to welcome the American entertainer. Danny had only time to change his tie and shirt before he was whisked away to the B.B.C. broadcasting studios to sing his songs for the millions of people who could not attend the royal command performance.

The next day was filled with tense and grueling rehearsal. Even such experienced British clowns as the Crazy Gang admitted that perhaps Danny did not want to be known as a clown but he was "funnier than any of the clowns who would perform for the King."

That night Danny was initiated into the Grand Order of Water Rats, the highest honor to be bestowed by the fraternity of British Variety Artists. In order to become a Rat, a performer must, first of all, be a "good chap" and, secondly, a recognized entertainer. Salary, top billings and reputation mean nothing unless the two prerequisites are recognized and the personal qualifications unquestioned.

Danny was introduced with the not-so-new play on his name, "Danny, you are okay," and lauded by a long and moving speech which reviewed his contributions to the English theater. Danny was touched beyond the point of humor. He answered the ovation with no gags, no jokes, no clowning . . . merely, "This is the nicest thing that has happened to me in a long time."

Then came *the* night. It was far from gay and carefree. Danny, so easy and relaxed when performing before the King and the royal family before, was anxious, tense and tired when faced with the command performance. Sylvia recalls the illustrious event: "I was amazed how much Danny had learned about British manners. He instructed me to curtsy first and then to talk when meeting royalty. He listed the members of the royal house who should be addressed 'Ma'am' and 'Your Royal Highness.' "

The curtain went up before a difficult audience, a stiff group of overdressed people who watched the royal box instead of the stage. Danny struggled to get the feel of the crowd, to lure their attention to the act, to break down the stuffy dignity of an evening that was proving to be more of a blue-blood social event than a gay night at the theater.

Timing was against him, too, for his act of only two songs came toward the end of the program, after a string of excellent entertainers. He was finished before he had scarcely begun.

"I was no court jester, but a flop," he said afterward.

In addition to a difficult audience, Danny had a bad break that night. Sylvia, rushing into his dressing room, told him firmly what she thought had been wrong with his fast delivery. Unfortunately, in the corner of the dressing room sat a London reporter, who released Sylvia's wifely criticism in the morning papers. Since that night Sylvia looks around very carefully before she gives a negative evaluation of Danny's performance.

But for all the bad breaks, the London public did not think Danny had failed at the command performance. Some felt there had been too many acts, too many songs, too long an evening, but no one said there was "too much Kaye."

The 13,000-mile round trip and performance took a little over five days. Then Danny reported back to Warner's to slip back into his role in *Happy Times*.

The next year Danny returned to the British Isles for the fourth time. Nothing had changed. The fog still rolled in and so did the customers.

On the night of his last performance in Glasgow the crowd followed him from the theater to the hotel singing "Will Ye Nae Come

Back Again?" a song written in the time of Bonnie Prince Charles, and seldom sung by the Scots unless with meaning and emotion.

Danny's performance had a new facet. There were, of course, the old standbys, "Minnie the Moocher," "Stanislavsky," "Tschaikowsky," but, to avoid repetition, he began to talk about Dena, to tell stories of her growth and yarns of her childhood. It was plainly obvious that Danny missed his young daughter. The audience, in full sympathy, felt they knew Danny as a person, as a father, a warm-hearted human being.

London, in 1949, was more than a series of lowering and raising of red velour curtains. There were several Danny Kayes: the lonely man without his wife and daughter; the inquisitive artist who "played hookey" on his time off and visited Paris, where he met Maurice Chevalier, with whom he is still in contact. He also yearned to meet the greatest Shakespearean player of the times, Laurence Olivier, and his wife, Vivian Leigh. His most unforgettable experience was a meeting with the cynic of the century, the brittle George Bernard Shaw, with whom he shot a private movie.

Stephen Winston, a talented and helpful neighbor of Shaw, arranged the meeting with the then ninety-three-year-old sardonic verbal master.

Danny remembers the details of that visit: "I walked through the village of Ayot St. Lawrence with Mr. Winston. No one knew me, and we were left alone. I stood in the grounds of a demolished abbey, and I never before had experienced such a deep peace—all created by a few simple stones.

"Then Mr. Winston took me to one of his neighbor's gardens to show me his wife's bronze of St. Joan. It stood there dominating a beautiful landscape. The bronze seemed to me startling and fierce with vitality at first, but as you look at it, the statue grows strangely calm and fills you with beauty. How Shaw must love it, I thought.

"My host showed me the small hut in which the great playwright composed his immortal plays. All I could think was: What a self-imposed penance! How can a comedian write away from people? I enjoy this quietness, but I also need the contact of the large crowds of people to stir me to do my best. I need the response of an audience, for they give me as much as I try to give them. And yet,

Bernard Shaw sits in that little armchair and makes the world laugh. I was almost envious.

"I enjoyed my talk with my host. I remember I expressed surprise that a squire would demolish an abbey, as had happened in this village, merely because he thought it was old-fashioned. I had not finished my thought when the side gate in the garden opened and Shaw walked in for a chat under the trees.

"I felt like a shy schoolboy as Mr. Winston introduced me simply as Mr. Kaye. The name meant nothing to G.B.S. Mr. Winston added, 'This is Mr. Danny Kaye, your brother-entertainer.' That rang a bell.

" 'I saw your name in the paper,' said G.B.S., groping to remember. 'In what connection?'

" 'I do a little turn at the Palladium,' I answered.

" 'Comedian?'

" 'No, a busker.'

" 'How long are you staying?' Shaw asked.

" 'As long as they will take me.'

" 'Humph, they still take *me* at ninety-three.'

"After that G.B.S. entertained us with stories, one after another. I just listened. The garden virtually vibrated with Shaw's beautiful voice as he orated, sang, recited Shakespeare.

" 'I can see, Mr. Shaw, why you despise actors,' I said. 'It is because there is not one equal to you.'

" 'I do not despise actors,' G.B.S. snapped back. 'People think I despise them, but when I was writing *The Doctor's Dilemma* I had the assistance of doctors. Only I said what they feared to say.' Then, as if to prove his compassion toward theater folk, he imitated the voices of the great actors, from Sir John Martin-Harvey to Henry Irving and his own first love, Barry Sullivan. 'You may call him a ham,' Shaw said, 'but I have never yet come across anyone like him.'

"I felt I had to show what I could do, so I mimicked Winston Churchill and told him about Churchill's visit to my dressing room and his quip that I should not compete in politics.

"Shaw wanted to know all about Churchill. 'Was he smoking a cigar? I have always wanted to know whether or not it was a real cigar. I have heard that it is a stage prop. You see, in England,'

Shaw explained, 'you have to prove yourself by doing something that people understand. Baldwin smoked a pipe; Churchill has to display a cigar. In America, I am told, Roosevelt gained his popularity because he insisted on holding up a child and kissing it in real English election style.'

" 'Some people in America think your beard and eyebrows are stage effects,' I tossed at the old man, wondering what the effect would be.

"My statement took him by surprise, but he added seriously, 'I've never thought of popular favor,' and then changed the subject by asking, 'Have music-halls changed much? I have not been to one for many years.'

"I told G.B.S. what I knew of modern music-halls and how I, personally, have tried to eliminate the iron curtain that separates the entertainer from the audience.

"Since he had no opportunity to see my program, G.B.S. asked me to describe exactly what I did at the Palladium night after night. I told him as best I could. 'I entertain my audience for something like an hour at each performance. When I am tired, I lie down flat on the stage, make myself comfortable and talk about things in general—about things that happened during the day. Tonight, for example, I'll talk about the peaceful English countryside. I don't prepare any program. I might get a rest by walking off the stage among the people, so I make them part of the act. I am all wound up when I come onto the stage, and as I unwind, I let go and give and give till I can go on forever.'

"The nonagenarian's eyes twinkled. 'I write plays, you know. When I started, I was told by successful playwrights that any speech longer than a few lines and lasting more than a few seconds would empty the theater. But my street-corner experience as an agitator taught me that when you have talked for an hour, you can discern a little restlessness, but if you go on, the audience gets a second wind, and then you *can* continue forever.'

" 'I've done it for as much as two hours,' I said.

" 'Your type of acting is of no use to people like myself,' said Shaw half teasingly, and shook his head. 'You take the bread out of our mouths and occasionally the words as well, by doing your own scripts.'

"I could not resist accepting the challenge. 'All right,' I said. 'Tonight I'll go to the Palladium and do *Man and Superman*.' "

Then they made a short movie in which Shaw tiptoed out of a fence of bushes, clapped Danny on the shoulder, embraced him and said, "I shouldn't like you, Danny. If you have your way, you'll do away with authors. You do whatever comes into your head."

Danny hung his head and replied, "Mr. Shaw, you're a better actor than all of us."

The three hours with G.B.S. seemed to Danny like three minutes, but the theater schedule called him back to the Palladium for the early evening show.

As he stepped into the country road, he was struck by a passenger car that seemed to emerge from nowhere, from somewhere beyond the blind spot in the narrow, curved road. The impact of the blow drove Danny's elbows sharply into his ribs. He called the theater, reported the accident and requested a doctor to await his arrival in the dressing room. A fast cursory examination disclosed no broken bones, and Danny had barely time to bullet onto the stage.

For more than an hour he went through his songs, dances and patter. Suddenly he winced in the middle of a number, and in spite of the glare of the spotlights and his thin make-up, he visibly paled. He hunched slightly and walked off the stage. The orchestra filled in with "God Save the King," but instead of standing in silence, the puzzled audience began to shout for Danny. They felt it was another of his gags.

A theater official came on the stage and gestured for silence. "Mr. Kaye was in a motor accident and made his appearance only in great pain." But even with this announcement the audience couldn't believe the fact. His stage smile had been as bright as always, the smooth patter of his songs and dialogue up to his usual high standard.

"If he was in pain," a member of the audience said, "then his performance certainly was a classic of the show-must-go-on tradition."

Danny was taken by Eddie Dukoff to the Middlesex Hospital, where his chest was taped from neck to waist. Two hours after he

had left the stage he walked on again, his usual smiling self, for his
late show.

A thunder of applause greeted Danny for the second time. But
those who had watched him backstage as he rubbed his hand across
his heavily taped chest knew that it was sheer will power that
pushed him back for the second show. He was irrepressible. "I've
never been so thrilled in my life—to meet Shaw, not to get hit by
the car," he said. "That hurt. I mean getting hit, not meeting Shaw.
That was wonderful!"

Watching Danny from the wings, the ventriloquist who preceded
him commented, "Perhaps this accident will give that ball of fire
a rest. I cannot understand how he keeps up that pace." A sage
British stagehand replied, "I have seen them all in the past twenty-
five years. Kaye would rather be a race horse and last a second than
a plough nag and go on forever."

But Danny surprised everyone by taking a couple of days' rest.
"You know," he told the gang at the Palladium, "you can't gun a
motor all the time . . . it has to idle now and then."

What did he do with his free time? The Brooklyn boy who could
never study medicine asked for the privilege of watching a surgical
operation. His avocational interest exploded in his face.

Danny explained later: "Ever since I was a kid, I wanted to be
a doctor, but my father suffered financial reverses. I have a tremendous interest in medicine, and it is nothing for me to go to New
York and watch a good operation. When we were in Newcastle a
surgeon called me and announced he was doing a gastrotomy the
next morning and wondered if I would like to see the different
operational procedures between England and America.

"I put on a gown, mask and gloves, and it was all very interesting.

"Well, two days later there was the biggest stink about it, and
the thing went to Parliament. Why was that music-hall entertainer
—'Music-hall entertainer,' like I was a Communist spy!—allowed
to watch an operation?"

Many members of the House of Commons rose to Danny's defense. One witty dignitary commented to the press, "Mr. Kaye had
come well recommended to the hospital. It is hoped that, since Mr.
Kaye attended the patient's opening, it will be possible for the

patient to attend Mr. Kaye's next opening." The case was closed.

Danny learned much about the British mentality and their humor, although he had never believed for one minute the common American fallacy that the Englishman is either mirthless or slow on the laugh. No less a known personage than Noel Coward was helpful with his wisdom on these points. Said Coward: "The popular notion, undoubtedly spread about by the same chap who convinced American cartoonists that all Britishers have walrus mustaches and go blind without monocles, is that Londoners have delayed reactions of from one to twenty-four hours to side-splitting jokes that would slay an American, a Frenchman or a native of Borneo in one second flat."

When Danny heard Noel's analysis, he was reminded of the standard story: "Never tell an Englishman a story on Saturday night."

"Why?"

"Because he will laugh in church Sunday morning."

But from his own experience Danny knew these comments held some of the real secrets of success in Britain. He had not kidded the Japanese in Tokyo years before or poked fun at the English now. He had never given a single performance which belittled the United States, for which everyone respected him. His is the art of caricature and satire, not needles and barbs.

Danny was deeply interested in the background and culture of the British Isles and talked and quipped about things the English people knew. He was not a smart alec, as some of his American entertainment predecessors had been, eager to criticize, quick to compare war-torn England with get-rich-fast Hollywood or Las Vegas. He was neither snide nor condescending, braggadocio nor apologetic. He was an American who sincerely loved his British cousins, and thereby forged an everlasting bond.

XV

Seeds for Mighty Enterprises

DANNY HAD BECOME ONE OF THE MOST PHENOMENALLY PAID entertainers in the world, a comedian who earned an average figure between $500,000 and $1,000,000 a year, not including Sylvia's substantial income as a song writer and co-producer.

By 1956 he had appeared in a total of twelve pictures, made hundreds of recordings and won the Hollywood title, "The Grand Young Man of Show Business."

Variety theaters, night clubs and fairs were willing to pay fabulous sums for glimpses of Kaye in the flesh. The motion picture companies insisted on his making personal appearances, since attendance skyrocketed as a result.

Danny was well advised by Sylvia, Dukoff, his lawyers and the William Morris Agency. His was a shrewd business operation, and Sylvia, again, should receive the laurels for holding out for big stakes. Her crystal ball predicted the future accurately and wisely, and Danny, following her business acumen, hired his own cast and musicians for his variety show at the Palace Theater on Broadway.

Building his own team was perhaps somewhat of a gamble, but before the doors opened to admit the first customer, the Palace Theater had sold $230,000 worth of tickets in advance for the first eight weeks. He grossed $744,692 within fourteen weeks.

Money per se perhaps did not mean much to Danny, but it is

ironic that the one great and enduring picture he has made, Goldwyn's *Hans Christian Andersen,* paid him less—$200,000.

The jangle of the cash register kept time to the steps of an impressive line of notable personalities who came to see his performance at the Palace. The roster of big names reads like the blue book of celebrities. The Duke and Duchess of Windsor made their glittering entrance, to be followed by Mrs. William Randolph Hearst, Jr., General David Sarnoff, Mrs. Walter Chrysler, Lily Pons and André Kostelanetz, Sir Gladwyn Jebb and Marlene Dietrich.

The audience stood to applaud Danny's entrance. Sammy Prager tweedled a two-finger tune on the piano—and Danny took off into his act like a guided missile.

The Kaye family was hit by an avalanche of income.

During the late fall of 1949, Danny completed *Inspector General,* a picture which brought in poor reviews but a neat bagful of money: $100,000 plus 35 per cent of the profits. In addition, his recordings, which included a wide variety of songs, scat numbers, ballads, children's stories and sophisticated comedy, sold in one year the amount guaranteed for two, netting a cool $50,000 per year.

In February, during a three-week, five-shows-per-day engagement at the Roxy Theater, contracted on a guarantee and profit-sharing deal, he collected $91,000, in one week alone producing a $37,000 income.

In March he accepted an offer for one short evening appearance in Montreal, for which he received $10,000. On this evening a cable arrived from London announcing the very happy news that the Palladium was completely sold out two months before he would appear. It was certainly a busy year of work, heartbreaks, personal trauma, tensions, successes, a pot-pourri of experiences which left him on the top of the heap—"the world's highest-paid buffoon."

The Royal Theater in Dublin paid him $25,000 for one week. A tour through the British provinces netted $117,000 in five weeks; a similar stay in San Francisco brought in $185,250; a tour through the Pacific Northwest $90,750, and one single date in

Dallas, where he performed as a one-man show at the fair, put $25,000 in his pockets for less than ninety minutes of work.

Princess Grace Kelly of Monaco remembers when the Prince tried to hire Danny for a special gala evening. His first offer was $10,000, then $15,000 and finally $25,000 for thirty minutes of entertaining. The last offer was delivered to Danny in Paris by a special courier who interrupted an elaborate dinner party with Maurice Chevalier and Marlene Dietrich.

Danny sent the messenger back to Monaco with the same answer he had given before. "No; I am having too much fun in Paris to leave now."

But the night of the gala Monaco party found the Kayes at Cannes on the Riviera. The temptation of a party was too appealing, so Sylvia and Danny "dropped in" and joined the audience at the festival.

Scarcely seconds after the two had slunk in to a small table in the darkened rear of the hall, the crowd spotted the familiar blond hair and long nose and set up a chant. "We want Danny! We want Danny!"

For ninety minutes the American clown was kept on his feet entertaining in his own inimitable way—and received for his efforts not so much as a Monaco stamp.

The publicity director for the principality and the local hotel public-relations representative were completely thwarted by the visiting celebrity. Thinking his appearance would boost the prestige of their tourist center, the two set out to get pictures of Danny lounging happily on the sun-drenched coast. But Danny saw them coming. He donned a raincoat, turned up the collar, held an umbrella high above his head and took on the countenance of gloom.

"Of course," moaned the publicity men, "we could not photograph Meester Kaye in such an attire. Eet would be bad for our beezness."

Unlike many entertainers, Danny did not throw his income away, throw lavish parties, hire planes or drink himself into a coma. Sylvia, now associate producer, kept a firm hand on the money, investing it wisely and allotting $100 a week allowance to her husband and the right to charge "within reason." Danny was convinced that it was the only way to keep ahead in the financial cauldron of Hollywood.

Danny, when in a gay mood, is a fun-maker in his private life. He plots and schemes, spends no little time to work out his gags, and pursues them with diligence.

Danny's best one-man audience is Jack Benny. Like a giddy adolescent girl, Benny can get uncontrollable giggles by merely glancing at Danny or hearing a single Kaye word over the telephone. Several times Jack has been reduced to a laughing heap on the floor, writhing with pain and begging for help, sick with helpless mirth. His usual procedure is to eat a large sandwich before joining the Kayes for dinner, since he is so often unable to eat in Danny's presence.

It isn't necessary for Danny to say a single word or tell a single story. All he has to do is to sit silently across from his guest and soberly give an imitation of a nervous eater; a man who never stops to breathe or to chew, who reaches out compulsively for an olive, a piece of bread, a dab of butter, a dash of salt, gulps down a glass of water, never looks up from his plate, but who uses both hands unerringly to fill his mouth.

It makes no difference to Danny whether he is a guest or the host; dinner parties are generally times of hilarity.

One night Danny was the guest of the eminent Dr. Charles Mayo of the famed Mayo Clinic. Slipping away from the guests, Danny called Dr. Mayo from the extension phone in the bedroom and, through a series of strange noises that sounded like a bad connection, announced himself as "Docteur Ravignac," a friend of Mayo's future son-in-law in France, and explained that he had promised to visit Dr. Mayo while in the United States.

"How very nice of you to call," responded Dr. Mayo, "and of course you must tour our hospital and stay here with me as my guest. When you reach Chicago, be sure *not* to take a train to Minneapolis. Take the plane to Rochester instead, and I will meet you at the airport."

"But I weeesh not to go to Minneapolis," said the French "Docteur" in barely understandable English.

"That's what I said," patiently repeated Dr. Mayo. "Do *not* go to Minneapolis. Take the plane to Rochester."

"Mais, no, I do not *weeesh* to go to Minneapolis."

This nonsense went on for twenty minutes, until Dr. Mayo was totally confused and frantic.

"Eeef you weeel be good enough to hold the phone, I weeel try to explain," said the Frenchman finally.

Dr. Mayo held the phone with bewilderment.

Danny tiptoed into the living room and stood behind the doctor, who still had the receiver at his ear. "And now, Dr. Mayo," he continued in his fractured English, "allow me to explain why I do not weesh to go to Meeneapolis."

Business manager Eddie Dukoff, who lived with Danny for "seventeen years in chaos" until their ways parted in 1955, has often been the victim of Kaye's telephone gags.

One day in Hollywood Dukoff received a phone call from a Londoner. The voice on the phone explained that, being new in the United States, he had dialed incorrectly and asked, "Sir, would you be so kind as to explain to me how to dial on this American phone?"

Eddie obliged. It took five minutes of explaining the American telephone system before it dawned on him that Danny had done it again.

Friends who call the Kaye home often hear the answering voice of a Japanese houseboy, an Italian cook, a Negro valet, an English butler or a Russian piano teacher, and are forced to wait while Danny calls himself to the phone.

Once in Hollywood he glued on a false beard, draped himself in tattered clothes and begged for food at his own back door. He was promptly kicked out by his own loyal cook. Living with Danny Kaye is not unlike exploring a store of gags, magic and tricks.

Sylvia is never safe. "Once," she says, "we went to Carnegie Hall to a Sunday afternoon concert. It was very dull—a pretty bad violinist played. All of a sudden out of the corner of my eye I saw Danny's face. He was reacting to every note of the music. He kept his body perfectly still—just moved his facial muscles. It was so funny I had to stuff my handkerchief into my mouth.

"The other people began to notice him, and soon half the

audience had turned round to watch Danny. I had to drag him out in the middle of the concert."

Eddie Cantor tells of the time Danny tricked him into a burst of very surprised laughter. "I was playing in the musical version of *Three Men on a Horse* in New York. Danny played at a next-door theater. He had a break in his show just about the time I did a number with six chorus boys. It must have taken Danny little advance time to plot this one. But one night Danny slipped out of his own show, made a split-second change into a chorus-boy costume and pranced out on the stage behind me. I was singing. As a grace note he took along a banana, which he ate during my routine. My number got laughs it never had before. What was up? I knew something must be happening behind my back. Every time I turned round the banana disappeared. I examined each boy sharply. Funny, I thought; that new chorus boy looks like Danny Kaye. The new chorus boy eyed me mildly with an affectionate look, the sort of a look you get from a loving but not too bright Cocker spaniel. I looked harder. Danny looked more lovingly and tossed first one foot and then the other—all in perfect timing with my own dance routine and the rest of the chorus. Finally I caught on—it broke up the show. It was too funny. It was a riot. Everyone loved it."

What are the satisfactions of a prankster's play? The psychiatrists explain that a comedian's brain is different; his emotions are acute and his senses alive. Boys who never grow up behave like Danny Kaye—if they have his charm, intelligence and talent.

Actually, however, although Danny Kaye retained much of his boyish verve, he grew and matured as a person and, as an entertainer, he was less dependent upon scripts and written gags. Today he sings better and dances better. He displays more natural warmth. He is more secure.

During the years, his intellectual taste buds were never sated. Danny's interests branched out into many fields, although medicine claimed most of his attention. During his travels Danny saw poverty, illnesses and suffering. He talked with welfare workers, doctors, psychiatrists—anyone who had a theory about the multitudinous ailments of human beings.

The comedian had his share of fun-making, money-making and

love-making. He enjoyed his rounds on the golf courses, luxuriated by the sides of pools and wore dapper clothing. But deep inside, there was a desire to do more than make people laugh for the sake of entertainment alone. There was a need to help others.

The thought was dim and unclear, the stirring yet uncrystallized. But he needed and wanted to follow the stream of humanitarianism.

Pop Kominsky, guardian philosopher, had moved to California. California with its terraced hills of pink geraniums guarded by gray-green eucalyptus seemed to the aging man a new kind of paradise. He had known Florida, but California was different. Tourists were not so dominant. People worked hard, and even the garment industry had started a new center "out west." Some of his old Brooklyn friends were migrating to the Pacific shores.

Mr. Kominsky had grown old gracefully. There was much to be thankful for, he thought—Danny's success, Sylvia's kindness and the goodness of life.

He wanted to be remembered as a man who was never a burden, never a fifth wheel, never an intruder in his son's life. There were other old fathers who walked in the parks, played cards, compared the successes of their sons, talked of the old days in Europe and Brooklyn and enjoyed the easy life in the warmth of the California climate.

As he grew older, Mr. Kominsky was even more closely bound to his religious beliefs than he had been before. The temple was an integral part of his life, and the Jewish holidays were revered. Whenever possible, Danny insisted that his family join his father in these observations. Until this day, Danny refuses to work on Jewish holidays in deference to his father and his traditions.

Pop Kominsky was often seen at the Farmers Market, wandering with friends among the stalls of foods and fruits, buying great loaves of bread and sampling the variety of meals spread on the counters.

He was impressed with Danny's success and standing in the Hollywood community, but he was also a human being who was unimpressed by the conspicuous display of wealth and the lavish life of the film colony and its imitators. He believed in hard work and its products.

"I'm glad for you," Pop said to Danny; "I'm glad for you for what you have achieved. But in my generation we always wanted more than to make money. We wanted to help others—to help others who were less fortunate. We all tried somehow to make a contribution to society. Believe me, Danny, we talked more about ideals than about mink stoles."

"Dad, I agree with you," said Danny. "But I am just a stupid entertainer. What on earth can I do?"

"Duvidl, what you can do? I won't tell you. Rabbi Akibah has taught us to search ourselves . . . then we will find."

XVI

The Prankster

CREATING FUN NIGHT AFTER NIGHT, MONTH AFTER MONTH, YEAR upon year, without being repetitious, is a most difficult task. Some of Danny's critics complain that his personal appearances are really the same old routine and his repeat shows are weak. In spite of new numbers and new routines and scripts, there is a public demand for those "traditional" songs which have become Kaye's stamp. There are few audiences which would let him leave the stage without singing "Ballin' the Jack" or "Deenah." They have become as classic as Cantor's "Susie" or Jolson's "Sonny Boy."

The dangers of repetition Danny knows only too well. He minimizes the problem with the statement, "If you don't vary your stuff, you're sure to bore the orchestra, and why should the paying customers laugh when the musicians are sitting around with a long face?"

So he continues year after year, making fun, keeping a skeleton of classics and nightly putting new flesh on the bones to fit the mood of the situation.

"I'v got a strong gambling instinct," he explains. "Outside of my business I wouldn't risk a dime on the turn of a card or the roll of dice, but on the stage I take chances.

"Like the night in Philadelphia. They gave me the big introduction—then the ta-ra-ta-ra-ta-ra—and out I came. But when I got to the mike I saw it was unsteady because one of the screws was loose. So right then and there I clowned around about the loose screw and asked for a screwdriver and spent four or five minutes fixing the thing.

"Now, there isn't another performer in the world crazy enough to try that. I could have died right there, but the audience loved it.

"Then, when I finally got the thing fixed, I realized that the impact of my introduction was lost, so I asked for another introduction. I went out into the wings again and then made another grand introduction. The crowd howled."

Kaye's insistence that he does not and will not gamble brings to mind his victory over Ludwig Stössel during the filming of *A Song Is Born*. The film, planned to be a "carnival of laughs," was not a great picture in spite of its prominent cast, including Benny Goodman on the clarinet, Tommy Dorsey on the trombone and Louis Armstrong on the trumpet. Danny Kaye and Virginia Mayo were unable to rescue the tired plot and thin script even with such expert help.

Mr. Ludwig Stössel, one of the great Berlin actors in the pre-Hitler days and a moderate success in the United States, had a small role in *A Song Is Born*. He played it quietly, with distinguished reserve and brilliant conservatism.

In addition to his fine acting, Mr. Stössel exhibited another outstanding ability on the Goldwyn lot. His supremacy as a gin rummy player was unchallenged. He won against Virginia Mayo without appearing to be thinking, beat Hugh Herbert while glancing at a magazine and collected a round sum of money from directors, camera-men or anyone else who would play with him.

Everyone on the staff was angry. Everyone had lost money. Everyone grumbled to Danny. For several days he viewed the series of badly matched card games and then confided to three of the actors. "I have an idea. Think I will fix Herr Stössel once and for all. After all, in *Walter Mitty* I was a cardsharp, and I think I can give him a first-rate Mississippi gambler treatment."

With that, luck changed. Stössel lost. Danny won. Game after game, the same thing.

Stössel put down his magazine, furrowed his brow and began

to play with a new concentration. But Danny was unbeatable. He won every day of each week in the month.

It soon became a general suspicion that something was wrong. It was a shocking thought that the honest Danny Kaye would or could be cheating. No one dared to voice their distrust, but the sensitive Kaye knew that the time had come.

"Bring me a brand-new deck of cards," said Danny finally. One of the actors produced a sealed pack. "Some people will do anything to win," he said, and drew another half-dozen cards with a lightning-like flip of his long fingers and stashed them in a hand already bulging with illicitly acquired cards.

There was an unheard gasp from the onlookers. Everyone, with the exception of the preoccupied Mr. Stössel, knew that Danny was cheating flagrantly. "What will happen next?" was the thought that flashed through the minds of each of them. "Danny Kaye a card-sharp? What a pity! What a scandal!"

Danny did not say a word. Yes, he had cheated and won back the money which had been lost by the actors and crew during the past weeks. His fellow actors in on the secret spread the word that Kaye was just having his fun and, in a way, meting out his form of justice.

Danny picked up the money from the last game and without moving a muscle said to the group in general, "I've sent all the. money to the cancer fund—including Mr. Stössel's."

A sigh of relief followed by many chuckles cleared the emotionalized air. The rummy champion, Mr. Stössel, had met his match —even if it required the slick tricks of the prankster, Danny Kaye.

Faithful and jovial Sammy Prager has suffered his share as the butt of Danny's practical jokes. In Philadelphia one night Danny leaped out on the stage, came to a halt and stared at Sammy. Suddenly the pianist was assailed by the terrifying thought that a joking wager had been made that morning on the golf course. If he lost, the role in their act was to be reversed. Danny would be at the piano and Sammy would sing and dance.

Sammy looked at Kaye and began to laugh. Danny looked at Sammy and slapped his knee. They both broke down at their own gag. The puzzled audience was caught in the breeze of merriment and began to chuckle too. The chuckle moved to their middles. And soon everyone was convulsed. Eventually Danny and Sammy regained control and started the program all over again, with a new entrance.

"But," says Sammy, "my birthday knocked out everything. We were playing the Palace when Danny arranged a surprise birthday party for me in the dressing room after the show. When I entered, the room was dark. Suddenly the lights went on and I saw a mammoth cake with seventy-two candles on it, a special order from Lindy's. The gang sang 'Happy Birthday' and I got sorta limp and wet with sentimentality. Just as I leaned over, per Danny's order, to blow out the candles, *someone* slipped a thick juicy cream pie under my nose and pushed it into my face. My brand new tux was a complete mess, but we had a wonderful time, and I now know how those characters in the old Mack Sennett films felt."

In the life story of Danny Kaye there will always be a special place for Sammy Prager. He is more than an accompanist, more than a co-funmaker, travel companion, golf partner and sounding board. Sammy is a close friend. The two men have gone through trials, even dangers, together.

The bond was established when Sammy replaced Sylvia at the piano. In a way, the two musicians were rivals. Sylvia lost her job of directing Danny. Sammy filled in, but he never forced, commandeered, or held the reins of the performances.

The fact that Danny Kaye has arrived in the Hall of Fame is evidenced by his effigy in Madame Tussaud's world-famous London waxworks. When the plans for his statue were being discussed, Danny insisted, "Don't put me near the boiler. I'd hate to be reduced to a grease spot on the floor."

Danny's tailor delivered the correct measurements for his clothing. His oculist verified that the glass eyes were correct in color, size of pupils and position. Sylvia sent from Hollywood, via airmail, two complete sets of underclothes to give his outer wax appearance the "right perspective."

When Danny saw himself in wax, he was almost speechless—"This is me?"

Danny can be as intense in serious moments as he is in humorous ones. When Sid Field died in London, Danny, with no concern for time or expense, flew to England to participate in a benefit for Field's widow. The show was staged from midnight until three in the morning and the tickets cost twenty guineas—a steep price in London. The entertainers included Sir Laurence Olivier, Vivian Leigh, Orson Welles and Judy Garland. The glittering list of entertainers brought in some $42,000.

That night Mrs. Field had in her purse a letter Danny had once written to her husband, which ended "I love you, Cocky." "And that was the way Sid saw you, Danny," said Mrs. Field. "He used to say to me 'Danny Kaye gives everything he's got. He doesn't just *like* you—he *loves* you.' "

Many hospitals remember similar benefits. Not a single call for help from any medical research center or organization dedicated to aiding children has ever been rejected by Kaye.

Who would know better than this funniest of all funny-men that laughter and tragedy are twin brothers? The more a man can laugh, the easier he faces the deadly side of life. Korea was certainly macabre enough to need Danny Kaye to bring the bright beam of laughter into the fields of destruction.

So in the front lines of Korea, he, along with Monica Lewis and June Bruner, played before large audiences—15,000 at one time. On several occasions he and his audiences were protected by anti-aircraft guns and a patrol of fighter planes. Following one long show, he ate a hasty lunch and then took off in a jeep to visit those troops in the foxholes who were too occupied behind their guns to attend his personal appearance. For each of these small groups he gave a special show.

Sammy Prager comments, "Actually Danny disobeyed army orders. He crept on his knees and often slithered on his belly to the front lines to clown with the fighting men. Guess he figured they were the ones who needed a laugh the worst.

"I shudder when I think of it. Danny climbed to the top of a besieged hill just to see what a fighting front looked like. At one time he was less than thirty yards from the enemy.

"There wasn't a front-line division that he missed. He took pictures of the kids, got their autographs and walked miles with the soldiers on stretchers. At the end of the first day he was so dirty and torn that he looked like one of the soldiers who had been stuck in a hell-hole for days."

In one area Danny talked the colonel into letting him get near enough to the battle-grounds to shoot a motion picture of the attacking Communists. He recorded a scene of the Red Chinese withdrawing from their bunkers under United Nations fire.

On this episode Sylvia commented, "I nearly fainted when I saw the film. Danny, you were too close." Danny grinned with the smile of a mischievous urchin. "It's no use talking to him," she continued. "He's nosey. But, if he weren't, I suppose he wouldn't be Danny Kaye."

Danny visited the Belgian, Greek, Thai and South Korean troops and totaled twenty-three shows.

Back in the United States, Danny received a heart-warming letter from a Korean veteran which gave dramatic proof of the value of front-line entertainment. The letter, written by Lieutenant Bruce V. Reagan, Jr., of New York City, detailed how he, commanding a rifle platoon on Hill 424, an outpost of the 24th Division, sent a third of his best men to see the show Danny Kaye put on in Korea for the troops.

According to Reagan, "The men were battle weary and dog tired when they left their slit trenches. During the afternoon we saw the beginning of a Chinese build-up. I prayed for a short show. Had you run fifteen minutes longer, it would have been too late. No one moves in the lines after dark.

"The morale of the men who returned from your performance was sky high. Their tales of the show would have gladdened your heart. At 11:30 we were hit by a battalion plus. Our hill was the initial objective. We were lucky—phenomenally lucky—no casualties.

"I still think about that night. Thanks for sending them home happy, Danny."

Why do people laugh with Danny Kaye? This man who has been able to stay on the top of the heap of laughter defies definition and description.

The publicity agents have their versions.

Eddie Dukoff considered Danny not just a person, but "a

nation, or at least a fair-sized principality, with coastline, discernible topographical features and diplomatic relations."

A secretary of the William Morris Agency seemed more down to earth in her analysis of Danny's success.

"He's very sexy looking," she said, and, after a second's pause, added, "Of course, in a very clean-cut way. Some men are good looking and dense. Danny's good looking and bright."

Profilist Gilbert Millstein of the *New York Times* gives a more substantial analysis, saying: "Aside from his clean-cut sexiness and abnormally developed perceptive mechanism, Kaye's indubitable assets include a face, individual parts of which he is able to manipulate with a kind of insane precision while the rest of it remains quiescent; a tongue so quick that he is able to give the impression of speaking English, French, Spanish, German, Italian or even Volapuk, either together or separately; a baritone voice with a range of two octaves, which permits him to imitate a German lieder singer or a coloratura soprano or simply sing well; a pair of legs that would be adequate on a chorus boy and are more talented than those of a good many; and an awesome gift for mimicry. With this basic equipment, he has evolved, in the past dozen years or so, from a comedian who depended largely on special reference and limited audiences, into what an associate has characterized, in a rather overblown way, as 'America's first genuine international entertainer.' "

But all these are only partial answers. Danny had grown as a person, as a human being. There is a human warmth that radiates from him on or off the stage. His informal manner of performing, his casual dress and his boyish naturalness are genuine characteristics of Danny—as natural as the times when he stops to play with a group of unfamiliar boys; to feed the pigeons in the park of a strange city or to give chocolates to children in Okinawa.

An audience can't be fooled. They have as much of a radar-sense for the warm-hearted man, Danny Kaye, as he has for the ticket-buyers in the music-halls or movie houses.

Director Charles Vidor summed it up once: "Besides being able to tear up the stage in comic routines, Danny, as a restrained sensitive actor, has learned to tear at your heart."

The First Fourteen Pictures

A PERPETUALLY FILLED WELL IS PROBABLY FED BY THE SPRING of giving. The more one gives, the more he has in store to share with others. Danny, who made the transition from a stage buffoon to a motion-picture actor of stature, seems to want to give himself away to others.

His technique varies with each task and new picture. But common to all of them is his superhuman drive, bringing about a self-emptying process which is found only in top-flight performers. A part of his natural technique is an incredible mastery of time and timing.

An analysis of Danny's first fourteen pictures shows his alternating rhythm between two extremes: on the one side, his ad lib fun-making, for which one really needs a stage; on the other, the many characterizations of the maladjusted jester. The narrow or the wide screen still has its limitations, and the trouble with Danny Kaye as a movie comedian, actor and singer lies in the fact that his humor is so fast and graphic that it is difficult to capture on film. To increase his problems, many of his pictures had poor scripts. Sylvia's comment, "It is so hard to find a script for Danny," is a partial alibi, but no more than that.

It is doubtful that Danny will ever be a great motion-picture actor, although thousands enjoy watching him on the screen. It is unlikely that the stiff, unbeautiful but highly treasured "Oscar" will ever stare out from his fireplace mantel. He needs the wide open spaces of a theater stage, where, like the prairie flower, he can "grow wilder by the hour." To confine him to the camera's cold and heartless technicolored eye, to substitute the whirr of wheels for the clapping of audiences produces a Danny who will never be greater than his script.

Elliot Nugent, who directed Danny's first picture *Up in Arms* for Sam Goldwyn, tells the story of his life with Danny and Sylvia during that period. Listening to his report, one is reminded of Alfred Hitchcock's repeated claim that he is not a director, but a midwife who faces all the pains of the birth of a picture. Mr. Nugent says wryly: "Knowing that Danny Kaye is a genius as an entertainer, a director might be justified in assuming that there would be great stretches in a musical picture during which he could sit back comfortable in his canvas chair, admire Danny's diabolical technique and watch the ripe bank checks drop like magnolia petals to the sun-kissed earth of Hollywood. But no! The most tried-and-true of the Kaye routines played violently, not only up my spine, but in my face as well. He has a dozen ways of doing each transition.

"Faced with this demoniac energy, so alien to the semi-tropical calm at Santa Monica Boulevard, even a refugee from Broadway becomes invigorated. Before a half-month of preparation had passed I was a raging lion. Frustrated by Kaye's superior savvy of contrapuntal lyricism, I fell back on my hard-earned lore of the camera and lenses, levers and lights. But here was a new foe. This was a technicolor production. There were pastel shades, and they did not go with Danny.

"It is hard to plant a die on quicksilver, and Danny's personality is mercurial. He was a frightened pupil one day, a good practitioner the next. I thought my stay in Hollywood would be a vacation. I was wrong. I finished the Kaye picture admiring but exhausted. I needed a vacation after I was through."

Elliot, as well as other directors, and Danny Kaye himself have admitted movies do not necessarily improve an actor. In many cases the canned world of make-believe proves a deterrent. There is never enough time to experiment with characterizations, to grow into a role, to embroider a screen personality. Each moment lost in trial means thousands of dollars in production cost and expensive delays in schedule. No one ever has the time or opportunity to mature in a role.

Danny's own analysis of some of his pictures is worth noting. "Each picture has taught me something," he says seriously. "They were educational, perhaps not for those who saw them, but for me who made them. Even a picture like *The Inspector General* (with Walter Slezak and Elsa Lanchester) taught me never to make another movie like that." (Having two such able comics as Kaye and Elsa Lanchester play against each other was a great mistake.)

"My first picture, *Up in Arms,* had in it a musical number, 'The Lobby Number,' a satirical song about the movies. Before Sylvia and I could compose a song about pictures, we had to know more about the business than a couple fresh from Brooklyn had any right to know.

"So we saw just about every musical picture ever made. We gained a knowledge of musicals that helped us create what I still think was one of the best numbers I have ever performed.

"The one factor that has made movies so educational for me in particular is the fact that I am so frequently called on to satirize or spoof some serious occupation. This first happened in *Wonder Man,* when I had to sing a burlesquing operatic aria. Before I started burlesquing opera, I wanted to know a little bit about the subject. So I studied opera for several months, actually learning several operatic roles. From what I learned, I was then able to sing operatic gibberish that sounded close enough to the real thing to be funny, even to those people who understand opera.

"Out of all this I gained a really deep love for operatic music, and I now have a collection of recorded operas that is one of the most enjoyed of my possessions.

"Thanks to Sam Goldwyn's *Hans Christian Andersen*—and I was really happy to do another picture for Sam—I learned not only all about the fabulous world of Hans Christian Andersen, but I learned a tremendous amount about Denmark and the rest of Scandinavia, with its wonderful people and customs, that I will never forget.

"In *Knock on Wood* I did a satirical ballet, composed by

Michael Kidd. In order to make fun of ballet, it was again necessary to learn the subject, so for months before the start of the picture I was executing *entrechats* and *jetes*.

"But, frankly, all of this was a cinch until Norman Panama and Melvin Frank came up with the idea of having me portray a guy who is hypnotized into thinking he's the world's greatest swordsman—in *The Court Jester*. Now I was really in trouble. I had to actually learn to fence well enough so that even experts in the audience would be fooled. It took months of training under Olympic coach Ralph Faulkner, but I finally managed it."

Those who stood out of range in safe territory say that Danny took his fencing lessons seriously. While he learned the ancient art of self-defense with agility and speed, there arose at the school a new slogan, "Slash and Slay with Danny Kaye," and he acquired a new title, "Fency Dan." In a dueling sequence in *The Court Jester* he sustained a slight concussion from a fall, a wrenched thumb and a torn fingernail. It is questionable that the ever learning Danny considered these casualties of the profession also "educational." As a matter of fact, when asked about the hazards of fencing, Danny answered, "There are some places I draw the line. Recently Panama and Frank approached me with a new story idea. 'This will be a hysterical comedy,' they assured me. 'You play a circus performer who gets shot out of a cannon.' I never heard the rest of the story. I'm still running."

While Danny had done little running away, many substantial plans flitted past him with the transitory flight of a swallow.

He had not run away from Sam Goldwyn but was lured by Warner Brothers, who promised him not only much more money, but also better scripts and greater roles. There was the promise of the part as Don Quixote which never materialized. Guthrie McClintic was enthusiastic about Danny's doing the lead in *The Pirate,* but it was only a pipe-dream. Gabriel Pascal visualized Danny in *Macbeth,* an idea that died in the embryonic stage. Oscar Serlin insisted that Danny should play a straight dramatic role, but the plan was aborted, and this time sooner than the rest.

The Metropolitan Opera spotted Danny as the perfect Figaro, but the deal ended at a pleasant luncheon with Edward Johnson and was forgotten. Rudolf Bing offered Danny the role of Dr.

Frosch in *The Fledermaus*. Danny was thrilled, but rejected the suggestion, not on the basis of the scant money offered him, but from the standpoint of time. He would have had to wait thirteen days between performances, since *The Fledermaus* was not on the daily repertoire of the Metropolitan Opera.

Ideas by the dozen poured in. Suggestions were made for his doing Huckleberry Finn or the Pied Piper, but each ended in stillbirth.

"The man of action," however, showed up at the opportune time. Sam Goldwyn asked the prodigal son to return to the celluloid folds of Metro to play the greatest role yet to materialize: that of Hans Christian Andersen, one of the greatest storytellers of all times.

It was to be a straight role with no funny business, no acrobatics, no scat-singing—a melodrama about the beloved fairy-tale writer: a film about children and romance.

"Children?" asked Danny unbelievingly. "Real and honest scenes with kids? Not just another musical?"

"No," was the answer, "this film will be different. A fairy-tale about children for children. You will be the hero among the youngsters."

No more needed to be said. Danny knew this was his picture.

Goldwyn was serious and intense in his preliminary sessions with Danny. "This picture," he said, "will be the fulfillment of a sixteen-year-old dream. In 1936 I had the idea of creating a full-length motion picture around the ageless fairy-tales of the great Danish writer. If you think you are going to have a tough role in the picture, let me tell you that translating my original idea into something that can be done in a picture is the most difficult task I have ever tackled.

"I don't want just a screen biography of Andersen. I hope to catch the warm philosophy expressed in all his stories. Nothing less than a great tribute to the captivating tales that have become a treasured part of the world's cultural heritage will satisfy me."

Almost without waiting for Danny's final acceptance, the wheels of the publicity department were set in motion. Announcements began to blast the world outside the studio. "Danny," said fatherly Goldwyn, "this will be my most ambitious picture, and you'll be in it. I know you will be great. I want this to be sort of a monument, for it is my eighty-eighth picture in my thirty-eight years of making movies."

Danny knew this was Goldwyn pep-talk, a product no doubt of an enthusiastic press agent or cooperative yes-man, but the idea of the film was a challenge. Today, when the producer is shooting *Porgy and Bess,* he is no doubt saying the same things. Danny took the assignment with more than usual seriousness.

The enterprise was a sort of reunion. Danny was again working and planning with the man who had "discovered" him for the screen. Moss Hart, his friend from the days of *Lady in the Dark,* was writing the sentimental, sensitive and heart-breaking script around Hans Christian Andersen's life.

Sam Goldwyn, producer, Michael Curtiz, director, Moss Hart, writer, and Danny Kaye, star, turned back the clock to over a hundred and thirty years ago in Denmark, 1830. There they told through the media of song and ballet the story of Andersen's unhappy love, his difficulties as a schoolteacher and his never ending love for children. No one could have been cast better than Danny Kaye, whose rapport with children is not too different from the storyteller who preceded him.

During the sixteen years that *Hans Christian Andersen* was in the "brewing" stage, countless writers worked on the script. In Goldwyn's desk drawer lay twenty-one completed screen plays, each written by able and experienced craftsmen, and each representing thousands of dollars. Each, however, had been rejected, and it was not until the summer of 1951 that Moss Hart agreed to take on the task. The Hart touch had the "heart touch," and Goldwyn was so deeply impressed and thoroughly satisfied with the new script that shooting began a short six months later.

The end product was a controversial but entrancing picture of truly rare beauty. To take Danny out of his customary entertainer-comedian role was sheer inspiration. He characterized Hans Christian Andersen just as those who love his fairy-tales imagine the immortal Danish writer to be. He brushed the role with naïveté and sincerity, spiced it with fantasy-filled stories and filled his interpretations with gentleness and restraint.

Danny, although he looked a trifle like a Danish Walter Mitty, put aside all his clowning, and whether he flew a kite, sang with children, chatted to an inchworm, talked to a dog, was on his way to jail or busily transformed his thumb into a tiny girl called Thumbelina, he was every moment and every bit a conjurer of the charm of a child's story-book world. His was the magic realm of slippered ballerinas, pouting princesses, dreadful dragons, long green serpents, flowers that waltz and Dresden figures that fall in love.

Danny's story of the Ugly Duckling, told to a child who was miserable because he had lost all his hair, brought tears into many eyes in darkened theaters.

The beauty of the songs composed by Frank Loesser caused recordings of the movie's lyrics to sell better than any other of the Kaye albums either before or after. "The Ugly Duckling," "Wonderful Copenhagen," "Thumbelina," "The Little Mermaid," "No Two People," and "The Inchworm" became children's classics the world over.

But behind the picture's great success and "office-box hit" Mr. Goldwyn faced a barrel-load of problems in releasing the picture.

The Danes were "up in arms." The very thought that Hans Christian Andersen was to be portrayed by an American clown was an insult to their beloved national hero. The Danish government protested not only to Goldwyn, not only to the combined dignitaries of the Hollywood motion-picture industry, but to the State Department in Washington as well.

Great pressures were on Goldwyn.

It all had started after a Danish woman journalist visited the studio, returned to her native country and pounded out an irate article stating that nothing in the movie was true to Andersen's life. She flatly charged that the plot, the story, the décor, the music, and the costumes were contrary to Danish taste, culture and approach, and ended with the statement that the only thing that was Andersen was the opening "Once upon a time."

Following this histrionic outburst, Sigvald Kristensen of the Danish Foreign Office took up the cudgel: "Sam Goldwyn cannot be unaware that Denmark opposes his production of Hans Christian Andersen. When Danny Kaye was in England, we tried to persuade him to quit the role, but he told us he could not break his contract. And I think one of the script-writers resigned from the job as the result of our appeal that the Goldwyn version would insult the memory of the beloved fairy-tale writer."

Denmark's largest newspaper, *Politiken,* wrote a long editorial asking, "Is Hollywood really permitted to distort the life of a great man in such a reckless manner? It's a gigantic joke. . . ." For Sam Goldwyn there was the frightening possibility of losing the Scandinavian market or, even worse, of injunctions to prevent the showing of the picture in foreign countries. Although Goldwyn blasted his accusers by saying that their statements were irresponsible and astonishing, he also used a system of pacifying tact by inviting a Danish government delegation to come to Hollywood as his personal guests to review the film. He quickly hired Paul Bruhn of the Royal Danish Ballet to dance with the ballerina, Jeanmaire, and set up a staff of technical advisers from Denmark. With sage business strategy, he composed a preface to the film which said, "Once upon a time there lived in Denmark a great story-teller named Hans Christian Andersen. This is *not* the story of his life, but a fairy-tale about this great spinner of fairy-tales."

Goldwyn's canniness, coupled with the advice of his lawyers, saved him from disaster and heavy financial losses.

As beautiful as the picture was, there were, according to the Danes and to historians, many errors and discrepancies. Andersen was never a cobbler as shown in the film. Hans Christian Andersen would not have known the difference between a ballet slipper and a ballet slip.

The real man was fatherless at eleven, and enjoyed ignorance until King Frederick VI sponsored his education. By the time of his twenty-second birthday, Hans was embittered, disappointed, frustrated, beaten—a young man who almost hated children. At thirty, recognition came to him when he published his first fairy-tales. He was never in love with a ballerina, but harbored an unrequited adoration for the internationally known Swedish singer, the great Jenny Lind, who passed him by for an American tour under Barnum's auspices.

At sixty, Andersen fell out of his bed, suffering injuries which caused ill health until his death at the age of seventy.

Danny, of course, knew the film script had little in common

with the true story of Andersen's life, but he was attracted to the poignancy of the treatment. When the Danish press attacked him, his answer was straightforward: "I am playing the role as straight as I possibly can. After reading the script, I couldn't see any of my particular brand of comedy. I have as much respect for Hans Christian Andersen as the Danes, and as much warmth in my heart for his writing as the millions of kids who have enjoyed his stories.

"Of course, there are a few delightful moments in the film where I sing and dance with a group of children. If it becomes funny, it is naturally that way. There are also many fantasy sequences in the film in which I either sing or dance or both. I think they have been handled entertainingly and with a great amount of visual appeal. If the audiences find these routines delightful and chuckle, I can't see where this is an 'insult.' "

The political and legal issues had been cleared with the Danes, but not the moral problem of producing a picture which portrayed an untruth. When Danny's recordings from the picture were released, the Danes protested again.

They didn't like the words—or the Kaye pronunciations—or the idea behind the lyrics. In fact, they just didn't like the songs.

In the first place, the natives claimed, there isn't a maiden in the whole of Denmark who answers to the name of "Wilhelmina." They don't ride around on toboggans, either.

And they don't even pronounce Copenhagen "Copenhagen." In Denmark it comes out "København."

A spokesman for the Copenhagen Committee, a Danish Chamber of Commerce, apparently, sat himself down at a typewriter and pecked out a letter of protest to funny-man Kaye, who was then cavorting in Twentieth-Century-Fox's *On the Riviera.*

"Copenhagen is standing on its head!" wrote Trier Pedersen. "The tourist chief of Denmark is being threatened with dismissal. And a complete change in foreign publicity is contemplated.

"Also, your own reputation with the Copenhagen girls, which has been mighty good since they found out you have red hair, is in serious danger."

The whole ditty's a lot of "tomfoolery," according to Pedersen.

"A Danish girl doesn't say *'nein,' "* he complained. "She says '*nej*'—pronounced 'nigh'—if, that is, she doesn't prefer to say 'yes'—which is '*ja.*' "

The irate Pedersen also sent Kaye a book about Copenhagen. He suggested Danny read it and then pass it along to Mack Gordon, who wrote the lyrics in the first place.

"Unfortunately, there isn't much in it about Copenhagen's girls," Pedersen closed. "But they're certainly worth getting to know!"

The Danes, however, failed to tell America that the year the tune "Copenhagen" was released, tourism in Denmark increased fifty per cent. Copenhagen has never had so much publicity before or since.

The film was shown everywhere. For the most part, the reviews were excellent, but the more important and intellectual magazines sided with the good Danes and pointed out the fallacies of the film. *The New Yorker* blasted the Goldwyn boys: "Nobody connected with Hans Christian Andersen seems aware of the fact that the gentleman whose name is being so casually kicked around as the originator of characters now inhabiting the heads of most of the children of the Western world is . . . credited with a simplicity bordering on active idiocy.

"As Mr. Hart has it, Hans Christian Andersen was a shoemaker in a sort of community that the Shuberts used to construct when Romberg was lining out his song. With the Shuberts, of course, it was Alt Wien, but what the hell, Denmark's on the same continent."

The *Saturday Review* added: "Without any clowning to do, Danny Kaye is simply not very interesting, and it's hard to get worked up over his encounter with a ballet dancer in Copenhagen and his rather foolish mooning about her. The movie's neither truth, good fiction nor a good fairy-tale."

Danny's own daughter, Dena, joined the opposition by declaring, "I don't like the picture either. They put Daddy into jail, and I don't like that."

Now was the hour, deemed Goldwyn, to send Danny on a goodwill tour to Denmark, to apply his charm to salve the wounded temperaments of the Scandinavians, to regain the popularity that publicity had failed to revive. It was an admirable plan, a masterstroke of wisdom, for Danny received the most enthusiastic welcome in Denmark that any foreigner had ever enjoyed. The papers that had once attacked him, joyfully proclaimed that Danny had drawn out more people than Eisenhower had after the liberation.

The Danes were captured by Danny, his songs, his dances, his appealing manner and his sincerity. And the admiration was returned. Danny fell quite in love with this old democracy, its democratic royal family, its art, the program for adult education, the clean and tidy little country. After Danny was carried on the shoulders of a band of enthusiastic countrymen, he reciprocated their appreciation by laying a wreath on Andersen's grave and giving an outdoor benefit show for the Danish children charities which was attended by 75,000 people.

They all lived happily ever after.

But, Janus-like, Danny wanted, at the completion of *Hans Christian Andersen,* to return to comedy. He had no intentions of being bound and gagged by the success of a serious role. "I have no ambitions to be a great dramatic actor," he said. "If God has given me the power to make people laugh, I want, please, just to keep it."

So, with full fanfare and much to-do, he and Sylvia formed and launched their own motion-picture production company, following the pattern set by nearly all important Hollywood actors and actresses. Sylvia believed in harvesting the ripened acclaim for themselves. She knew the techniques of adroit management and planned to continue with her hawklike vision and booming press-agentry to watch over Danny's career. The revolving wheel of their relationships brought many changes, but Danny's chief concern lay in his freedom to select his own scripts, leading ladies and fellow actors.

Danny analyzed his motivation for this new step shrewdly when he said, "Why do I now enter the field of independent production —with all its attendant headaches—when I could continue to work for other producers and let them have all the worries?

"Well, I'll tell you. Working for myself gives me some control over what I do. *Knock on Wood,* for instance, is a movie I've wanted to make for five years. The idea was suggested that long ago by Norman Panama and Melvin Frank, and we batted it around from time to time until it took proper shape in our minds. I like it because for the first time in my career I can be pretty much myself on the screen and can get the real Kaye personality over. I've always liked personal appearances, such as my vaudeville act, better than movie-making, because on the theater stage I can be spontaneous while producers have always made me stick to the script in movies. But in *Knock on Wood* I'm my own producer and I let my own ad libs stay in the film. This gives it a lively quality which I think helps it greatly. Actually I do not intend simply to confine myself to independent productions.

"For instance, I also made *White Christmas* at Paramount. But from time to time I will certainly make my own movies, choosing my own subjects, having a say in how the script is written and how the picture is shot. Then, if my judgment is wrong, I'm the one who will suffer most. If it's right, I'll get the reward. And to my mind that is only right and reasonable. I think this first independent film of mine will be a success—knock on wood!

His first independent movie was a roaring comedy. Danny played a ventriloquist who became unwittingly hooked up with some spies and some women.

"The whole premise of the thing is to keep me in as much trouble as possible," explained Kaye. "But it's always funny trouble. Serious for me, perhaps, but funny for the audience.

"Actually, comedians need far more than a good sense of humor. Some of my best pals have a tremendous sense of humor— but they're doctors or attorneys who can't perform worth a hoot. A good comedian needs training and technical ability, too. You don't just decide you're going to be a comic and go out on the stage and be one."

Kaye, who has been called the comedian's comedian because of his excellence, dislikes the appellation.

"I'd hate to think I entertained only the comedians," he reasons. "To be successful, a comic has to entertain the whole broad public. True, fellow comedians may be aware of a colleague's special phrasing or technique—but the public only cares for one thing: Is the guy funny?"

Frank and Panama, Sylvia and Danny were now partners in the Dena Productions, with Danny controlling the majority of shares. Both Frank and Panama had written many scripts for Bob Hope, and were considered to be top comedy writers and producers in Hollywood. As Danny's partners in *Knock on Wood* and later *The Court Jester,* they are full of praise for their cohort, but their stories of how a writer, producer and director must work with this untamable comedian while shooting his pictures is a study in working relations. Their major problem seemed to lie in the need for daily changes in the script to keep up with Danny's constantly brilliant ad libs.

"We're never sure just what's coming next when Danny begins a scene," smiled Frank. "But then, if it weren't for his genius at improvisation, his pictures wouldn't be the hits they are."

Panama credited Danny's success to his "constant surprise and shock value," which often throw even experienced actors off balance.

"That's why we surrounded him almost entirely with veteran stage performers in *Knock on Wood.* Their experience has given them the ability to come right back with an ad lib of their own when he takes off with a new routine."

"Danny has such a creative mind," Frank declared, "that we kept a complete file of his impromtu gags. They came too quickly to be remembered, so we noted each in case we wanted to use it later."

Danny says he's happy with his own company, but claims he seldom thinks of the fact that he has his own money tied up in the picture.

"You know," he said, "there's no difference at all. Even though you're working for yourself, you're just as tired at the end of the day."

Did the headaches pay off in the production of a better film? The answer is in the affirmative. *Knock on Wood* was Danny Kaye's funniest picture and one of the most rib-tickling films to be released since the days of Chaplin and Harold Lloyd.

Danny plays one of the funniest automobile salesmen there ever was. Topped by a flat straw hat, Salesman Kaye dashed through thousands of feet of film driving a $100,000 automobile and sputtering out near-intelligible conversations about "vorhead underslung oscillating compression dreavinators."

Since playing many roles in a single picture has come to be a Kaye trademark, he was also a spy, a ventriloquist and a British explorer, who, when asked what he thought of the Himalayas, first looked flummoxed and then quipped, "Loved him. Hated her."

The greatest and most persistent argument during the filming of Knock on Wood involved the ballet. Panama and Frank were sure Danny could not dance at all. Danny concurred, "I would louse up any ballet. I never had a dancing lesson in my life." It was consensus—that is, all but Sylvia, who insisted Danny would make an excellent showing if given a chance. Against the opinions of every man on the set, she forced her point, and again made sense. Danny's ballet was a sensation.

Sylvia, who had written the music to Knock on Wood, not only insisted that Danny do the ballet, but also changed the plans for his costume. Danny was scheduled to appear in an elaborate suit.

"I said no," related Sylvia. "If Danny wore a beautiful, elegant costume he would become just that. He wouldn't be funny.

"So I insisted on a makeshift costume. I got him an old red union suit. I remembered a wonderfully ratty fur piece I'd seen at MGM, and got that too. I found the hat lying around Paramount. It was just right."

The ballet sequence in Knock on Wood was a ridiculous one, although it bore some distinct resemblances to both Scheherazade and Prince Igor. From a technical standpoint, Kaye's debut as a dancer was impressive. His support of Diana Adams in her pirouettes was excellent, and if he had not possessed his remarkable muscular intelligence, Miss Adams would likely have suffered a few broken bones.

The New York Times backed up Sylvia's insistence that Danny could dance with the statement, "He would have made a superb ballet dancer if he had been inclined."

Sylvia, pleased with her own insight and correct judgment, commented, "I'm probably the only person who knows the full range of Danny's talents. He doesn't even know it himself."

Knock on Wood was not even finished and Danny's world promotion still unformulated when Paramount offered him a dancing role, first projected for Fred Astaire, the greatest dancer in motion pictures, and later assigned to Donald O'Connor, who fell ill. The film? Irving Berlin's *White Christmas,* with Bing Crosby.

Danny got a bad case of "Dorchester" feet and was sure he couldn't fill Astaire's shoes, but Sylvia again was adamant: "Danny protested that he was a faker, not a dancer, and that the routine would have to be simplified for him. I told him he could do it."

White Christmas was not a great picture, but Danny carried away $250,000 and ten per cent of its considerable profits, which, partially at least, was consolation for the fact that he looked a trifle pale and weak by the side of such competition as Der Bingle and Rosemary Clooney. In spite of the excellent dancing acts, which spoof modern choreography, there was little of lasting value in this picture other than a close friendship with Mr. Crosby.

When asked what Danny thought of Bing Crosby, who had once been the idol of his youth, Danny said, "I loved to work with him. I had the feeling he was my close personal friend.

"The real truth is that everybody knows Bing, but no one knows him. Through the years he has created a legendary character that is so vivid, no one knows where the legend begins and the real Crosby leaves off. I thought I knew Bing—thought I knew all about him until we started to make *White Christmas.* Then I realized I actually didn't know the man at all.

"The truth of the matter is, there isn't a lazy bone in Bing's body. He works harder than any man I've met—but he does it with an easy casualness that makes him *look* lazy.

"Some of the routines Bing and I did were as tough as anything I've ever done. Not once, though, did I see him miss a rehearsal or say, 'Let's take a break.'

"Usually it was I who said, 'Man, let's sit this one out for a while—I'm pooped.'

"Another portion of the Bing Crosby legend that was destroyed for me during the making of *White Christmas* was the belief I held that Bing was aloof and a guy who liked to be by himself.

"To my surprise, I discovered him to be one of the most gregarious of individuals. He had a dressing room, but he only used it to change clothes. Between scenes, he likes to sit on the set with the rest of the guys and gals making the picture. Bing, Rosemary

Clooney, Vera Ellen and I even got together a quartet. You should have heard us on radio commercials: 'Sooper Suds, Sooper Suds, lots more suds from Sooper Su—uds.' "

In comparison with the happy, silly days of making *White Christmas,* Danny felt that the filming of *The Court Jester* was not so enjoyable. "The Governor," as they call him now, was a businessman, the keystone of Dena Productions, with its headaches and happinesses, repayment and remorse. Each hour of shooting cost somewhere in the realm of a thousand dollars.

"When I sneezed," Danny said, "the producer told me it cost us three hundred dollars."

In developing a sound track, a single song was redone many times. Sylvia prodded, "Danny, that last 'biddiddy, tiddildy wowo-wo' wasn't off-beat enough. Try a little more syncopation."

"Let me lead the orchestra in one take with no vocals," proposed Danny. "We'll be protected and I'll dub in the lyrics on a separate track later."

Danny, obviously a frustrated Toscanini, mounted the podium, put the orchestra through its paces and listened to the playback with obvious satisfaction.

"Listen to those fiddles," he said. "How wonderfully full! And that piano. What tone! Let's do one more take!"

But Panama and Frank jumped him on this.

"At these prices? We'll run over the hour, and it'll cost another $2,000. Don't forget you're a partner in this venture. Let's not spend all the profits before they're even counted."

"No, let's not," Danny agreed. "On second thought let's go home."

The Court Jester, his twelfth picture, cost $3,000,000 to produce and again was an inferior picture, and definitely not one of Danny's best. To this point the consensus seems to be that *Knock on Wood* produced the most guffaws; that the most unforgettable was *Hans Christian Andersen;* and the one which almost laid the financial egg, *Walter Mitty.*

The Court Jester was a knight picture to end all knight pictures. Danny plays the lover of a child—with a couple of cheesecake women on the side.

The plot was woven around a court jester who disposed of the usurper of England's throne and re-established the rightful king, a tiny baby whose identity was established by the birthmark on its bottom in Vistavision scarlet pimpernel.

Danny kept the child from danger, sang the little king to sleep with a sincerity, warmth and love that is seldom seen on the screen.

On the set co-workers shook their heads saying: "For everyone else the baby vomits—but for Danny it laughs."

After the critical reviews of *The Court Jester* in 1955 it took Danny three years to muster up courage to do another picture. Unfortunately MGM's *Merry Andrew* turned out to be a very unfunny tale about a mild professor who joins the circus. After this second frustration Danny chose a totally new role in *Me and the Colonel*. In this motion picture he played a bewildered Jewish refugee named Jacobowsky, who fled without a passport before the advancing Germans.

Me and the Colonel is a film version of Franz Werfel's great wartime comedy, *Jacobowsky and the Colonel,* a story which underlines the plot that there is always an alternate solution in life—if one does not like a single grave there is always a mass grave.

His fourteenth picture, the long delayed biography of the trumpeter Red Nichols, *The Five Pennies,* has been produced by Danny's own Dena Productions.

Danny says of *Me and the Colonel:*

"I liked the script. I'd been away from the screen for a long time and suddenly here was an excellent part. So I'm doing it.

"Particularly, I like this Jacobowsky. I don't know how it will do as a picture—there's no great violence in it, no love story. It's really just the story of two men—vastly different men thrown together. In some ways I guess it's the story of people in general, of how they can get along with others when they must.

"You know, there was a time when I couldn't see myself playing a part like this. It would have been wrong for me. I really think until I made the tour for the United Nations children that I would not have been able to do this part.

"I think it was what I learned about myself that made me ready for a role like Jacobowsky. Before that UNICEF tour, I would have had to reach—to play this part. Now I think I can understand him a little more because I have more understanding of myself. "I believe a guy like me needs to do things like this U.N. tour—for himself. And for his work. You can't be just set, you know. Talent isn't something you can just pull out of a box. You've got to work with it, build it."

XVIII

The Private World of Danny Kaye

MANY CONTRADICTIONS REMAIN WITHIN DANNY KAYE. HE GREW
strong in his relationship to the Hollywood motion picture industry and stronger still in his bond with Sylvia. Although he could
be strong as steel, he easily wilted when it came to the problems
of children or human emotions. This led him to appear in benefit
shows, to assist any cause slated to help boys and girls, and finally
brought him to the offices of the United Nations.

Hollywood viewed his activities with tongue in cheek.

"What is he—" asked critic John Erskine, "a comedian or self-
styled savior of mankind?" The columnist had the nerve to pose his
question to Danny in person. The actor's voice trembled as anger
swelled inside him.

"I cannot shut myself from the rest of the world. I cannot spend
the rest of my life merely being on the stage. When I'm off the
stage, I want to be a human being with decent and real values and
concern for others. Dena should be left a legacy other than
wealth."

Danny, like any other person in the limelight, was accustomed
to criticism, but when it was aimed at his ideals, it hurt the most.
A Hollywood producer said Danny lost money on *The Court*

Jester because his greatest interest lay outside his business in the film capital.

"That's ridiculous Hollywood thinking," said Danny. "The picture didn't make money because its production cost too much in today's inflationary market. Expenses got out of hand.

"I don't believe I'm hurting myself in trying to do something as a human being. Is it a mistake for comedians to give their talents to the City of Hope, to the Heart Fund or to the Cancer Drive?"

It is impossible to determine the exact moment when Danny donned the invisible uniform of a soldier for the United Nations. "I am going wherever they send me," he told a press gathering, "to Thailand, South Africa, Russia—to the end of the world."

Perhaps the death of his father had ushered in a new period in his life. The two, father and son, had been extremely close in spite of the long intervals when they were separated by the miles. Pop Kominsky's long illness had been partially stalled by Dr. Somach's operation which removed a section of his stomach, but the disease crept slowly on.

During a visit in the East with his other two sons, pain took over. He asked Larry to see if "my boy Duvidl can come."

Frantic but powerless, Danny took the first and fastest plane out of Los Angeles International Airport. He arrived one hour too late. Jakob Kominsky, Russian horse-dealer, corset sewer, earthy philosopher and patient father of a genius son, was dead.

It is certain that without the encouragement, the love and the belief of Jakob Kominsky, Danny Kaye would not be where he is today. A wise man had died, and Danny was proud to have been his son.

Whatever contradictions there are in the life story of Danny Kaye, it was his father who put the balance of the scales in favor of human values as opposed to personal success and satisfaction.

The private life of Danny at home vacillates from silliness to solitude. It is not always possible for a comedian to hang up his madcap at the studio and step out of his role as an actor. Everyday life with Danny is not too far removed from living in the eye of a hurricane or being tied to the tail of a flying saucer.

It is true that his marriage is a business partnership, although Sylvia is under contract to him in spirit, their marriage, as a whole, is a good one, in spite of past tempers, disagreements, separations and difficulties.

Hollywood press agents give their own well-gilded and over-simplified analysis of the Kaye team: "Sylvia is even tempered; he is volatile. She is analytical; Danny goes by instinct. She likes steaks; Danny goes for lobster. She walks; Danny runs. She talks; Danny listens. She is conservative with money; he is liberal. She works easily; he works hard. He looks twice at pretty girls, while Sylvia knows that one man like Danny is a full-time job. He is the artist; she is the craftsman.

"He loves to play golf; she prefers the indoor activities. When they met he was insecure and she was sure not much could go wrong. He had doubt of the past and present; she had the confidence of a person who has led a sheltered life. He was poor; she came from a well-to-do family.

"But they laugh at the same things and like the same people. Anyone who does not accept both members of this team will lose both eventually."

Such articles read well in the movie magazines, but in their superficiality they are more like horoscopes than good psychology.

There is no clear black and white in Danny's and Sylvia's make-ups; no such clear-cut opposition of qualities. Both have the touches of genius which inevitably lead to a contest. One doubts the pat assurance of the press that "Sylvia is deliriously happy." In public she has learned to smile and to gaze at Danny with sublime admiration. She too has become an actress.

There are undying loyalties and interdependencies in the Kaye family which outweigh the traumas arising from the problems of submission, domination and competition. Danny, as do all strong men, rejects Sylvia's belief that "there is not a woman in the world who doesn't think her husband is childlike."

Many of their past conflicts resulted from this philosophy, and it was a wise Sylvia who later modified her statement by saying, "Danny gets easier to live with as the years go on. He used to be shy and uncommunicative. I was brought up to drag problems into the open and work them out. It took me years to bring Danny to the point where he was willing to do that. But he still has a great capacity for living in a world by himself."

Sylvia knows best what makes the man tick, and she has discovered the great discrepancy between the inner and the outer man. In spite of his keen sense of the ridiculous, Danny is basically serious minded.

As a wife, Sylvia was forced to discard and disregard all concepts of a normal family life. One critic dubbed Danny "the first space man in the entertainment world," and Sylvia has had to adjust herself to many months of separation during his global travels and to live with the knowledge that Sammy Prager, as an accompanist, actually sees him for longer periods than she does as a wife.

Anyone who has observed Danny's life at home in Hollywood, in New York or London, realizes that Kaye's day generally starts the night before. His mind runs ahead of time.

Kaye leaves the set still wearing make-up on his face, enters the kitchen at home, prowls through the icebox, digging his fingers through every pot. Behind him are two energetic boxers and a delighted Dena, filled with her day's adventures. Danny, having built an ingenious "Dagwood" sandwich, sprawls his lean length in his favorite easy-chair, and is immediately overwhelmed by both dogs, who seem to harbor the illusion that they are lapdogs.

"Danny," comments Sylvia, "may decide he wants dinner to start with a cold soup that no one has planned. He'll start with a consommé, add beets, potatoes, sour cream, sample every step of the way and insist that everyone sample with him. By the time he's washed and we sit down to the table, he has very little appetite left. If Danny gets really involved in the kitchen, we set the table there to catch him while he is still hungry. He is a mixer and fixer of mysterious dishes."

Danny never overeats, and always leaves something on his plate to be sure he won't gain weight.

There was the evening when Danny unexpectedly brought home the entire Paramount orchestra. Sylvia, too, had invited guests. Amid the jam session going on, with Danny beating out a good drum, Sylvia phoned her guests to come a little later and notified the patient cook to plan dinner for some number between ten and twenty-five. At seven-thirty the drinks were served, and at nine, thirty-six people lined up at the buffet. By midnight more guests had been called and Danny exchanged his drumsticks for the trumpet which he learned to play with an eye to a new film, *The Five Pennies,* the Red Nichols story.

"We love parties of all kinds," concludes Sylvia. "Giving them and going to them. When we plan one, it's like staging a show, but no one is ever asked to entertain."

Sylvia, who never finished writing her husband's biography, is often called by reporters to comment on their living habits. She has learned to be careful in what she says, to avoid the negative and give Danny's public what it wants to hear.

"After dinner, Danny glances at his mail, starts dictating a letter to a friend in Pittsburgh, ends up calling him on the phone. Sometimes he wants to start rehearsing right after dinner. Usually, I play over what I've written for him and sing it once or twice. He sits quietly listening. But if what he hears excites him, he'll get up, start looking over my shoulder and begin to create.

"These are thrilling moments. I love watching something I've written come alive in him, in his face, in every gesture. I know what I've had in my head, but what he does is something better. Wonderful as a performance of his is in its final version on the screen, for me it's second to the first moments in our living room. When he's stimulated, anything can happen.

"After an evening of rehearsal he falls asleep, as he always does, like a child, the covers loose at the end of the bed, his feet sticking out. Or we both read in bed. In addition to everything else, he likes to read; he's mad for books on golf.

"Next morning he's up by seven to get into make-up at the studio by eight. He and Dena breakfast together, but unless I'm due at the studio early, I bury my head in the pillow and keep on sleeping.

"To run a house for the Danny Kaye family is not an easy task. Danny is completely allergic to anything domestic except cooking. He won't touch a dish, never hangs his things away and doesn't like to eat at definite hours.

"He hasn't the vaguest idea about his bank balance—he leaves that to his attorney and me, and gaily splurges on his allowance, which generally runs out before the end of the week. He's usually a very quiet guy—preferring to listen rather than talk—which is often taken by casual onlookers for a sense of superiority.

"He has a one-track mind, and when he's worried he just can't manage to be effusive. He rarely complains, is always late for dinner and always punctual for rehearsals. Almost anybody who talks well can convince him of anything. He is an odd combination of confidence and diffidence, and will take criticism graciously from anyone for whom he has respect."

Such thumbnail sketches fail to give an insight into the inner thoughts, aims and fears of the middle-aged man as he continues to fight for his professional career and personal fulfillment. Growing old is, at best, not easy. It is even more difficult for a star. How will the public feel about Kaye if he is ever forced to wear glasses? The idea has become almost an obsession with him.

An early-morning riser, Danny likes to catch the early rays of the sun, and this he does with a purpose. Many a morning he uses a steel mirror to reflect the sunlight into his closed eyes. "It is the best-known method of improving eyesight," he contends, and, to prove his point, has countless stories of men who improved their eyesight after having been rejected by the armed forces. These exercises, he believes, will prevent the necessity of ever wearing glasses.

Danny's taste in clothing is a study in contrasts. While he claims he is not particular, he buys only the most expensive suits and neckties and wears silk underwear. "He can come home," states his wife, "disheveled from a day of golf, and ten minutes later appear in immaculate evening dress, showered, shaved, studs in, hair shining.

"But essentially he shares the American man's passion for old clothes. He'll have a hole in each sock and we can't get the socks away from him. He has two hats he's devoted to, an old rain hat and an air force fatigue cap he got in Korea.

"There's just nothing pretentious about Danny. He'll be as fond of a two-dollar turtle-neck sweater he's picked up at the golf club as of a fine cashmere. As a matter of fact, he looks equally at home in the most dilapidated sweat-shirt or in the most formal attire, and equally at home at an impressive banquet or perched on the kitchen table."

But these finely phrased sentences tell nothing of the nights when Danny is not at home, nothing of the anxieties Sylvia feels when he is touring the world by plane while she takes care of their child, home and business all alone. The press accounts seldom mention that Danny worries; that he is all too often weary and even bored with his existence.

"I have read all the articles telling how funny Danny is at home," says one of his close friends, "but with people he knows well he does not perform. Often after dinner we move into 'Danny's room' and for several hours sit quietly and listen to opera recordings.

"This favorite spot for the whole family has acoustic walls and ceiling; shelves, covering the entire end of the room, for his records, which include practically every operatic recording ever made; two immense, low, long couches; several easy-chairs; radio; television set and tape recorders. Most of his orchestrations are done in this room. It's a place where everything is in easy reach.

"One night he played the entire Traviata album without saying a single word. The two dogs lay with ears cocked appreciatively. At eleven Danny carried Dena to her bed and announced that he had had a rough day at the studio and needed to go to bed too. These are the rare moments when Danny is totally relaxed. Another is when he is on the golf course."

But such an uninterrupted evening is uncommon. The Kayes are easy hosts and people like to drop in. Not even at home is Danny left alone. The phone rings constantly, and in spite of the protection Sylvia and the secretary try to give him, he usually takes at least a dozen calls during an evening.

The three windows from "Danny's room" look out on the patio with its large swimming pool, which Danny and Dena use during the summer, but leave, as Danny says, to the polar bears during the winter.

The living room is separated by wide doors. It, too, is a large room almost overfilled with sofas, lounges and chairs, placed so that you can fall into one from any place you may be standing. The tables are covered with massive ashtrays, disposable cigarette-holders, bowls of cigarettes and jars of candy. The walls are a restful green.

It is not a showy place. It lacks the typical Hollywood mirrors and glass brick, but it is comfortable, livable and thoroughly pleasant. An evening with the Kayes is a far cry from the publicized Hollywood drinking bouts and fancy-dress parties. It's one of the reasons the Kayes are such popular hosts.

The man behind the clown is a complicated and often difficult human being. His life of prolonged travel, enormous tensions and constant demands from an international public leaves him little solitude or time to reflect on the status of his nerves. A pause for contemplation is rare, unfortunately, for Mr. Kaye is a man who needs solitude in the same way a plant needs sunlight in order to flourish.

It is not uncommon for him to retire within himself and fail to share his experiences even with his family. Sylvia comments, "He gets awards and I don't know of it. Sometimes I go through his jewelry case and find things with inscriptions on them which I have never heard about."

Sylvia has developed an inner sense in her ability to cope with Danny's prismatic moods. She is willing to see a motion picture every night of the week, sit up to watch a midnight show on television, or stay at home for weeks when he is tired and travel weary. She keeps the larder stocked with the ingredients that may be needed for a Kaye experimental dish, for Danny's eating habits are very nearly as strange as his film characters. For a year he was obsessed by health fads and rejected liquor for celery juice. He later changed to a diet of cucumber sandwiches and orange juice with an egg in it. For months he was on a vitamin spree and carried large quantities with him, which he washed down with copious amounts of milk. Once in London it took days to find a store which sold buttermilk.

During the years of probing into the corners of the world, Danny has become a gourmet in his own right. Following a tour through France, Art Buchwald of the *New York Herald Tribune* asked in an interview, "What is the best way to eat one's way through France?"

"It's a matter of parlaying your restaurants. For example, when you visit a good restaurant in Paris it is always better to come on behalf of someone. Say you come on behalf of Bing Crosby or Rosemary Clooney or Irving Berlin. The French restaurant owner may not know who these people are, but he would never admit it. So you are greeted as a long-lost American cousin. After the meal is over you kiss the chef on both cheeks. It's his garlic, so it shouldn't bother him. Then you tell him you are going on a vacation to the 'Souse of France.' Does he know anyone along the road who has a restaurant maybe half as good as his? The chef gives you the name of his friend who owns a restaurant, and you're off. You then arrive at the restaurant bringing kisses from the friend in Paris. At the next place you bring kisses from the last place, and so on all the way to the Riviera."

"What do you order at a three-star restaurant?"

"Each restaurant has its own specialty. The only danger in this is that the restaurant where you dine may have the same specialty you ate for lunch in the previous restaurant.

"It is most important for an ignorant American to make sure the chef of the restaurant doesn't think he is an ignorant American. This can be done with a few well-chosen words.

"For instance, when discussing the first course with the chef you might tell him: 'Mon chèr chef, you must understand I don't want the taste of fish so much as a fishlike taste.' Or for the main course: 'Do you add cognac before or after you kill the poulet? I always insist my poulet is given the cognac while he is still alive. It's less cruel that way and the cognac is absorbed in the blood.' A few statements like this will make the chef realize he isn't dealing with an amateur. Once you have shaken his confidence you can order frankfurters and he'll make them for you.

"Some three-star restaurants wish to take credit for their oysters, but they don't deserve it."

"Who should get the credit?"

"Other oysters."

"Should one pinch a waitress in a three-star restaurant?"

"Of course. It is one of the reasons a restaurant has three stars. Not only that, but waitresses expect it. It keeps them on their toes. Of course, it must be done discreetly, away from probing eyes.

In France we call it the *finesse de pincer*. The best time to pinch is when the waitress is bringing out a soufflé. It is at this time that everyone is watching the soufflé and the waitress has her hands full."

"Why does pinching help a meal?"

"It is what we French believe gives ze zest to the meal. The sauce may be perfect, the duck may be exquisite, the *petits pois* may be *petit,* but it's that extra pinch of something which gives the dinner that *je ne sais quoi* feeling."

To all of this Sylvia merely listened with an amused smile on her piquant face, never betraying the thoughts that danced through her busy and brilliant mind. None of the *restaurateurs,* waitresses or news reporters knows the real Danny Kaye, the problems and joys of cooking for him and creating a home, a setting for this genial and "crazy" funny-man.

Sylvia is still as much in love with Danny as she was the day they married. The long separations are difficult for her and Dena, but they try to span the distance by phone, thereby running up bills that look somewhat similar to the national defense appropriations. Phone calls are a necessity, both to keep the family united and also to coordinate the business aspects of their lives. Sylvia, having her finger in each and all of the pies of Danny's career, often has an urgent need to reach him in Paris or London or Johannesburg or Helsinki.

"The strange thing," comments Sylvia, "is that no matter where I find Danny—Bangkok, Tokyo or Dayton, Ohio—two times out of five he'll say, 'Just a minute, there's somebody special here who wants to talk to you.' In Dayton I reached him at a restaurant. I got this usual 'just-a-minute' routine, and then a gay warm voice with a French accent started talking to me.

"You can never be sure whether it is really somebody else or Danny being a mimic, but after a few sentences I knew it was really Maurice Chevalier. He had flown to Dayton from New York just for one evening, because, although they are great friends, he had never seen Danny in the theater."

Sylvia is often worried. And what wife wouldn't be—with a husband who insisted on being taken to the Mau-Mau centers in

Nairobi for an interview, which he tape-recorded with a Mau-Mau leader shortly after two British citizens had been killed by the angry natives?

The Kaye family life is also blessed by a warm and tender romance between father and daughter, a loving bond clouded only by the persistent question which Dena flings at Danny as soon as he returns from a trip, "Daddy, when are you leaving again?"

During their days together, Dena and Danny are inseparable. She attends the previews of his movies and exerts severe criticisms of many scenes. She sits in judgment during his rehearsals and enters into many of the recording sessions. Recently the two made a platter of "The Little Child," a song with poignantly charming lyrics of a father's answers to his daughter's philosophic questions.

"How do you like the record?" Danny asked when the finished product was played back.

"I don't like it at all," replied Dena with the same critical judgment she displays toward her father's pictures. "I think I sound better off the record than on it."

"She is really twenty-four, and not ten," commented Danny out of her hearing. "She doesn't fool me for a minute."

The little girl who once wept when others laughed at her daddy has become a sophisticated young lady who enjoys riding with her father, joins him on the golf course, sings in perfect pitch, is careful not to wrinkle her party dresses and walks with regal straightness.

She is overconscientious about her studies and once, when Danny suggested a long week-end in Palm Springs, flatly refused to miss school on Friday. "I cannot be absent," she declared seriously. "We have a new project in school. We have just finished studying the citrus industry in California, and are ready to move on to something else that is important to the state. Not the motion picture industry—that will be dull when we get to it later—but something else. No, I can't go with you."

Dena, a product of pampering in Hollywood, has been spoiled in many ways. Nervous and demanding, she has learned to rule her father when it is necessary to gain his attention. She is bright, quick and unselfish, but the pressures of the theatrical life around her resulted in her first visit to a psychoanalyst at the age of six. She has seen and heard too much in the dizzy adult world of the movie colony. Result? A sort of precocious "Eloise in Hollywood." In spite of all the efforts of both Sylvia and Danny to keep her from the emotional upheavals of glittering lights, their one and only child has been surrounded by press agents, reporters, glamorous and not-so-glamorous stars, and the fame of being the daughter of the popular Danny Kaye.

For Sylvia, here, too, was a contest for Danny's time and affection. And who can win when pitted against a growing daughter?

In November of 1955 Dena and Danny were invited to join the Thanksgiving parade in New York on a float designed to promote the film, *The Court Jester*. Making the arrangements entailed a phone call to catch Danny in Finland. Danny answered, "Well, it is all right with me if it is all right with you, Sylvia, and with Dena."

Sylvia asked Dena.

Dena hedged, "Do you want me to be on the float?"

"Only if you want to," Sylvia replied.

Dena thought for a moment and then asked, "But why didn't they ask you?"

Pleased, Sylvia explained there was not room on the float for two "queens," and that Dena was the royal personage the parade officials really wanted. Dena was satisfied and accepted enthusiastically.

Later the two, mother and daughter, boarded a plane for New York with long red underwear tucked carefully in a bag so Danny would not be frozen by the stiff cold wind off the Hudson River. On the float Danny and Dena played various gags from the picture.

Dena, when surrounded by the attention of writers, producers, United Nations officials or reporters who gush their approval of Sylvia's abilities, reminds them firmly, "My mommie has really only *one* job—and that is taking care of me."

Dr. Irving Somach remembers with a smile the day when Dena was a tiny baby and Danny raved with fatherly pride because "Dena has my hands."

"Oh, stop it, Danny," he laughed. "All babies' hands look alike You are merely being a typical new father."

Seven years later, when the doctor lunched with the Kaye family, Danny suddenly reached out his hand and Dena's. "You must see it now," he said; "our hands are alike." It is true. Both have long, thin fingers, narrow palms—and both are missing one joint on their little fingers.

When Danny is at home, he makes a special world for his daughter and himself. Child that he often is, it is easy for him to join Dena on the playground, to play checkers with her, although he has been forced to abandon "the easy way" for a serious adult game, since she has been known to beat him roundly and soundly. When the B.B.C. arranged a transatlantic interview with Danny on a Sunday that was scheduled for a school picnic, he unhesitatingly canceled the broadcast in order to take his daughter to the outing.

The man behind the clown, the man at home, is a full-sized human being who enjoys his home and family and maintains a humble gratitude for the gifts of life.

XIX

I'm Their Kind of People

DANNY KAYE WAS NEVER CUT OUT TO BE THE RESCUER OF MAN-kind. Nor is he a crusader with the sacrificing ardor of an Albert Schweitzer.

The seeds planted by his family took twenty years to mature into the demand that he, the entertainer, with the talents and tools at his command, contribute more than the usual share to society.

The talents and the tools were meant to produce laughter. Per-haps Danny sensed more than any of his critics that the reason for his failure in early life was that he played only for adults. To make children of us all has become his forte.

"Danny is an overactive and underwise adult," said one studio executive recently. But with children he is neither unwise nor adult. The spontaneous laughter of a ten-year-old, the delighted coo of a baby, the amused grin of a tottering infant of any race or country have helped to replenish his creative springs and set a purposeful cause for being.

Mr. Kaye likes to discuss children. He becomes relaxed and sincere, as if completely convinced that youth is the only real value worthy of life-long dedication. At least, it is for him.

Children are difficult to fool. They seem to possess an uncanny protective power of sensing when the adult world approves or rejects them; so it is no wonder that children fill Kaye's matinees and file in noisy lines to see his pictures.

When playing the Paramount on Broadway, Danny began a jam session at eleven-thirty in the morning. During one show he looked down to discover a small plastic box on the apron of the stage.

"What is this?" he asked into the theater's darkness, and, upon opening the box he found six pancakes with a poem:

> We're thrifty folk at our house
> I'd like to point with pride,
> Our pancakes are so thin, by gosh,
> They only have one side.

A small amount of detection disclosed the story behind the pancakes. One small girl had stood in line since nine that morning in order to assure a front row seat so she could get the box to her hero. After Danny thanked the youngster, she piped in a shrill voice, "May I have the box back?" Danny promised it would be at the stage door at the end of the performance.

Since his entire life has been influenced by a sensitive love for children, and much of his professional satisfaction derived from the appreciation of his small-fry fans, Danny's views of youth come as no surprise.

"I like children, but I don't like every single one of the thousands I meet. That would be a phony thing to say, and there's one thing for sure about children: they can spot a phony a mile away. Some kids I don't like, and some kids don't like me, which is the way it should be. Saying anything else is false.

"I got a theory about kids and grownups. Children have no pretense and no shame about behaving like children. I know they pretend to be cowboys and pretend to be spacemen and all that, but they are well aware they're pretending. Now, adults—well, lots of adults are really children, but they've got to at least put on a pretense that they're adults and behave like adults. Doing that gives them a guilty feeling, and they know they're faking. Oftentimes I think children can see right through a fake. I know this is kind of complicated, but it's a theory I have."

One day in 1955, as the result of a warm invitation, Danny revisited his old Brooklyn high school. There was still a sprinkling of his old teachers.

"Danny, it is great of you to come back and see us," said one. "I get a great kick out of telling people that you used to be in my class. Things haven't changed much around here since you left—same buildings, same kind of people here. Of course, thousands have come and gone. Some of you have become successes, but I just stay on here, getting grayer and older by the year. Makes me feel good, though, when I can tell people that I taught Danny Kaye!"

In the assembly hall, the student body was set for a show. The excitement of anticipation produced a loud buzz and stirring. When Danny walked out on the stage, the applause was deafening. He raised his hands for silence. "Young ladies and gentlemen," he began, "it is a very real privilege to be invited back to talk with you here where I received much of my education. I'll bet I know some of your fathers and mothers, grandfathers and grandmothers, because I was born here in Brooklyn. And I want you to know that Brooklyn isn't just a city. It's a state of mind."

The youngsters, after the first shock of hearing a serious Danny Kaye, were delighted.

"After all," he continued, "has Manhattan ever been able to produce such an all-round, wonderful, brave, courageous team as 'Dem Bums'?"

The teenagers applauded madly. Danny was in.

For the next twenty minutes, Danny gave a serious talk. He recalled his early life of poverty; the satisfactions of growing up in a hodgepodge community; his struggles as a boy when he thought he was gangly and unwanted. There were sparkling witticisms in what he said, but toward the end of the talk no one laughed very loudly. What he was saying was too close to their problems, and his sincerity was clear.

Then Danny leaped into nonsense, sang his famous songs and waved his audience out as the final class bell rang.

Danny was besieged by autograph hunters that day, until the principal inquired if he would like to be relieved. "Doesn't your hand ever get tired? Wouldn't you like me to send these kids away?"

"I should say not," said Danny. "What if this sort of thing should stop? What if kids no longer wanted to see and hear me?

It would mean I was washed up. I'd like to believe I'm their kind of people."

Often when Danny makes a contribution to the fields of charity or humanitarianism, the wheels of press-agentry quickly grab the details for their own purposes. Agents exploit the situations in order to provide columns designed to promote a new Kaye picture. The fact remains, however, that Danny's good deeds are motivated by his sincere desire to help others and are not stunts fabricated in some publicity office.

Both Dr. Somach and one of the studio men traveling with Danny's entourage tell the same story: "One of us on tour with Danny had a six-year-old son whose hearing was rapidly going bad. We were talking about the situation one night in a hotel room in Danny's presence. He had no comment to make at that time, and the boy's father forgot all about the conversation. At the end of the trip Danny returned to California.

"Imagine the father's surprise when he was notified that Danny had made arrangements for one of the best ear doctors in New York to operate on the boy! Not only that, but Danny also flew across the continent to watch the operation."

From Kaye's warmth with children to his closeness to adults is only a small step. Life cannot be devoid of jealousies, and although the entertainment profession possesses perhaps more than its share of bitter tongues, as a whole Danny has built many lasting friendships.

During the early years of his career Danny signed no contracts, in the belief that a shake of the hand was a bond of gold.

His judgment in choosing friends has proved infallible. His loyalty to them is unshakable. When Louis Mandel, his lawyer, faced the death of his mother, Danny canceled all his engagements and spent twenty-four hours near at hand. When Frank Sinatra lost his voice through an attack of laryngitis, Danny immediately volunteered to replace him.

One of the managers of New York's Waldorf Astoria Hotel tells of a remarkable event with an amusing ending. "Danny was with a party of six at the Empire Room to see a singer who suddenly fell ill and had to cancel his performance. Kaye volunteered to substitute and entertained the night club customers for almost an hour. We were most grateful, but imagine my embarrassment when I discovered one of the waiters had given Mr. Kaye a bill for his party with the statement, 'Because you were so nice, we've removed the cover charge.' "

Friendship is deep and lasting with Danny. Lilian Waldman Schary was asked to decorate one of the Kaye apartments because she and Danny had been friends in the days when both were struggling to see some light in the gloom of the beginnings of their professions.

Sammy Prager and Danny have developed an almost Castor and Pollux-like affection, which is equally strong on or off the stage. Before the footlights Danny makes sure Sammy receives his share of the recognition and applause. On the golf course they are friendly rivals who compliment each other on well-placed shots.

The Kayes number among their friends such notables as the Oliviers, Maurice Chevalier, Marlene Dietrich, Goldwyn, Goetz, and Liebman. But theirs is also the talent of giving and receiving warmth and affection from the "little guy."

There appears to be no class- or race-consciousness in the lives of the Kayes. They entertain with equal graciousness diplomats and students, workers and nobility. Their friends and guests come from Lapland or South Africa—from the Pacific shores or from India.

Danny often sits down with his doctor friends in Hollywood or New York to attempt to find a medical cure for a certain friend in London, Melbourne or Cape Town. Following Sir Harry Lauder's advice, Danny adheres to the idea, "Don't try to be anyone else." Fortunately, the real Danny Kaye is a humanitarian.

His co-workers appreciate his kindliness, realizing that there are times when he should and must be left alone. But even when preoccupied, Danny is fair, polite and helpful. As one of the theater managers once said, "Danny believes in self-sustaining democracy. He never refuses to work with a performer, even if he disapproves of him or her. There are many entertainers, and even just plain people, who could learn manners and kindness from him."

In his own shows Danny goes out of his way to give a build-up to acts that precede or follow his own, and in many cases has introduced British artists into the United States.

One of Kaye's cherished possessions is a shiny golden plaque, presented at the end of the filming of *The Court Jester,* with an inscription which says:

To
Danny Kaye
for being the biggest fool
of the year and doing his own stunt work.
The Crew

However, one close business friendship did come to a sudden end. Eddie Dukoff, who had served as business manager and confidant since 1938, left him and the Dena Productions to strike out on his own in the television and motion-picture world.

The parting was not without some bitterness, but outwardly, at least, the two have tried to patch up their separation. It is certain that Danny was not responsible for the break. At first the situation was difficult and uncomfortable. In London the two cut each other when they met at social events and each tried, like a nervous girl, to find out if the other was to be at a party before he accepted the invitation. With the passage of time ruffled feathers have fallen into place, and the two men are again friendly, although each goes his own way.

Wally Westmore, Paramount's famed make-up man, who puts faces on faces and makes old stars look young, says that Danny is a shy person, without the flattered ego of so many film stars. Kaye's most appealing characteristic to Westmore and his co-workers is his genuine interest in their lives, worries and careers.

"Unlike some of the others," says Westmore, "he treats us as equals—not as servants to his glory. He wants to know details about us—where we live, what flowers we grow, how many kids we have—and never fails to ask about our wives.

"Danny Kaye is so modest he wouldn't even autograph a photograph for me because he didn't want to be hung in my Rogue's Gallery on the wall. To my thinking, he is one of the great stars who is not temperamental in spite of his tremendous energy and perfectionism. He is kind over and beyond what anyone would expect. For instance, at the end of each picture he gives everyone on the set a present—not just the usual run-of-the-mill sort of gift, but something that shows he knows the guy or gal to whom he is giving it. Each one is a real token of friendship; very personalized and picked with love—and observation.

"For instance, we were talking about gold-mining, and I received a real gold nugget. I am quite sure he doesn't own a gold-mine. Some of the others were given initialed cuff-links and special jewelry. This sort of thoughtfulness doesn't happen very often in our busy-busy business."

His reading is constant, despite the demands on his time, and consists not only of the so-called "good books" and golf books, but scientific and medical magazines as well. This capacity, coupled with his phenomenal memory, makes for a mine of information.

Politics, as such, do not captivate the Kayes, although both worked actively for President Roosevelt's election campaign in 1944, with Sylvia writing a few parodies and Danny serving as the treasurer for the Hollywood Democratic Committee. During this period Sylvia also served as an executive board member of the Independent Citizens' Committee of the Arts, Sciences and Professions, an organization later infiltrated by pro-Communist elements.

During the dark and disgraceful days of "name-calling" in the United States, some extremists and "super-patriots" called Danny a Communist. He, by instinct rather than legal advice, did the only thing that could succeed against irresponsible defamation. He rebutted by saying that his accusers were fanatic liars and confused extremists. He stated conclusively and convincingly that he never was and never would be a Communist.

None of his accusers dared to sue Danny for libel, and the topic was forgotten until Danny traveled for the United Nations Children's Fund as its ambassador. Then the same political forces exerted themselves again and pointed fingers at Danny as a member of the team of the "Communist-dominated United Nations."

It was a clever Danny who did not, this time, reply. The campaign of slander fizzled out into oblivion.

Danny is aware that everyone in the limelight has to guard

against being hurt by disgruntled people—the scandalmongers and the hide-skinners. Off stage he speaks with deliberation, measuring each word as if it cost him $100 per syllable.

His spontaneity is matched by his caution when it comes to public issues and the world press. Any actor is, in the long run, at the mercy of columnists, reporters and biographers who can hammer a victim to death under their typewriter keys—or build him into a hero in print.

Danny's "at home" language is more colorful than that before the footlights. Once, at a party, Danny analyzed the coordination between his mind and his tongue with the statement, "I'm a guy who sometimes thinks dirty—not very often, though. But when I am on the stage I only think clean. That is what saves me. Much of my act is impromptu, but when I'm behind those footlights, the four-letter words just don't occur to me."

There was only one time when an audience ever heard Danny swear. Danny, wanting to make every member of his audience a part of the show, spotted a grim face within the range of the lights.

"Hi, you, everything all right?" he inquired.

"Naw," came back the sloppy answer of one obviously pinioned under the weight of Bacchus.

A drunk in the audience can kill any show. The best performer is helpless, and no entertainer should be asked to cope with such a situation. Danny tried to avoid the mush-mouthed heckling of his alcoholic problem child. It didn't work. The more he tried to rise above the imbecilic mutterings from the floor, the louder the taunts became. People shushed and waiters attempted to calm the situation, only to make matters worse.

For Danny, making love to an appreciative audience is far less difficult than inducing one inebriated customer to be attentive.

"Oh ——!" said Danny and stomped off the stage.

Sylvia followed her husband into the dressing room and urged Danny to return to the stage. After all, she reasoned, the entire audience should not be penalized for the misbehavior of a single person. Danny returned for the second show, but not before.

From that night on Danny has refused to appear in night clubs. He knows the drunks are a part of night-club life. His face and antics have never appeared, even in the Las Vegas casinos, where fabulous fees are paid to top-bill entertainers in order to lure customers into the gaming halls.

Danny also resents people who walk up with the request for him to turn on the spigot of humor, and those who solemnly "quarterback" his wit, as well as ill-informed, casual laymen who proffer unsolicited advice. With intelligent, cognizant individuals, however, he is eager to hear any and all suggestions and slow to react to negative criticism.

In the lights and shades that make up the unpredictability and sometimes inconsistency that is Danny Kaye, one can never be sure whether Danny will meet a situation with sage consideration or, on the other hand, turn on the bright light of tomfoolery. When he is working with his own crew on a set, he may burst into an unexpected *"O sole Mio"* out of tune, drink a warm Coca-Cola, play a deliberate game of checkers with Dena, or sing the Wagnerian aria he listened to the previous night. With full knowledge that all this wastes valuable time, he behaves in a manner that makes Jerry Lewis look like a prim schoolteacher.

These are moments of either temporary relaxation or high-geared concentration, much like the unconscious singing of a happy child or the heavy hum of a dynamo. One stanza of a song during rehearsal may have to be sung over thirty times until Danny and Sylvia decide it is perfect.

To watch Danny during such a rehearsal, or while he is preparing a recording with his "bamperamperamperas," is a real sight. Generally, he wears old sneakers, a comfortable sweat-shirt and a red, misshapen, felt hat. He is often out of tune, and Dena shudders while Sylvia reminds him how the song should be sung according to their planning of the night before. Danny checks on Dena, takes a sip from her coke, grins at Sammy Prager, waves a hello at a newspaper reporter, laughs at the conductor and goes on with another trial run. Finally, weariness takes over. Weariness for whom? Not for Danny!

He suddenly bursts out with an unexpected routine, filled with grimaces and monkey-business, which sets the entire orchestra into such an explosion of laughter and amusement that the members are unable to continue.

After the relaxation that comes from easing out the wrinkles of tension by laughter, the recording goes on, to the relief of Sylvia, new owner of the recording company, who realizes the end result will be good.

"My tongue is getting like cotton," says Danny.

"Little wonder," think the rest of the group, "and it is a marvel you don't have a cramp in it from the tongue-twisters you have been executing for the past hours."

Three tries later Danny rips off his red hat, throws it, without real anger, on the floor and says, "I think I am out of schmaltz!"

Again the chaos of laughter.

Repeat. Dena listens. Sylvia corrects. Sammy improvises a ditty at the piano. Sound experts explain their problems. Two hours past lunchtime Dena is restless from hunger and some foreign correspondent is impatient.

"Gosh, guys," says Danny, "let's knock off until Monday. It's past lunchtime for you all." And Mondays sees the birth of a new recording which millions will hear on their radios, record players and in corner drugstore jukeboxes.

To the question posed by one of the exhausted crew, Danny answered, "I never get tired of doing a show or a song. Sometimes I get tired of the stage-floor. That's the best I can explain."

Kaye, who circles the globe with astonishing speed, knows that it is impossible to please all people. His life is public domain, and any reporter can write a "confidential" which exposes some of his faults. It is necessary to develop a thick intellectual and emotional hide, and yet to be able to evaluate each remark carefully and thoughtfully for its merits.

Negative criticism is not easy to take. One night at the London Palladium, Kaye overheard the comment of a critic: "Kaye's act ran eighty minutes. Far too long—much too long. Who does he think he is? Victor Borge?"

XX

Ambassador-at-Large

IT WAS JUST ANOTHER BENEFIT SHOW. ONE MORE ORGANIZATION
had reached Danny with the usual, "Would it be possible for you
to come and entertain our staff?"

Inside the spectacular United Nations building Danny had found
a group of milling people which was like many other assemblies
he had met. However, this gathering had more people of different
races and nationalities than he had seen in a long time.

As far as Danny knew, the United Nations was a bold, exciting
adventure to keep the world together by settling arguments at the
conference table. The United Nations subagencies, with their
imposing arrays of alphabet names, meant very little to him.

Dag Hammarskjöld, Secretary General of the United Nations,
had decided to give a party for his hard-working crew at headquarters, and invited an impressive list of entertainers to donate
their talents. Among the notables were Ezio Pinza, Marian Ander-
son—and Danny Kaye, with Sylvia by his side.

When the evening was over, Danny was thanked by Dag Hammarskjöld and Ralph Bunche for his generous performance, to
which Danny replied: "It was wonderful to be here. The work you
are doing is inspiring, and if I can ever do anything for you again,
please call on me."

At one o'clock the next day Dag Hammarskjöld and his co-worker, Maurice Pate, executive director of the United Nations Children's Fund, called Danny and asked for a conference.

"Aren't you going to South Africa?" inquired Mr. Pate when Danny arrived.

"Yes," replied Danny. "I have some promotional theater appearances to do there."

"We have little money and few people we can call on," continued Pate. "While you are in that area, would you be willing to visit our UNICEF installations and photograph the work being done?"

"What is UNICEF?" Danny inquired.

"That array of initials stands for United Nations International Children's Fund," explained Mr. Hammarskjöld.

"Gee, that sounds like a fine idea," exclaimed Danny. "If I can help kids, I'm all for it."

Twenty-four hours later the meager request that Danny take some pictures with his Rolleiflex of UNICEF installations in the South African area had grown into a gigantic round-the-world project.

For Danny, upon returning to his hotel, began to mull over the idea. Two hours later he had called Paramount in Hollywood and lined up a camera crew of two, complete with the latest in camera equipment. He convinced the studios that this was their contribution to the kids of the world. Both Prager and Dukoff agreed to join the expedition.

South Africa seemed too small a district for their activities, and Danny's next step was to suggest that he and his entourage return to Hollywood the "short way," via Asia—at Danny's expense.

Pate was overwhelmed, and Hammarskjöld delighted.

Danny was briefed by Paul Hoffman at a private luncheon and plans took final shape.

For Danny, it was new and exciting. He had spent years with kids who had the money to visit him in theaters, kids who understood his language. Now he was to meet the dirty children, the helpless ones, the urchins, the children in the shadows of disease and starvation.

During his first briefing session, Danny was shocked to learn that two-thirds of the world's 900,000,000 children lack adequate food, shelter and protection from disease. The result is a high mortality rate.

"You, Mr. Kaye," said Maurice Pate, "can directly or indirectly help to vaccinate some 50,000,000 children. You can also help to cure a few million cases of yaws. I need to warn you that your trip will not be easy. You will be in areas of the earth that no tourist has ever seen. You will be uncomfortable. You will miss your warm shower and good food. You yourself will not always be safe against disease. Think it over again, but know this: Yours would be a tremendous contribution."

Danny did not think long. "This is exactly what I want to do," he said.

Danny, who had never known the deck-chair apathy of many globe-trotting tourists, was suddenly in the midst of a most intricate game of cat's-cradle with the forgotten children on the earth. Feeling his own insignificance in so great a project, he recollects: "I confess I didn't quite appreciate the seriousness of the assignment until I received my written 'orders': 'The United Nations Children's Fund has the honor to appoint you its Ambassador-at-Large, charged with making known the needs of children throughout the world.'

"My first reaction to this can be summed up in two words: 'Who, me?'

"I have never been accused of being the most diplomatic person in the world, but, fortunately for the solemnity of the mission, I was received, not for myself, but as the representative of two institutions that are held in affectionate respect throughout the entire world—UNICEF and the motion-picture industry."

He followed a gargantuan path of humanitarian relief work and medical help. His need to contribute more than laughter to the world found its first outlet and burst with the force and power of a river that has broken its dam.

The result? Danny, the man of many emotions, experienced the emotional heights of his life while bringing light into the huts of darkness and silence, suffering and poverty.

Danny tells how his work began when he reached Asia: "My UNICEF work started in India with a visit to a tiny village many miles inland. This was a village selected as a typical example of the UNICEF tuberculosis vaccination program at work. Days before we arrived, teams of UNICEF workers had circulated leaflets telling about the program and inviting all mothers to have their children in the village square on the day our team was to arrive, for the vaccination.

"My job was primarily to film the work being done, but once in the midst of such exciting work it was impossible to remain a disinterested observer. As soon as a small crowd assembled in the square I began to do what I could to entertain them. No one there had ever heard of a guy named Danny Kaye. I don't think anyone there had ever seen a movie. They didn't speak my language. I didn't speak theirs.

"But I jigged through a couple of dances, shouted a couple of songs, got the children clapping their hands in accompaniment and pretty soon the crowd doubled, redoubled and redoubled. Kids came flocking from all over the village to find out what all the commotion was about. They stayed to receive a lifesaving injection of T.B. vaccine, courtesy of UNICEF.

"The long lines at the vaccination center are probably the most rewarding tribute I have ever received for my peculiar ability to make funny faces.

"And, after all, what's the use of being a comic if you can't amuse children? It didn't make any difference that the village kids in Burma, Thailand and Japan had never heard of me either. I made funny faces. I clowned through the villages, trying desperately to play a new kind of Pied Piper. And the children, sensing that here was someone more simple-minded than they, laughed and followed. Nobody fears a clown.

"In New Delhi I attended a diplomatic reception given in my honor by that great humanitarian and wonderful all-round human being, Madame Pandit, and attended by her brother, Prime Minister Nehru.

"Outside of Rangoon, in Burma, I jibbered through three choruses of song and danced a clog in a rice-paddy before an audience of deadpan children."

In New Delhi, UNICEF's program was to test approximately one million people for tuberculosis. Danny accompanied the

UNICEF doctors and regional health officers to the crowded fly-ridden city districts, into the outskirts of town and to the neighboring villages. Everywhere they went there were swarms of people, children, adults—the lame and the blind. The methods of the UNICEF team was not unlike those of a traveling circus. There was a band with its drummer to attract the crowds, followed by a jeep with a loud-speaker system which explained the medical program, told of the T.B. tests and urged those who were found to be infected to return at once for vaccination. Unorthodox tools of medicine, but they worked.

Later, the UNICEF team was split into five units of twenty-five persons each. Danny divided his time among them through India and most of the other Asiatic countries.

It was a massive program. Each unit tested approximately 32,000 people, and in a single day eleven doctors in New Delhi examined 16,000 children and followed up the next day with vaccinations. It was a race against disease and death. One doctor alone tested 5,500 children in a single day.

The news of these achievements was broadcast day and night all over India.

A new world opened its doors to Danny Kaye, a world he knew existed but which before had little meaning for him. Few people have the imagination or the bravery to visualize so much human suffering.

Danny, who traveled through twenty-seven countries for UNICEF, can report for hours on his experiences, the people he met, the conditions he found.

Danny Pied Piper Kaye believes, "You cannot bring health and happiness to a million children by talking about it, signing a paper or waving a wand. It has to be child by child. It has to be done personally and with love. And that's the way UNICEF works.

"In Thailand I acquired a new fan. I'm sure of it, because my own heart went out instantly. This was a two-year-old Siamese baby that I would have adopted, surely, if I could have. I made faces and she laughed. And every time she laughed her eyes closed tight, and her whole body shook. What a darling!

"I must have been quite moved, or I would not have been so sharp with a neo-Malthusian I met en route to Japan.

" 'But, after all,' he argued, 'isn't the disease of the Near East —the malaria, tuberculosis, starvation—nature's way of taking care of overpopulation. I don't mean to sound cruel, but—'

" 'That's a very logical argument,' I said. 'Why don't you put it to the test next time your own child gets sick?'

"On my tour I visited hospitals and clinics in big cities, wayside stations in jungles, portable vaccination units set up in villages. In Thailand I saw a kid with great ulcers all over him from yaws. After two shots of penicillin he was completely cured. These people had never seen penicillin before. In Indian and Burmese villages I saw children line up by the hundreds for BCG inoculations that would protect them from tuberculosis. (And an Indian youngster is just as scared of his first vaccination as any other kid in the same spot!) At first the children, shy of us strangers, often tried to hide from the cameras. I would make an unexpected funny face, wink or make some comic gesture that would intrigue them. Then another face or two, and I would get them laughing. We would start clapping hands, and before long we would be playing follow-the-leader down the lanes, all over temples and pagodas. They would let me hold them, even feel their tummies for the telltale malaria-enlarged spleen. Children are the same the world over. They ought to have a chance to live."

In Thailand Danny met his first, but not last, leprosy case. He, like the other UNICEF workers, was impressed by the now-famous story of Kao Ket Sin King, the eighteen-year-old boy who traveled thirty miles from his village to receive sulphone to cure his leprosy. After two years of treatment, the boy was cured but refused to go home.

"But why not?" Danny asked the field director, Simon Polak.

"We have cured Kao, but we haven't cured superstition yet," was his answer. "He says everyone in his village hates him except his mother." I asked him if he had committed a crime or done something bad.

"Well, did he?"

"Of course not, but the villagers will not believe he is well again. They fear that if he returns, they will all get leprosy. This fallacious belief is held by many people in even our 'enlightened' United States."

Of all the many friendly things said about Danny Kaye, he seemed to appreciate most the comment of "Shrimpie," the tiny young Chinese maid of the Polaks, who has been one of his most devoted fans since she saw his performance in an imaginary pet shop in *Wonder Man*. She said (in Cantonese): "When we see most big shots, our hearts remain closed because we know that behind their smiles they are thinking up ways to increase our taxes. But when this clown smiles, we feel that he is our friend, and our hearts are opened." She also added, practically: "The best thing is that, as he smiles here at the airport, we can have fun too, without buying a ticket." For this he picked up all seventy-five pounds of her in his arms and kissed her. She also kissed him. When asked why, she said, "He asked me to."

"But you speak no English and he no Chinese."

"It's not our Chinese way to kiss," she said, "but I've been to enough movies to know what are good manners in America."

"How does it feel to be a United Nations ambassador?" a reporter asked Danny after his trip.

With his usual serious clowning, Danny answered: "First of all, it's great. I carry a United Nations document so big you have to fold it six times to get it in your pocket. It's very effective with customs guards, from Algiers to Bombay. But I've found out that all its fancy language means simply, 'Let this bum t'ru.' Next, as an ambassador, I learned a very important rule: Always observe protocol. The best way I can define protocol is to illustrate. In Vienna, I called on the late Austrian president, Theodor Körner, at the Imperial Castle. That day I had paid my respects to the mayor, the minister of social welfare and the minister of finance. My feet were killing me. When Herr Körner came into the hall to greet me, he stood and talked. When my feet could no longer take it, I asked him, 'Wouldn't you like to sit down?'

"He was flabbergasted. 'But I'm supposed to ask you that,' he said.

" 'So ask me,' I replied, grinning. This is known as protocol.

"Perhaps the most important ambassadorial rule of all is this:

Neglect no one. In Bonn, UNICEF officials gave me a banquet. One by one those at the head table rose and proposed a toast to the guest of honor, me. Each time, when the toast ended, we all stood and drank. We were two-thirds of the way through the brass when I jumped up, raised my glass and shouted: 'To the gentlemen who serve UNICEF! The waiters!' And so everyone stood and drank a toast to the waiters.

"By now I hope you realize I'm jesting. I know no more about protocol than what common sense tells me. You couldn't get a top hat on my head because a golf cap is usually there already. As for foreign languages, I don't know them—not even French."

And then, becoming serious, Danny continued: "All this means much more than just what appears on the surface. The world's less fortunate people are beginning to understand that the more fortunate want to help them. To the Nigerian or Moroccan this is overwhelming knowledge. For perhaps the first time, he can see a life of work instead of beggary. The people I have met are proud people; they'd rather work than beg. Now that they are being helped, they are beginning to help themselves. They are taking independent measures to protect their health.

"One of my firmest beliefs is that there is no common formula for happiness. Each human being finds happiness in his own way and time. To a Nigerian leper the idea of mingling with non-lepers is happiness. I remember a welcome I received at a leper settlement in northern Nigeria. The lepers formed a large, thick circle, and when drummers set upon their drums, some children began to dance. I felt like dancing too—so I got up and started dancing with them. Suddenly out from the crowd came a young lady—a leper—to dance with me. We faced off, shuffled feet, swirled and circled as though we had rehearsed the dance for weeks. I had a great time, and so did my partner. So did the audience—laughing at us."

XXI

Juggler of God

THE ROLE OF AN AMBASSADOR WAS NEVER A COMFORTABLE ONE for Danny's informal personality. He hates to dress up and to be surrounded by diplomats in striped pants and cutaway coats. It took years for him to learn the protocol of official audiences. But, for UNICEF, he was willing to undergo even these "ordeals."

He has never thoroughly mastered any foreign language, although he knows a smattering of many. Danny says:

"An ambassador may be called upon to speak any language from Tagalog to Thai. But don't let this scare you; languages are a snap. I wasn't in France more than a week, for example, when I was able to say to a U.N. benefit audience in Paris, *'Je ne pas trense electrol ensi tren toi.'* Pretty, eh? Imagine my dismay when the audience laughed. It was all straightened out when a friend explained that what I had said was, 'I can't help the train although the rattlesnake is limping.'

"Not knowing languages, you can, of course, use an interpreter. But you must know how to use him. I advise breaking your sentences into even fragments. In Spain I used an interpreter because my Spanish is not as good as my French. Greeting the audience, I said: 'I . . .' The interpreter translated: *'Yo.'* I said: 'Am.' The interpreter said: *'Soy.'* I said: 'Very.' The interpreter said: *'Muy.'* I countered: 'Glad to be able to meet with you ladies and gentlemen to talk to you about the great work being done by the United Nations International Children's Emergency Fund.' "

Indeed, Danny has become an ambassador, even if he is limited to the small but bright world of laughter, the laughter which he took into the lives of thousands of children in the hospitals of Yugoslavia, the polio wards of Greece, and the trachoma stations of Thailand. He jigged his way into the hearts of thousands of Moroccan children. With them he fought a constant battle against swarms of large crawling flies that clustered around the eyes, at the corners of the mouth and on the children's ears. Brushing them off was a futile task, for they returned immediately.

Danny played ball with children who were learning to catch with the stumps of their arms, and he ran races with hopeless cripples. His was a function quite different from that of world politicians at diplomatic conferences, but he got to the heart of the matter—the hearts of the next generation.

Danny reports, "I'd walk funny and make faces. I'd get mixed up in dances. I'd mimic every kid I could. If he covered his mouth, I'd cover mine; if he waved me away, I'd wave back. And I'd listen hard to get the rhythm and sound of his language, because among other things I learned in my UNICEF travels is that people flip if you utter so much as a single phrase of their tongue. At a show in Belgrade, the biggest laugh I got all evening came after a chorus of little Yugoslav girls sang a song about a little doll, which in Serbo-Croatian is *lutka mala*. All I said was: '*Lutka mala.*' In a Roman polio ward, I watched a nurse leading a group of little boys in abdominal exercises. At her count of 'one,' the youngsters, lying on their backs, would arch their bodies. At her count of 'two,' they would relax. '*Uno . . . due,*' she said; '*uno . . . due.*'

"I asked if I could count too. She said I could. I counted: '*Uno . . . cinque.*' Just that delighted those little boys.

"I went to Zagora in French Morocco. It's a tiny town of 667 people who live in an ancient fortress built on the desert. Zagora in the summer is frighteningly hot, dusty and insect-ridden—a climate favorable to conjunctivitis, an eye inflammation that usually paves the way for a contagious disease called trachoma. Trachoma strikes mainly at children. In many cases, it blinds them. In some southern areas of French Morocco, it blinds them all.

"Three years ago, after a government study of preventive treatments, seventeen teams of health workers spent five months in heat that reached 115 degrees, treating the entire population of one foothill area. Twice a day for half a year, they treated the eyes of 114,000 people with antibiotic ointment. That summer, there was no conjunctivitis in the area.

"I can't forget Luc Dulière, one of the doctors in this campaign. A young man, he came from France to devote his life to the trachoma program. I can't forget him because every three or four weeks he gets conjunctivitis himself. He cures himself and he keeps on working. Because of devotion like this, Morocco's war against trachoma is on the verge of success. Once all but a few of the country's three million children had an eye disease of one form or another. By 1960, UNICEF expects to be giving them all preventive treatment.

"But UNICEF personnel—and local officials and World Health Organization experts with whom they cooperate—cannot easily step into a community and go to work immediately. Often they must first overcome ancient fears. UNICEF workers four years ago set up a maternity and child health center in a small Syrian village. They were ready for business, but they had none. Their methods were foreign. They were suspect.

"One evening a nurse midwife, trained by UNICEF, was roused from her bed by an insistent knocking at her door. Several Arab men stood outside. 'Come quickly,' one of them urged. A cow was calving and in trouble. If UNICEF knew all about delivering babies, here, said the men, was a chance to prove it. The midwife rushed off with them to the scene of the difficulty. There was little she could do, but she did that little. In time the calf arrived. The next day there were women and children at the clinic.

"I found perhaps the most striking story of the fight against superstition in Nigeria. The man who leads this fight is a fifty-year-old Irish doctor who could very well double for Barry Fitzgerald—droopy spectacles and all. His name is Charles McConnaughy Ross. Ross went to Nigeria twenty-eight years ago to fight leprosy.

When I asked him if he intended to stay for the rest of his life, he looked at me as if he didn't understand how I could ask the question.

"If he lives long enough, Dr. Ross may well see the end of leprosy. A relatively new group of drugs—sulfones—has revolutionized the treatment of leprosy. Until a few years ago being a leper meant social and economic ostracism. Today lepers have begun to walk among their people. The new drugs reduce the symptoms and in many cases hasten recovery. As a result, lepers who had stayed in hiding for fear of being ostracized—and had unwittingly endangered their families—are now coming out of hiding for treatment."

It was a new and different Danny Kaye who delivered such a touching travelogue, his descent into the modern inferno of misery.

The first UNICEF tour took Danny and his crew into twenty-four countries and covered some 40,000 difficult miles often in remote areas. To those with malicious tongues who claim that the gesture was merely a promotion gag, it should be pointed out that the trip was not without its hazards. Many United Nations and UNICEF workers have been killed either by accidents or by the diseases they set out to cure.

Many tools were used by UNICEF to lure the often suspicious children into the hospital tents. Danny was not always enough. In Asia old Tarzan pictures were shown before the vaccinations were given. The vaccinations were followed by the distribution of balloons, pink lemonade and candy.

The need for help seems, at times, endless. The corners of the world must be cleaned—from Guatemala to Morocco, Thailand to Brazil, Tonga to Nigeria.

In Indonesia UNICEF came armed with penicillin to combat the dreaded yaws. "The first time I saw a case of yaws," says Danny, "I almost fainted from horror. It is one of the most awful diseases to see. Yaws are boils, one right after another. A person has them for years. If they break out on his feet, he can't walk—on the hands, and he can't work. And think, one single shot of penicillin can cure the infection.

"My job was to keep the kids laughing while the nurses and doctors filled the hypodermic needles."

The word spread. Children told their parents, and parents told their grandparents. They told of the funny man and showed where their yaws had been. A miracle had been performed.

In many sick communities there was suddenly more man-power, greater harvests of rice, and laughter once again. Tears of pain were replaced by gratitude and happiness.

Korea, which Danny had known from the war years, was in the process of recovery. The devastation had been drastic and cruel. There was an incredibly large number of orphans in need of food, especially milk. UNICEF established two thousand distributing points and two million children received milk. For many it was a new drink—one they had to learn to like. "Milk for two million children," comments Danny, "is a godsend, but the sad part is the total picture. UNICEF never has enough money. Seven million children in Korea needed milk. There was not enough to go around."

The films taken on the trip were edited into a short documentary, called *Assignment Children,* which was shown all over the world. The money from its rental went into the never-steady UNICEF account and amounted to several million much needed dollars to carry on the gigantic humanitarian work which holds only one restriction—the recipient must be a child.

Suddenly the world met the unique manifestation of a great personality. In large cities the theater audiences expected to see a howling dervish, but found a clown with a sometimes sad or bewildered face making serious speeches. This struck home. People were touched, and every place he went the crowds paid tribute to Danny Kaye. From the polio wards in Yugoslavia to the hospital tents in Burma, there was Kaye with kids, kids, kids.

His arrival at Johannesburg touched off one of the wildest demonstrations in the memory of the local police officials. Danny was met at the airport by a civic delegation headed by the mayor. He was taken to the city by a motorcycle escort. Crowds lined every inch of the sixteen-mile route to the hotel. Inside the city the crowds broke through police lines several times, halting the cavalcade in a sea of humanity. Police estimate more than 50,000 persons took part in the welcoming demonstration.

Outside Kaye's hotel a mob of 12,000 people chanted, "We want Danny! We want Danny!" until he made a speech from the balcony of the hotel. He had to repeat his songs three times before the audience dispersed.

Three months after his departure on the first UNICEF tour, Danny, Sammy Prager and Eddie Dukoff completed their deviational round-the-world tour and landed in a tired heap at the Honolulu airport, where they fell into the anticipatory arms of their respective families. Their physical weariness was less than their emotional depletion.

The press that met Danny and his cohorts in Honolulu, and later in Hollywood and New York, found a new Mr. Kaye, a man who could still laugh and clown, but who was serious and sober when he thought or talked of the scenes he had witnessed: children, the innocent victims of man's ignorance and nature's cruelties. His laughter had a different tone; his remarks lacked their past flippancy. The toomler had become a missionary.

The world's first children's ambassador was created by the United Nations, and this trip was the beginning of an extended project to help unfortunate youth.

Said Danny: "I intend to fulfill my commission, and talk and preach about UNICEF as much as I can—even at the risk of boring people. I warn everybody—I'm not very funny on the subject.

"The extent of UNICEF services, however, is beyond any ordinary imagination. I have new respect for the United Nations as a result. If it gives birth to nothing but UNICEF, it will be worth the effort, the meetings, the arguments, the vetoes and the confusion involved in setting up any kind of world-wide organization.

"I'm not in politics. Nor are children. I do not like it when they are sick and hungry. The greatest organization the world has ever created to prevent this is UNICEF. I think more people should know about it."

His contribution to the children's cause was not overlooked in America. On the contrary. The public of the United States honored him for his message and his selfless activities. The motion-picture industry saluted his crusade. Awards were heaped on him, including an honorary degree bestowed by the American International College in Springfield, Massachusetts, and the title "Humanitarian of the Year" from a Denver hospital. Mrs. Roosevelt presented him with the United Nations citation of the American Association for the United Nations.

"Don't ask me what I will do in the future," he said after receiving one of the awards at Brandeis University. "I'm just an entertainer, a kid from Brooklyn—not a missionary. I don't know what I'll do next."

Back in Hollywood, Danny completed *The Court Jester* and established a recording company with Sylvia. He invested his savings in stocks and bonds, made personal appearances at theaters, and gave all his available free time to his rapidly developing daughter. Then came the next call from the spectacularly modern building in New York, the United Nations headquarters.

UNICEF needed him again. Danny left a few days later.

Danny never mentions it, and the newspapers have never published the statistics, but a charming secretary in the overworked and financially hard-pressed UNICEF office will tell an inquisitive questioner, "Nearly all our work has to be done by volunteers because we have no funds to pay employees. Most of the things done in this office are accomplished by men and women in New York who come up to see if they can give their time and abilities, and believe me, we can always put them to work.

"Danny Kaye? What a help he has been! Every cent for his tours has come from his own pocket. He has paid all the expenses for himself and his co-workers. From the films he brought back and his other activities for UNICEF he has raised money to care for thirty-two million children. Just think, one man helping thirty-two million youngsters!"

It was in 1956 that the third call came from New York, stating the urgent need for another tour, this time to be joined by Ed Murrow of C.B.S., the dean of American news commentators. Another 32,000 miles was covered in only seven weeks.

He sold laughter, kindliness—and UNICEF.

"Children are the world's one common denominator," he says.

"If they perish, the world dies. UNICEF has only one purpose: to help kids grow up and be healthy adults."

Wherever Danny went he captivated audiences with the same typical Kaye japery that has made him a favorite throughout the world. In Israel he conducted the Israeli Philharmonic in numbers such as Sousa's "The Stars and Stripes Forever." In Belgrade he joined a group of Yugoslav folk dancers and led an august Belgrade concert audience in a community sing.

One of the high spots of Kaye's tour was a personal interview with Marshal Tito of Yugoslavia, during which Tito expressed the appreciation of the people of Yugoslavia for the work done in that country by UNICEF in the field of nutritional aid.

In Greece "Ambassador" Kaye talked with King Paul and Queen Frederica; in Israel with President Ben-Gurion; in Turkey with President Colal Bayar; with tribal chiefs of Nigeria; in India with Mr. Nehru.

While in Italy he was granted an audience with Pope Pius, with whom he discussed the problem of caring for children in the less fortunate countries of the world.

"Politics are not for me," Danny commented, a bit sadly, and then his face brightened. "You know what I am interested in. Everyone who knows me knows that; but does everyone interested in children know the seven achievements of UNICEF?"

This is what UNICEF has accomplished: (1) Sixty million children vaccinated against tuberculosis through UNICEF-aided campaigns; (2) Ten million persons treated for yaws with UNICEF penicillin; (3) D.D.T. and related supplies for campaigns against malaria, to protect some 20 million persons in 1956; (4) Milk and other diet supplements for over 7 million children and nursing and pregnant mothers in 1956; (5) Over 120 powdered milk and milk pasteurization plants in operation with UNICEF equipment; (6) Basic medical equipment for nearly 10,000 maternal and child health centers; (7) Expanded training facilities, within their own countries, for thousands of rural health workers.

Ed Murrow called his ninety-minute television report on UNICEF "The Secret Life of Danny Kaye." The two had grown close during their many weeks of travel together. It was Kaye's television debut. In the past he had consistently refused to appear on television, and had turned down enormous fees. Even his old friend Max Liebman had failed to lure him to the new field.

Hearing this, Murrow quipped, "Don't blame you, Danny, I permit my own son, Casey, to watch television only a half hour a day."

The television film on UNICEF was circulated around the world, shown in twenty-four countries, and brought in urgently needed funds for UNICEF.

The Murrow-Kaye team was a natural. At forty-nine, Murrow, who is a top TV figure, combines brains, integrity and showmanship. With Danny's added contributions the two produced an unbeatable show. It was estimated that approximately nine million people in North America alone viewed the film. Murrow's saturnine good looks and doomsday voice telling about the heroic work of UNICEF helped the over-all presentation considerably.

Danny was shown as a modern-day Hans Christian Andersen, soft-shoeing it down the steps from their plane, dressed in old clothes, tired tennis shoes and carrying his worldly goods wrapped in a red bandanna handkerchief tied to the end of a stick.

After the initial showing of the film on television, 4,500 letters poured into the United Nations offices in New York. Some merely expressed their delight, but most included gifts of money, ranging from five cents to five thousand dollars.

There was one letter among the 4,500 which Sylvia removed from the UNICEF files and took home. A Catholic priest from Ohio had written Danny personally to thank him for his work. The show, said the priest, had given him a "renewal of spirit." He went on to say: "Any fool can be solemn, but only a saintly person can be a fool—in the medieval sense. I think of the Juggler of God whenever I see you."